PROTESTANTISM AND THE NATIONAL CHURCH IN
SIXTEENTH CENTURY ENGLAND

PROTESTANTISM
· and the ·
NATIONAL CHURCH
in Sixteenth Century England

Edited by
PETER LAKE and MARIA DOWLING

CROOM HELM
London • New York • Sydney

© 1987 Peter Lake and Maria Dowling
Croom Helm Ltd, Provident House, Burrell Row,
Beckenham, Kent, BR3 1AT
Croom Helm Australia, 44-50 Waterloo Road,
North Ryde, 2113, New South Wales

Published in the USA by
Croom Helm
in association with Methuen, Inc.
29 West 35th Street
New York, NY 10001

British Library Cataloguing in Publication Data

Protestantism and the national church in
    sixteenth century England.
    1. Protestant churches — England —
    History — 16th century 2. Reformation
    — England 3. England — Church
    history — 16th century
    I. Lake, Peter II. Dowling, Maria
    280'.4'0942   BX4838
    ISBN 0-7099-1681-7

Library of Congress Cataloging in Publication Data

ISBN 0-7099-1681-7

Printed and bound in Great Britain by Mackays of Chatham Ltd, Kent

CONTENTS

PREFACE

The English reformation has emerged from recent research as a divisive and contested event. And yet if the triumph of protestantism was not the simple product of the onward march of modernity and print culture for which it was once taken, it still happened and the fact that it happened (however contingent its causes) surely means that any attempt to write the history of the English reformation without due regard for the spiritual dynamic of protestantism resembles nothing so much as the proverbial attempt to write Hamlet without the prince.

However, it has to be admitted that the present volume represents no sort of attempt to write Hamlet at all. Rather it is a collection of essays designed to make available to a wider (undergraduate) audience the results of recent research into sixteenth century English protestant ideology. As such it is intended to fit inside the recent wave of 'revisionist' writing that has emphasised the status of the reformation as a contested event and to examine the problematic relationship established by the minority of protestant engagés with the wider society in which they had to survive and which they were trying to convert.

What coherence the volume has stems from the engagement of each of the contributors with that relationship between protestantism and the national church. Whilst the focus of the collection is primarily on protestant ideology – the self image of English protestants – it contains (most notably in the contributions by Andrew Hope, Maria Dowling and Ron Fritze) material of a more positivist nature and the aim throughout has been to relate protestant thought to the practical situations in which protestants found themselves and had to operate.

While some attempt has been made to provide a smooth chronological coverage, there are obvious gaps. The thought of the Henrician protestant exiles (which is currently under examination by Bryn Morris of the University of Sheffield) is perhaps the most glaring example, but it might also be argued that too little attention has been paid to the 'imperial' theme in protestant ideology. Certainly a full scale analysis of protestant treatments of the Christian prince would have been nice, had any of us been qualified to produce it. As it is, the papers by Catharine Davies, Jane Facey and Peter Lake all contain some discussion of what remained a central theme in protestant polemic throughout the century.

Spelling and punctuation have been modernised throughout and dates are in the new style. The book was published with considerable financial help from the Isabel Thornley bequest, as befits a volume composed of the results of research largely undertaken at the Institute of Historical Research in London.

The final version of the book was typed with exemplary accuracy and patience by Miss Christine Stephenson.

Chapter One

LOLLARDY: THE STONE THE BUILDERS REJECTED?

Andrew Hope

In the play <u>Sir John Oldcastle</u> (1599) a bishop says of the Lollards '"They give themselves the name of Protestants, and meet in fields and solitary groves"'. (1)
It was, of course, the Elizabethans who gave Lollards the name of protestants, a term which the Oxford English Dictionary is unable to find used outside a German context before the reign of Edward VI. The Elizabethan apologists for the reformation however established an historiographical tradition which has proved remarkably persistent. Nor were they entirely disingenuous. Many aspects of later medieval English heresy would not have seemed foreign to Elizabethan protestants: the Bible-reading, the denial of the miraculous in the mass, the opposition to Rome and the papal hierarchy, a certain reserve in attributing a spiritual status to the clergy, and the elimination of a whole class of holy objects and holy activities from the spiritual life. Were Lollards then protestants? The question is still an anachronistic one. The word 'protestant' has acquired so many cultural and religious accretions that its use poses difficulties even when applied to the earliest reformers, let alone groups of pre-reformation heretics. In any attempt accurately to delineate Lollardy, its use will, on the whole, be unhelpful. (2) Yet there was one generation for whom the question was not so anachronistic. Lollards born in the last decades of the fifteenth century were, in their adulthood, to have to face the question of whether for them the reformation represented the fruition of their hopes. These transitions cannot be understood solely by matching up doctrine against doctrine. The continuities and discontinuities had as much to do with aspirations and allegiances which spanned social life, liturgical preferences, and the

1

Traditionally Lollards have been seen as being 'poorer artisans'. Their links with the textile industry have been explored, (3) but often their contemporary descriptions as 'fishmonger' or 'baker' are vertical classifications which can comprehend extremes of wealth, so that it is necessary to go beyond the trial records to discover the social background of Lollards. The geographical distribution of Lollards presents less of a problem: most could be found either in London or in a scatter of provincial towns and their hinterlands, although Lollard traditions may also have survived in individual aristocratic households.

An account of Lollardy in the half century or so before the reformation should begin in London. London presented unrivalled opportunities both for the exchange of clandestine ideas and for evading authority. In addition it made manifest in an exaggerated form many of the ecclesiastical abuses of which Lollardy complained. Nowhere else was the contrast between the wealth and pomp of the ecclesiastical establishment and the poverty of the poorly beneficed or unbeneficed quite so striking. In addition the social conditions which could be catalysts for heresy – the anonymity combined with a wider range of social and intellectual contacts – could undermine the ideas of a celibate priestly caste. (4) It should be noted however that complaints about the shortcomings of the clergy do not in fact figure very prominently in Lollard depositions: Lollards offered most often in justification of themselves a devotional life and a set of religious priorities in part at least outside the prescribed rhythms of the sacraments. The social background of London Lollardy is poorly documented, but heterodoxy infiltrated the livery companies at the highest levels. In 1495 Joan Boughton, a woman in her eighties, and subsequently perhaps her daughter Lady Young were burned for heresy. Lady Young was the widow of Sir John Young, a grocer and former Lord Mayor. That they were part of a wider group was demonstrated after Joan's execution when her ashes were surreptitiously removed, to be found later being venerated as relics. (5) Information about Lollardy in the Goldsmiths' Company is more detailed. The house of John Barrett, a well-to-do goldsmith, and his wife Joan became a resort for Lollards in the first decade of the sixteenth century. John knew the Epistle of James by heart and would recite it at meetings of Lollards in his home. He taught his

2

apprentices their religion as well as their goldsmithery. Two went on to spread their views in the Chilterns and to find martyrdom there, William Tillesworth in 1511 and John Scrivener in 1521. Conditions before the <u>magna abjurata</u> of 1511 were looked back upon with some nostalgia: 'Ah, good Lord!' said a fellow Lollard to John Scrivener, 'Where is all our good communication which was wont to be among us when your master was alive?' (6) Barrett's apprentices were not the only London Lollards who brought their message to the provinces. Evidence given to John Longland, bishop of Lincoln, in 1521, names a further five or six, including Thomas Philips, the veteran John Hacker, and Thomas Geoffrey, then of Uxbridge, who brought Chiltern Lollards to St. Paul's to hear Colet preach. (7)

It is easier to arrive at a social profile of Lollardy in provincial towns. Both Tillesworth and Scrivener resided in Amersham, where two major heresy investigations in eleven years combined with the survival of the 1522 certificate of musters and the 1524-25 subsidy assessment reveal many details of Lollardy, normally obscured. (8) The persecution by William Smith in 1511 was followed by that of Longland in 1521, the latter taking the initiative within months of his consecration. Longland used the device of demanding co-operation from those who had abjured in 1511 as evidence of the sincerity of their abjuration. If they did not co-operate they would be considered relapsed and liable to be burnt. This proved a most effective tool in persuading witnesses to speak and no one was able to withstand it. It is not to Longland's credit that after witnesses had testified he refused in some cases to accept this as sufficient evidence of their sincerity and burnt them anyway. In burning Thomas Holmes he burnt his major witness, and someone who had brought on himself the enmity of many Lollards by the alacrity with which he co-operated with the authorities: so much so that Foxe is at a loss whether to count him as a true martyr. (9) The result of Longland's procedure however is that we seem to have a relatively complete picture of Lollardy in the Chilterns, and especially Amersham, in the decade after Smith's persecution. One measure of its success was the evidence which emerged of irregularities in the 1511 persecution. These had provoked Thomas Holmes ruefully to remark at the time that 'the greatest cobs were yet behind'. And so they were: Thomas Grove and his wife Joan, and Richard Saunders, had each bribed Dr. Henry Wilcocks, Smith's commissary, with £20. (10) Longland was more

3

rigorous. Evidence emerged against between 350 and 400 people in the Chilterns of whom over eight were from Amersham or its immediate environs. When these are compared with the Amersham tax lists, it is found that about 15% of taxpayers engaged in Lollard activities or had Lollard interests, a number necessarily excluding those who were executed or who had died or moved away. The percentage in, say, 1518 would have been higher and in 1510 probably higher still. Such lists however include perhaps only the richer two thirds of the population: the percentage of Lollards in Amersham as a whole could have been nearer a tenth. (11)

Lollardy was disproportionately strong among the wealthy. Of the twenty richest inhabitants in 1522 ten were Lollards, and they included Richard Saunders, assessed at £300 and by far the wealthiest man in Amersham. Any average assessment would be so weighted by his wealth as to be unrepresentative, but the median assessment for Lollards was £10 and for the town as a whole £3. Incidence of Lollardy decreases strikingly going down the social scale. From half among the most wealthy, it falls to a quarter for those assessed at under £10 to £5, and a tenth for those assessed at under £5 to £2, and nil below £2. (12) The well-to-do could, and did, use their patronage to favour Lollards. After the 1511 persecution Richard's wife Alice Saunders boasted of how her husband had 'brought to beggary' those who had co-operated with Smith. The 1522 assessment was made apparently after the executions consequent on Longland's 1521 trial (there were six of which at least three were from Amersham) but before the penances or other penalties were carried out. Foxe heard from a very aged informant of the penury brought to some of those convicted and this can be confirmed by comparing the 1522 muster certificates with the 1524-25 subsidy. Appeals for over-assessment had been allowed and many were successfully made. Richard Saunders' fall from £300 to £200 may be due to this, but hardly that of Richard Bartlett. A Lollard neighbour had once said of him that he was a good man 'but he hath so much mind of buying and selling and taking of farms'. In 1522 he was assessed at £24 and ranked 12th in the town. Two years later he was worth a mere £1 3s 4d and had dropped to 72nd. Foxe's informant specifically cited Richard's brother Robert as 'a rich man, who for his profession's sake was put out of his farm and goods, and was condemned to be kept in the monastery of Ashridge ... the space of seven years'. Robert was assessed at £40 in 1522 and is missing from the 1524 assessment. The number of Lollards among the 20 richest fell from ten to six, and the median assessment for Lollards from £10 to £5, while that for the town as a whole fell from £3 to £2. (13)

The Chiltern Lollards were not exceptional. A group of Lollards has been identified in the civic and mercantile elite of Coventry, in existence at least from the last decades of the 15th century to the persecution of 1511 and beyond. It included Richard Cook, a leading member of Coventry's ruling oligarchy from Yorkist times and mayor in 1486 and 1503, and M.P. in 1491-92 and 1495. Their spiritual inspiration seems to have come from James Preston, an Oxford doctor of theology and vicar of St. Michael's. (14) A similar group probably existed in Colchester. Colchester escaped large scale persecution until 1528 when it was revealed that London evangelists such as John Hacker, forced out of the diocese of Lincoln by Longland, had been vigorously at work in Essex. Positive identifications of Lollards with members of the town hierarchy are difficult to make, but many names of leading Colchester families recur. At least one town councillor, Thomas Matthew, was deeply implicated, having held conventicles in his house, and members of his family knew large parts of the Bible by heart. (15) According to Foxe the Cowbridge family had been Lollards from Wyclif's time. Its senior representative at the beginning of the sixteenth century, Robert Cowbridge, was elected one of the two bailiffs - the town's highest municipal office - in 1501-02, and re-elected in 1507, despite arrests and trials of Lollards from Colchester and its environs the previous year. Robert died untroubled, but his widow Margaret was accused of heresy in 1528. She mobilised a formidable string of compurgators to attest her innocence and thus acquitted herself. Their son and heir, William, was less fortunate, despite being able to call on even higher support. He lacked discretion and under the compunction of a wayward inner life gave away to his sisters and relatives the fortune his father had left him and became an itinerant preacher. Although unordained, he established himself as parish priest at Wantage (a peculiar of St. George's, Windsor) and taught and administered the sacraments there 'a long season' before the authorities caught up with him, and even then it may have been his growing mental instability rather than his heterodoxy or irregularity which betrayed him. He was imprisoned in

Oxford, and tried and condemned by Longland. Lord Chancellor Thomas Audley, a former recorder of Colchester who was probably acquainted with Cowbridge's parents if not with Cowbridge himself, entered a plea in his behalf, but it was ignored. Cowbridge was burned in Carfax in 1538. It was the first and only martyrdom John Foxe witnessed and earned Longland a stinging rebuke from Cromwell. (16)

Many towns where Lollards were active had a hinterland of villages where Lollards could also be found: in East and West Hendred east of Wantage, Woodrow and Penne outside Amersham, Benenden and Rolvenden and other Wealden villages near Cranbrook and Tenterden, Godmersham outside Canterbury and so forth. Neither recent characterisation of Lollardy as predominantly rural (17) or as a product of urban conditions (18) is satisfactory. Generalisations on these lines are almost impossible, although it might be suggested that Lollardy tends to be stronger in areas where the traditional manor is weak. Even here, however, there were exceptions, since a third milieu in which Lollardy may have survived - or perhaps lingered - is that of the gentry or knightly household. Lollardy had initially enjoyed much success among such classes but associations with social radicalism and the military debacles of 1415 and 1431 frightened and repelled many. (19) However, heresy investigations continued to uncover shadowy households where meetings were taking place or irregular opinions were expressed. Rarely were these followed up and it is difficult not to recall the pliancy of Henry Wilcocks, although the sheer weight of social position or family connections may have been sufficient to deflect prosecution. (20)

The career of William Sweeting, one of the Colchester Lollards abjured in 1506 between two of Robert Cowbridge's spells as bailiff, contains hints that there were those in the gentry or aristocracy who did not view Lollardy with disfavour. Sweeting was probably brought up in the household of Lady Elizabeth Lucy (he refers to her by her maiden name, Elizabeth Percy) at Dallington in an old Lollard area in Northamptonshire. When Elizabeth died in 1455 her husband Sir William Lucy remarried Margaret John, daughter of Sir Lewis John alias Sir John FitzLewis, and Anne Montagu, daughter of Sir John Montagu and Lollard Earl of Salisbury. (21) Sir Lewis left a will in 1442 in which he spoke of his 'wretched' body in the manner characteristic of committed Lollards. (22) Sir Lewis's first wife had been Alice de Vere, sister of the Earl of Oxford. The earl's grandson

Richard de Vere married Elizabeth Lucy's sister
Margaret. Sir William Lucy was killed at the Battle
of Northampton in 1460. Sweeting subsequently
settled in Boxted where he worked first as holy water
clerk and then at the manor of Rivers Hall as bailiff
and farmer to Margery Wood, wife of rising Yorkist
administrator Sir John Wood the Elder. Sir John
became speaker in Edward IV's last parliament, was
Richard III's first treasurer and died a year before
Bosworth. The first evidence of Sweeting's Lollardy
emerges at this time when he was holding discussions
on the sacrament of the altar and reading the gospel
of St. Matthew with William Man. After Sir John's
death Margery remarried in 1489 Sir Thomas Garth, a
member of Parliament and an accomplished soldier.
(23) At the same time Sweeting moved on to St.
Osyth's, a house of Augustinian canons near
Colchester, an appointment he probably owed to de
Vere patronage as the steward of the priory was Sir
George de Vere, brother of the Richard who had
married Elizabeth Lucy's sister. Sir George left a
will stipulating that prayers at his funeral should
be said in English. Sweeting converted the prior,
George Laund, to his Lollard views. (24) Among the
other monks in the house at this time may have been
William Barlow, the future bishop of St. Asaph,
through whom the Church of England was to claim
apostolic succession. (25) Sweeting and Laund were
arrested with four other Colchester Lollards, sent to
London, and did penance at Paul's Cross on 15 March
1506. (26) Sweeting and another of the Lollards,
James Brewster, were condemned to wear a faggot badge
on their left arm or shoulder for life. However,
before two years were up both had had their badges
removed by their employers. Sweeting, after some
wandering, had returned to Colchester and found work
in his old occupation as holy water clerk at St.
Mary Magdalen, a small and poor parish outside the
walls on the St. Osyth road. It was a dependency of
St. John's Abbey in the town, with whom relations
were not always amicable. (27) The parson evidently
found Sweeting's faggot badge an embarrassment
rather than an impediment, and removed it. Brewster
worked - he was a carpenter - in the household of
John de Vere, Earl of Oxford and Sir George's eldest
brother. The comptroller of the Earl's household,
possibly Philip FitzLewis of the same FitzLewis
family, removed Brewster's badge. Sweeting and
Brewster were both again apprehended in a drive
against Lollardy in the diocese of London in 1510-11.
They had, with others, been holding services in the

fields outside Chelsea. They were burnt together at Smithfield on 18 October 1511. (28)

One case of Lollardy among the gentry which was investigated was that of Alice Doyly which came to light in the course of Longland's 1521 persecution. Alice came from the otherwise unidentified Glyddesdall family. Her first marriage was to John Wilmot of Stadhampton in Oxfordshire, who died in 1508. (29) Her second husband was William Cottesmore of Brightwell Baldwin and Britwell in Oxfordshire. The Cottesmores had established themselves through a Chief Justice of the Common Pleas in the first half of the fifteenth century. The family was apparently of an orthodox piety until the arrival of Alice. Alice expounded her views to those over whom she exercised some authority, her step-children and servants, and in due course, we may suppose, her own children. Her Lollardy expressed itself in a belief in the futility or inappropriateness of certain traditional devotional practices. (30) Whilst visiting the Barentines, a neighbouring gentry family at Little Haseley, (31) she pointed out Lady Barentine's images 'new gilded' and said to her servant Elizabeth Whithill, 'Look, here be my lady Barentine's gods.' Elizabeth replied that they were there for her remembrance of good saints. Alice said that if she was in a house with no images she could remember to pray to saints as well as if she saw them. Elizabeth replied that images provoked devotion, so eliciting from Alice the full Lollard litany against them: 'Ye should not worship that thing that hath ears and cannot hear, and hath eyes and cannot see, and hath mouth and cannot speak, and hath hands and cannot feel.' John Hacker was her mentor at that time. Alice thought him 'very expert in the gospels, and all other things belonging to divine service', and recommended him to Elizabeth, saying 'it would do one good to hear him'. She was impressed, as others were, by his use of prophecies, and his ability to tell 'what should happen in the realm'. She enjoined Elizabeth 'that she should tell no man hereof ... for hurting the poor man', though in the event it was probably Hacker who detected Alice. (32)

Alice was literate. She possessed a coffer containing 'divers books', which included a book of the creed and the 'Legenda Aures'. However, what the 'black book which she set most price by' was, we do not know. She raided the 'Legenda' for confirmation of her views, and once had the parson of Brightwell, Sir John Booth, read a saint's life to Elizabeth and

then explained how this supported her view against
pilgrimages. It was a pilgrimage which brought
matters to a head in the Cottesmore household. Some
time before 1519 William Cottesmore fell seriously
ill and made a vow to undertake a pilgrimage to our
Lady of Walsingham, but died before he could fulfil
it. The death thus of her husband could only confirm
for Alice the inefficacy of such things, and when Sir
William's chaplain required her to send her servant
John Stainer on the pilgrimage in her husband's
stead, she refused. Pilgrimages then seem to have
become an issue in the household, with Alice
justifying herself to her servants. None of this
emerged at the time however, and perhaps within a
year Alice had remarried.
        She had been wooed by Thomas Doyly,
unimpeachably orthodox and head of one of
Oxfordshire's most ancient and prestigious families.
It was however a family rebuilding its fortunes after
a disastrous lawsuit early in the previous century,
and Thomas's interest came, as Alice's brother sourly
put it, because he 'perceiv(ed) right well the great
substance of the said Alice', estimated at £1,000 in
movables alone. (33) After her marriage Alice
maintained her contacts with a group of Lollards
among whom she was known as 'Mistress Cottesmore
alias Mistress Dolly'. However, as we have seen,
evidence about her activities soon emerged in the
course of John Longland's 1521 drive against heresy.
The investigation of her case was entrusted to Dr.
John London, the future warden of New College, and a
native of Hambleden, where the Doyly's had their
principal seat. (34) Evidence was also produced
against Master Cottesmore, probably one of her step-
sons. No sentence against her exists, and her case
seems to have been hived off from the general run of
Chiltern heresy processes taking place at the time.
There must be a suspicion that there was some attempt
to limit the impact of this particular prosecution.
        Nevertheless, it proved too much for their ill-
found marriage, and Thomas's subsequent treatment of
her forced her to retreat to live with her mother. A
reconciliation was finally arranged in 1528 through
the rising lawyer, Thomas Cromwell. (35) She outlived
Thomas, who died in 1545. His will commanded his son
John to maintain a yearly obit in Hambleden church
for the health of his soul, and threatened him with
the judgement of God if he should neglect to do so;
as well Thomas might since John had already enriched
himself with the religious spoils of the 1530's.
Alice had five sons and eleven step-children. Many

9

of them rose to importance in county affairs. Her son Thomas Doyly became high sheriff of Oxfordshire and died of the pestilence at the Black Assizes at Oxford in 1577. It was on such as he that the Elizabethan settlement rested.

The evidence for Lollardy in gentry households is fragmentary. It is however difficult to believe that Sweeting, who did not shy at attempting to convert an Augustinian prior, would not have introduced his ideas to Margery Wood and others he came across. There is the further problem of the provenance of Lollard manuscripts. The magnificent Bibles and sermon cycles survived the fifteenth century in somebody's possession, and the poorer Lollard craftsmen's dwellings would afford few hiding places for such treasures. Hardly any appear in Lollard trials, where the literature in the possession of the defendants usually consists of single gospels, or other brief biblical extracts, or else short tracts. Some major manuscripts survived in monastic libraries, but the proportion of the whole is small. When, with the reformation, they emerge into respectability, they often do so in gentry households. The de Veres owned a Wycliffite Bible for example, and the Gates family had possession of a copy which may have belonged to John Purvey. (36)

Households were important however at all levels of Lollardy. They were the lowest unit within which Lollard discourse was freely possible, and provided the context of strong affective bonds within which heresy could be broached, taught and discussed. Children and servants might on occasion be excluded. Old Durdant of Iver Court near Staines, presiding at dinner with his children and their wives, first sent out a servant before reading from the Epistles of Paul and the Gospels. (37) Thomas Collins of Ginge, near Wantage, and his wife maintained an orthodox façade in the presence of their children. About 1513 he attempted to outline his real beliefs to his son John, who became very disturbed, especially by his father's views on the sacrament of the altar, and but for the pleading of his mother would have betrayed him to the authorities. In time however he became a trusted Lollard. Biological blood, as it were, proved thicker than sacramental. (38) Children were often educated in the households of others, a general fact of Tudor life. Isabel Tracher purposed to send her daughter to Alice Harding, (39) saying that she could better instruct her than any other. (40) John Edmunds put his daughter Agnes in the service of Richard Collins to be instructed in God's law. Roger Dodds

10

was set to service with Sir John Drury, the Lollard
parson of Windrush, Gloucestershire. Drury first
swore the boy on a book not to tell of what he saw or
heard, and then introduced him step by step into the
duplicitous life of a Lollard priest: showing him
Lollard books, introducing him to the woman he called
his wife, ritually breaking the church's fasts,
reading to him from the 'ABC' and the Apocalypse,
attacking images and pilgrimages, and discoursing on
the gullibility of his parishioners. Dodds became a
Lollard. Drury abjured at Burford in 1522. (41) We
have seen how the master-apprentice relationship was
used by John Barrett: there are parallel cases in
Essex. John and Thomas Hills were apprentices to
Christopher Raven, a Witham tailor, who had abjured
under Fitzjames and was in trouble again before
Tunstall. Thomas became an associate of John Tyball
at Steeple Bumpstead and accompanied him on his
famous visit to Robert Barnes.

Another relationship appropriated was that of
the spiritual family of godparents. Some Lollard
women seem to have taken it upon themselves to
initiate the rising generation into the group's
beliefs. (42) One such was the Colchester Lollard
Alice Gardiner. She was chosen, perhaps in the
1490's, by another Lollard, Ellen Tyball, to be
godmother to her son John. Alice also set John Pykas
on the road to heresy, discussing with him in his
early adolescence the Lord's Prayer, the Creed, the
Ave Maria, and the Epistles. Pykas went on to attend
Thomas Matthew's conventicle, and, like Tyball, to be
one of the first to possess Tyndale's printed New
Testament. (43)

It was imperative to find marriages for children
within the circle of shared dissent. Not only was
this so, but it was known to be so. Agnes Welles,
sister of Robert and Richard Bartlett, was
specifically asked by Longland 'whether she knew such
a law and custom among them, that such as were of
that sort did contract matrimony only with
themselves, and not with other Christians?' Robert
Bartlett was asked if he knew his wife Isabel was a
heretic when he married her. He said he did, but
added gallantly that he would have married her anyway. Marriage outside could present problems as we
have seen in the Cottesmore and Doyly families. John
Morden waited until he was dying of the plague
before, in 1514, entrusting his son-in-law Richard
Ashford with his true thoughts and a precious book.
Ashford went on to abjure before Richard Fox, Bishop
of Winchester, in 1521. (44)

11

Protestant historiography has traditionally assigned a prominent and heroic role to Lollard evangelists. Important as they may have been in reality the transmission of Lollardy both through time and geographically required in the first instance a solution which came to terms with, and if possible exploited, the realities of early Tudor family life and domestic traditions.

Lollardy can thus be located geographically and socially, and its transmission discerned. Is the noun itself however an historical illusion, a useful construct demanded both by the categoric demands of legal processes and by the logic of Foxe's argument, but corresponding to no very solid historical reality? The word here has hitherto been taken to be synonymous with those convicted of, or on apparently good grounds, accused of or detected for, Lollardy. To what degree these heretics possessed a coherence and self-identity will have been implicit in some of the examples cited. Although isolated prosecutions for heresy took place, the vast majority were of groups of associated individuals. For prosecutions of which detailed records survive - such as the Chilterns in 1521 or Essex in 1528 - these groups can be tracked changing through time with losses for example through death or persecution, or gains through migration or conversion. Similarly their geographical interconnections can be plotted. Most frequently these are between London and the provinces, rather than between the provinces themselves. Such links were not unknown however and could be activated especially in time of necessity. In persecution Chiltern Lollards were given sanctuary in East Anglia. (45) In about 1523 John Tyball helped a Colchester grey friar to escape from his house and his vows. He turned up at Tyball's house in secular dress and his head was shaved by Tyball to obliterate his tonsure. He stayed for a few days before leaving for Amersham where he subsequently married a girl who had followed him from Colchester. (46)

At the same time Lollardy was far from the exclusive and highly secretive world of the dualistic heresies of southern Christendom of earlier times. Lollardy was never without a penumbra of the sympathetic and interested, drawn by the new or the unusual or by resentment at material, legal, or spiritual clerical privilege. Thomas Man and his wife were accused of claiming that they had converted six or seven hundred people to their heresies. Man denied the charge, but while the number may be an exaggeration and the term 'converted' too strong, they probably had spread their views widely if thinly through the Chilterns. (47) Most Lollards would have been more cautious. There are many examples of secrecy. Robert Bartlett said of meetings at Amersham that 'if any came in amongst them that were not of their side, then they would say no more but all keep silence'. (48) We have seen how John Drury swore Roger Dodds to secrecy, and Old Durdant asked servants to leave. Books were particularly feared for their potential as incriminating evidence. Robert Freeman, the Lollard parson of Horton by Colnbrook, was caught reading a book 'which book when he perceived it to be seen in his hand, he closed it and carried it to his chamber'. (49) Humphrey Monmouth, the patron of Tyndale, indignantly defended himself by claiming that supposedly suspect books were not concealed in his house, but always freely available for anyone to look at. He did not explain why they had been bound with false titles on the spines. (50)

Nevertheless, it is wrong to view Lollardy as existing only behind a wall of secrecy and dissimulation, breaches of which were followed by immediate prosecution. If nothing else, the psychological tensions created by public acquiescence and private denial must have demanded some release. They may provide the context for the anti-clerical or irreverent remarks recalled at many trials. While true that neither anti-clericalism nor irreverence constituted heresy, they could serve as a means of public discourse when other expression was unacceptable. 'God speed, Father Bartlett,' said a passer-by to the Bartletts' father as he was threshing, 'ye work sore.' 'Yea,' he replied, 'I thresh Almighty God out of the straw!' (51) In Amersham the implications of such a joke would have been clear.

Such marks of disrespect were refined into a style of life by Robert Rave of Dorney. When he abjured in 1511 he celebrated the occasion by binding his faggot with a silken lace. (52) He was sentenced to complete a pilgrimage to Our Lady of Lincoln once or twice a year. He used these as opportunities to regale his fellow pilgrims with his Lollard views. He held forth against pilgrimage in general and when they met a party coming from St John Shorne called them fools and pilgrimage idolatry. When they passed a ruined chapel he said 'Lo, yonder is a fair milk house down!' implying it was where people went to be milked by the clergy. When they arrived at Lincoln and were at mass in the chapel he misbehaved himself in such a way that Foxe gives merely his excuse, 'that he did it of necessity'. However there was more to Rave than such crudity. He gave one of Lollardy's less straightforward arguments against the Real Presence: 'Christ had ascended to heaven and was at the right hand of the Father, and has said he had been once in sinners' hands and would come there no more.' These events can be dated to either 1512 or 1513. Rave's penance was subsequently relaxed so that he was required to go only to the nearer shrine of Great Missenden. (53) No action was taken against him though many must have witnessed his indiscretions. The story only emerged in 1521 with the accession of a bishop determined to make an assault on heresy in his diocese. Rave was convicted and burnt in 1522. There is no description of his demeanour at his execution. (54)

For a view of Lollards from the outside it is possible to turn to the evidence given in 1521 by Thomas Halfacre of Amersham. He is the only witness who gives extensive evidence about Lollardy without himself confessing either to be or to have been a Lollard and without being accused by anyone else of Lollardy. In his evidence Halfacre gave the court the current Amersham gossip. Katherine Bartlett being in good health came but seldom to church but feigned herself sick. Robert Pope fled at the time of the great abjuration and possessed English books. John Milsent and his wife, Roger Harding and his wife, Thomas Africk and his wife (and so forth: six married couples, a widow and probably two widowers) came to church and especially at elevation time would say no prayers but sit mum like beasts. William Frank married his wife Agnes knowing her to have been before abjured. And so forth. Thomas Halfacre knew well enough who were Lollards in the town, but knew insufficient seriously to incriminate anyone. (55) Perceptions of Lollards could vary: the Coventry Lollards were remarked upon for their apparent devoutness. (56) This need not have been insincere as a number of Lollards commented respectfully on the sacrament of the altar, while failing to give it the interpretation orthodoxy demanded. (57) No doubt different Lollard groups evolved their own responses to the rites of the church: but no doubt too the same behaviour could be perceived and interpreted differently by neighbours with different preconceptions.

How did Lollards view the church and its hierarchy? Reactions are often extreme. The church is often characterised in depositions as a synagogue, and the pope as Antichrist. These may not have been mere empty terms of abuse. Both have the connotations of either that which had been the vehicle of God's word and had failed; or that which might have been such, but which by treachery was not. The wife of David Lewis of Henley-on-Thames held ideas of a 'fall' of the church, such as were to become important in later protestant historiography: 'The churchmen in the old time did lead the people as the hen doth lead her chickens, but our priests now lead the people to the devil.' (58)

However, just as in practice the response of orthodoxy to heterodoxy could be muted, so Lollards too had to come to terms with the presence of the parish church and its liturgical round. A literary source is here instructive. The Lollard tract The Lantern of Light was composed sometime before 1415, but was still circulating at the end of the century. It distinguished three aspects of the word 'church'. First it was a material place 'made by man's craft, of lime, of timber, and of stone'. As such its elaboration and decoration may have evoked little enthusiasm, (59) but its necessity as a building was recognised: the 'Lantern' observes 'For man's profit this place is made'. Secondly, the church was a 'coming together of good and evil in a place that is hallowed, far from worldly occupation, (where) sacraments (shall) be treated and God's law both read and preached'. (60) Optimism for reform was probably greater in 1415 than it was eighty or a hundred years later, yet there are indications that Lollards still, for the most part, participated in this 'coming together'. Some found ways of registering dissent: feigning sickness (as we have seen), or small gestures such as that of Agnes Frank who turned her face from the cross as it was carried in Amersham church on Easter morning, (61) or absenteeism on major festivals. (62) On the key point of whether Lollard meetings were held at the same time as church services evidence points both ways. Thomas Man was consistent in his denigration of church services and held meetings which clashed with them, but other conventicles seem to have met after the Sunday service. For some Lollards the church exercised a fascination. We have seen how Sweeting returned to be a holy water clerk despite both the humiliation of a local abjuration and the danger of the proximity of church authorities, and how William Cowbridge actually installed himself as a parish priest. At Steeple Bumpstead John Tyball converted the local priest, and then secured the election of himself and

15

another Lollard as churchwardens. The commitment of
Lollards to this 'coming together' and their refusal
to cut themselves off from the generality of
Christians is seen in the occasional exception made
of Ember day fasts when fasts in general are
denounced. (63)

Yet it is with the third aspect of the
'Lantern's church that we approach the heart of
Lollardy. This church is 'Christ's little flock',
'the congregation or gathering-together of faithful
souls that lastingly keepen faith and truth, in word
and in deed, to God and to man'. (64) Agnes Ashford
of Chesham, probably the mother or stepmother of
Richard Ashford, knew Matthew 5 by heart, and would
teach it to others. The passage however which she
took most care over was this:

> We be - not as the Wycliffite and successive
> translations have 'ye are' - the salt of the
> earth: if it be putrefied and vanished away, it
> is nothing worth. A city set on a hill may not
> be hid. Teen ye not a candle, and put it under a
> bushel, but set it on a candlestick, that it may
> give light to all in the house. So shine your
> light before men, as they may see your works,
> and glorify your Father that is in heaven. No
> tittle nor letter of the law shall pass over
> till all things be done. (65)

The Wyclif version has 'lantern' for 'candle' so that
it is 'Christ's little flock' which is the true
'lantern of light'.

The problem of the historian is to penetrate
this 'little flock' (or, these 'sects of Antichrist's
hounds' (66)) with more success than Thomas Halfacre.
(67) How did they mark themselves off from those who
were not of their way? There are two areas where the
answer can be sought: first in the formal apparatus
of initiation, membership, and organisation, and
secondly in the articulation of their beliefs in a
distinctive literature, theology, and liturgy.

There is no evidence of independent rites of
initiation into Lollardy. Had there been such they
would have been of prime interest to inquisitors.
Instead there were attempts to reassess traditional
Christian initiation rites in the light of Lollards'
spiritualist ideas about the church. The subject was
discussed among Colchester Lollards in the 1520s
where a difference arose between those who maintained
that water was a token, real baptism being with the
holy spirit after the age of discretion; and those

16

who believed that the outward sign should have ceased
with the advent of Christ. (68) Rebaptism was not
considered as an option. As has been observed, there
is every reason to believe that membership was a hazy
affair. There were simply gradations of interest and
commitment. Lollardy was not, nor could it have been,
anything resembling what we would recognise as a
denomination. (69) Nor is there any evidence of
formal organisation (70) although it clearly would
have been within the capabilities of many. There were
of course less formal hierarchies among Lollards.
(71) Socially there were those of wealth and
consequence such as Richard Saunders in Amersham, who
used their influence to patronise, protect, and
promote the interests of local Lollards.
Functionally there were those articulate and
sometimes literate or semi-literate Lollards who
taught, read, and recited, and who acted as hosts for
meetings where such activities took place, and of
whom John Tyball is a good example in this period.
Superimposed on these from outside came the Lollard
evangelists such as John Hacker and Thomas Man. They
might have connections with widely scattered groups,
and were given hospitality and shelter as the need
arose. They were much revered. Two witnesses recalled
Robert Pope as 'the devoutest man that ever came in
their house: for he would sit reading in his book to
midnight many times.' (72)

Lollards therefore had little in the way of
formal institutions by which to define themselves.
They were bound by common ideas and attitudes,
transmitted through a common literature and finding
on occasion perhaps a liturgical expression. At the
same time of course they were subject not just to the
slowness and exactitude of fifteenth century book
production or oral instruction, but to persecution in
which their literature was subject to destruction and
their teachers to execution. There was therefore a
constant tendency for groups to become isolated and
to develop their own emphasis. (73) The ease with
which links with other Lollards and with the past
could be severed made books - often no more than a
few leaves - desperately important in their lives.
The Lollard who defended himself by saying that he
burnt his books rather than have his books burn him
was responding to genuine criticism. (74) The
vernacular Bible and the vernacular discussion of
doctrine broke new ground, but despite this there was
little in the way of a literary tradition independent of orthodoxy. Ideas could be generated in
one and come to fruition in the other. Whole books

could slide from one to the other, or be so corrupted
by interpolation and development as to lose sight of
their origin. 'The Poor Caitif' and 'Dives and
Pauper' cannot be assigned exclusively to either
tradition. The orthodox origin of Richard
Ullerston's defence of Bible translation was
obscured and finally lost in the Lollard form in
which it circulated. (75) Other orthodox works such
as the 'Ancrene Riwle' or 'Rolle's Psalter' underwent
Lollard modification. By condemning the Wycliffite
translation of the Bible in 1407 the church left
these waters very muddy indeed. Did readers of it
become tainted with heresy? Henry VI and Richard III
do not seem to have thought so, nor did Thomas
Eborall, a mid-fifteenth-century expert on heresy,
who inscribed a copy with a kind of <u>nihil obstat</u> for
a worried owner. (76) Nevertheless possession of a
Wycliffite Bible or part of it, continued to be used
as damning evidence up to its supercession by
Tyndale. The transmission of the sermon cycle,
Lollardy's other great literary achievement, was in
contrast exceptionally straightforward, with few
intrusions from, or into, other collections. Yet here
its very basis was the orthodox church year and
lectionary, and it was in this sense thoroughly
conservative. (77) The difficulties and misunder-
standings to which this process could give rise -
both from church authorities then and historians now
- can be illustrated by the case of William Pottier.
Pottier was accused in 1511 of affirming that there
were six gods. He is not however therefore to be
assigned to the lunatic fringe of Lollardy as a
superficial reading of the source might suggest.
Pottier's six gods were: the Trinity (3), the devil,
the priest's concubine, and that which a man setteth
his mind most upon. (78) He had almost certainly
derived this idea from a passage in one of the
ubiquitous Lollard tracts on the Ten Commandments. In
its commentary on the first commandment the tract
asks 'who breaketh the first commandment?' and gives
the answer 'proud men, worldly men, and fleshly men'.
Proud men are those who 'maken the devil their god',
fleshly men are those who 'maken their womb their
god' (this having connotations of both gluttony and
lust), and worldly men are those who 'maken worldly
goods their god'. These categories exactly
correspond to Pottier's second three. The tract
derived from a work which gave the same three sorts
of offenders against the first commandment,
prefacing them with the remark that 'men shoulden wit
that what manner thing that a man loveth most, he

18

maketh his god'. (79) However this Lollard's work was not original, but was an expansion of a pre-existing tract. Its textual history is most obscure, but seems to take in the 'Catechism' of John de Greystoke, Archbishop Thoresby's 'Ordinances' of 1357, and Archbishop John Pecham's 'Ignorantia Sacerdotum' which had propagated the programme outlined by the Council of Lambeth in 1281. This in turn was the first effective English response to the educational demands set out by the Fourth Lateran Council in 1215 called by Innocent III. (80) William Pottier, who was associated with the group who met with William Sweeting in the fields outside Chelsea, was almost certainly unaware of the long literary tangle stretching over three hundred years of reforming writings, both orthodox and heterodox, which lay behind his ideas. It was often the Lollard context which made them objectionable. This corruption or adaptation was common at the end of the fourteenth and the beginning of the fifteenth century. Lollard writers would interpolate passages into orthodox works leaving the basic structure unchanged and so surreptitiously give their views currency in orthodox circles. The Lollard wit who corrupted Greystoke's 'Catechism' added an indulgence of forty days to all who should learn it. Two points emerge. First, Lollards could be asked to abjure views which were in origin orthodox, but whose context or mode of expression rendered them suspicious. Secondly, if the Lollard corruption of texts circulated heterodox ideas among the orthodox, it also circulated orthodox ideas among the heterodox. (81)

Often it was Lollardy's use and interpretation of its literary tradition which was most alien, as can be seen in its use of the Bible. Lollardy did not use its possession of the vernacular Bible to revise the inner canon of books which had pre-eminence in the liturgy and theology of contemporary orthodoxy. This consisted of Genesis and Exodus, the Psalms, and the Gospels and Epistles, with centrality being accorded to the passion narrative. These are also the books most often in the possession of, or cited by, Lollards, although Revelation exercised a lure for some as it did in orthodox circles. It seems striking that later Lollards seem not to have known of, nor appropriated to their own use, the Old Testament prophetic indictments of image-making and of ceremonial religion as against righteousness and law observance which would have well suited their purposes. It was the law, both in the form of the Ten Commandments in the Old Testament and the Sermon on the Mount in the New, which was vested with new importance. As has been seen, tracts on the Ten Commandments were widely disseminated. The gospels which are most often encountered are Luke and Matthew, the two in which the Sermon on the Mount occurs, and of these, Matthew, the most anti-Pharisaic of the gospels, seems to have been most popular. Moreover, as is well-known, among the epistles it was the practical pieties of James which held most appeal.

If law enjoyed an elevated position among Lollards, the whole sacramental backdrop to Catholic orthodoxy was jettisoned. The bread and wine remained bread and wine; blessings and indulgences were of no effect; saints and priests were redundant as intercessors; the paraphernalia of Catholic devotion – processions, fasts, images, candles, pilgrimages – were at best 'not profitable for a man'; and so forth. Such denials are prominent in depositions because they were what was of most interest to the court, and of most need of record. However, underlying these denials was often an attempt to re-invest them in meaning, or to filch from them their rich associations of religious value and commitment and to re-apply them to those spiritual themes and neighbourly charities which lay at the heart of Lollard concern. The result was the true-false polarity which recurs in Lollard thought and writing. (82) True fasting for example was to fast from sin. Thomas Geoffrey maintained that true pilgrimage was barefoot to go and visit the poor, the weak, and the sick; for they are the true images of God. (83)

Thomas Beele of Henley (84) taught:

> Christ feedeth, and fast nourisheth his church with his own precious body, that is, the bread of life coming down from heaven: that is the worthy word that is worthily received, and joined unto man, to be in one body with him. Sooth it is, that they may not be parted: This is the wisely deeming of the holy sacrament, Christ's own body: this is not received by chewing teeth, but by hearing with ears, and understanding with your soul, and wisely working thereafter. (85)

It is tempting here to see the word usurping the place of the sacraments, and the law that of the hierarchy: the word underwrites the law, as the sacraments did the priesthood. If this is over schematic it is at least an antidote to the view of

Lollardy as no more than a conglomeration of
attitudes. (86)
     Specific and unique theological ideas were
developed and articulated. Thomas Man had spent time
in Henley almost certainly with Beele or his pupils,
and echoed some of his thoughts. He affirmed 'the
word of God and God to be all one, and that he that
worthily receiveth the word of God, receiveth God'.
He maintained an original and ingenious view of the
sacrament of the altar. He argued that 'the Father of
Heaven was the altar, and the second person the
sacrament; and that upon the Ascension Day the
sacrament ascended unto the altar, and there abideth
still'. (87) Here the mass becomes a memorial not of
Christ's sacrifice but of his ascension enacted in
the priestly gestures of the mass. The sting of this
interpretation is in the tail: 'and there abideth
still'. It was a common argument among Lollards that
Christ could not be corporally present in the mass
because his physical presence had departed at the
ascension and that he had said that he had been once
in sinners' hands and would come there no more. The
very actions of the mass were made arguments against
transubstantiation. (88)
     Did these communities and their beliefs find
ritual expression? The church courts do not seem to
have been much interested whether they did or not. It
would however have been surprising for groups to have
met for religious purposes with some regularity over
a period of time without evolving some ritual
structuring of these occasions. Some services are
known about. Brief descriptions exist of two Lollard
weddings. (89) A liturgical fragment is perhaps
preserved in the Sweeting-Brewster trial. At the
conventicle in the Chelsea fields James Brewster
would say, 'Now the son of the living God help us.'
To which Sweeting would reply, 'Now Almighty God so
do.' John Hacker could recite the words of
institution, and although it occurs in the context of
a discussion about transubstantiation, the words may
have been employed ritually: 'Christ made his Maundy,
and said, '"Take this bread, eat it: this is my body.
Take this wine, drink it; this is my blood"'. (90)
There are a number of possible allusions to Lollard
masses, but here, perhaps more than anywhere,
Lollards keep their secrets. (91)
     In the same week in 1521 that the trials of
Hacker and the other Chiltern Lollards opened in
Lincoln, mass ceased in the Augustinian cloister at
Wittenberg. (92) Luther had already been challenged
by Aleander, 'Has the Catholic church been dead for a

21

thousand years to be revived only by Martin?' and
been pressed to endorse the errors of Wyclif and
Huss. (93) Eck had made the same point against him at
Worms earlier in the year. (94) Bernard of Luxembourg
in his 'Catalogus haereticorum' of 1522 saw Wyclif as
a forerunner of Luther. (95) The challenge was
accepted. Wyclif's 'Trialogus' was printed in Worms
in 1525 with Wyclif commended as a 'true and pious
witness of Christ', and an abridged version of the
'Opus Arduum', a commentary on Revelation believed to
be by Wyclif but perhaps by Nicholas Hereford, was
printed at Wittenberg in 1528. (96) In the same
period at Cambridge the first English reformers began
to establish tentative links with Lollards, and
Lollards with them. Bilney preached in Lollard areas
in East Anglia. Hacker was so taken with Bilney's
preaching that he said he would go twenty miles to
hear him. (97) John Pykas probably accompanying him,
found Bilney's sermon 'most ghostly'. (98) Robert
Forman, President of Queens', left Cambridge to
become rector of All Hallows Honey Lane, and to turn
his rectory into a storehouse and distribution point
for reforming literature. From there books, and
especially Tyndale's New Testament, were parcelled
up and sent to Thomas Matthew's and other
conventicles, in East Anglia, or up to the growing
colony of Lutherans in Oxford centred on Cardinal
College. Part of this chain was John Gough who had
published both the General Prologue of the Wycliffite
Bible and the Lollard tract 'Jack Upland' by 1541.
(99) Indeed the reformers' consciousness of what
might be called this new tradition is most visible in
the publishing programme adopted by Tyndale,
Coverdale (100), Joye, Crowley, Bale, and others.
(101)

The initiative was not all on one side.
Chiltern Lollards, still incorrigible even after
Longland's persecution, met at Hitchenden to hear a
report from Nicholas Field of London of events in
Germany. (102) Thomas Lound, a priest who had been
with Luther in Wittenberg for two years, instructed
John Ryburn, another Chiltern Lollard. The amalgam of
ideas showed in Ryburn's confession before Longland
in 1530: 'The blood of our Lord Jesus Christ hath
made satisfaction for all ill deeds that were done,
or should be done; and therefore,' he added, 'it was
no need to go on pilgrimage.' Ryburn also advocated
liturgical reform, but was conscious of continuity.
After he described to his sister how he wished to see
elevation done away with, she said, 'And what service
shall we have then?' to which he replied, 'That

service that we have now.' (103) Thomas Harding, a
stalwart of the Amersham Lollards for many years, was
found on his arrest in 1532 to possess Tyndale's The
Obedience of a Christian Man, The Practice of
Prelates, and his English New Testament, as well as
Fish's 'Sum of Scripture'. (104) Thomas Philips of
London was a close associate of Hacker from his
Chiltern days. Deposed against in 1528, he was
arrested by Stokesley in 1530 and kept in the Tower.
After complex legal battles he perhaps made a virtue
of necessity and became a gaoler there. In this
position he was able to help incarcerated reformers
including John Frith. (105) Philips may have been
associated with Frith's fatal manuscript treatise on
the mass addressed to someone who 'for his
commendable conversation and sober behaviour, might
be better a bishop than many that wear mitres' and
who knew already the 'spiritual and necessary eating
and drinking of his body and blood, which is not
received with the teeth and belly, but with the ears
and faith'. (106) The closeness of Frith's language
here to that of Thomas Beele is inescapable. Philips
for his part assimilated reformation theology.
Making his will in 1541, he 'trust(ed) to be saved
only by the merits of the passion shedding of the
blessed blood of our saviour Jesus Christ'. (107)
John Tyball offers perhaps the best example. Sometime
in the early or mid 1520s he moved from Colchester to
Steeple Bumpstead. Not content to establish a small
heretical conventicle, he aimed at the whole parish.
To this end he set about the conversion of the parish
priest. The first two rapidly left, but he made
headway with the third, Richard Foxe. At this point
he was joined by Thomas Hilles, a former servant of
the Witham Lollard Christopher Raven. In September
1526 Tyball and Thomas Hilles travelled to see Robert
Barnes, then under house arrest at the Friars
Augustine in London. Tyball and Hilles desired Barnes
'that they might be acquainted with him; because they
had heard that he was a good man; and because they
would have his counsel in the New Testament'. They
told him of their attempts to convert their priest,
and Barnes wrote Foxe a letter and sold Tyball and
Hilles two copies of Tyndales's New Testament.
Returning to Steeple Bumpstead Tyball bombarded Foxe
with his opinions now backed up by his letter from
Barnes, and biblical and other Lollard literature. In
time he brought Foxe to his 'learning and opinions',
and early in 1527 took Foxe off on a tour of the
Lollard communities in Essex. Miles Coverdale
subsequently arrived to preach Lent sermons; and

Tyball and another of his converts, Thomas Hempsted, were elected churchwardens. Secrecy could not be maintained in the face of such success and the following year Tyball and his associates were arrested in Tunstall's sweep of his diocese for heresy. Tyball's examination reveals him as a thoughtful person and unexpectedly eclectic in his ideas. When he quoted the Bible from memory it was the Tyndale version which came to his mind. He was banished from Steeple Bumpstead and gravitated to London where he fell in with John Frith shortly before the latter's arrest, after which he disappears from notice. (108)

However, there remains something insubstantial about Lollardy on the eve of the reformation. It lacked the weight to make an appeal beyond the limited circles of those who were disillusioned with the church or sceptical of its claims or who felt rejected by it, or who sought a faith verbally rather than symbolically expressed. There had been no significant Lollard literary output for nearly a century, and even the copying of manuscripts was reduced to a small fraction of what it had been in Lollardy's heyday.The reformation brought print and a compelling soteriology, and the Lollards embraced both. There seems to have been little of the reluctance of future generations to endorse a new Bible translation 'of more cleaner English' as Barnes described it to Tyball. Acceptance of the reformation may have been helped too by Lollard prophecies which looked forward to a climactic time when the hegemony of the clergy would be overthrown. (109) Many Lollards may have felt, like Simeon and Anna, that they had lived to see the long awaited hour of fulfilment. (110)

For the reformers, the discovery that there were after all prophets in Israel who had not bowed the knee (111) was an important one, both in the context of the growing propaganda battle and of their own interpretation of their experiences. Before the burning of Thomas Hitton in 1530 most of the reformers' references to historical persecution - such as John Clerk's vivid evocation of what awaited him to the young Anthony Dalaber - were probably derived from the Lollard persecutions of 1511 and 1521. When in 1528 Thomas Davy wrote to his fellow Cranbrook merchant Richard Harman, Tyndale's host in Antwerp, of the tribulation of God's children, he was drawing on a shared memory of a persecution they had both witnessed. (112) There were doctrinal continuities, supremely in the importance of the word

24

over and against both the sacraments and other
traditional forms of devotion. However Luther's view
of the law was very different from that of the
Chiltern Lollards, as their varying estimates of the
Epistle of James bear witness. This could probably be
glossed over by emphasising the redundancy of the
ceremonial law and the priority over it of practical
charity and social justice. When however in Mary's
reign John Bradford contended with his free-willer
fellow-prisoners, it may well have been that this
divide was opening up again. (113) Nevertheless, in
the 1520s and 1530s it was perceptions which were
most important and the roles which each could fulfil
for the other. Experience was constantly
reinterpreted and restructured in biblical terms,
and for each there were biblical prototypes. In each
too was an element of the Prester John caste of mind:
the unknown hidden faithful surrounded by hostility;
and the unexpected aid which would bring help and
salvation from beyond the horizon.

Notes
    1. Michael Drayton, 'The Works of Michael
Drayton', (ed.) J. William Hebal (B. Blackwell,
Oxford for Shakespeare Head Press, 1961), vol. 1,
p.400. The work was a collaborative riposte to the
Oldcastle-Falstaff portrait in Shakespeare's <u>Henry
IV Part 1</u>. See Rudolph Fiehler, 'How Oldcastle became
Falstaff', <u>Modern Language Quarterly</u>, vol. 16
(1955), pp.16-28. The note in Jonathan Rittenhouse
(ed.), <u>A Critical Edition of 'I Sir John Oldcastle'</u>
(Garland, New York, 1984), p.116 compounds the
anachronism of which it complains.
    2. As will 'puritan' and 'fundamentalist'.
Some Lollards were very suspicious of the arts in
religion, and others were literalist in their reading
of the Bible, but both have to be seen in their late
medieval context. 'Puritan' and 'fundamentalist'
conjure up other Christian traditions.
    3. John F. Davis, 'Lollard Survival and the
Textile Industry in the South-East of England' in
<u>Studies in Church History</u> (E.J. Brill, Leiden, 1966),
vol. 3, pp.191-201.
    4. Susan E. Brigden, 'The Early Reformation
in London, 1520-1547: The Conflict in the Parishes'
(unpublished Ph.D. Thesis, University of Cambridge
1979), pp.13, 23-6.
    5. <u>The Great Chronicle of London</u>, ed. A.H.
Thomas and I.D. Thornley (Alan Sutton, Gloucester
1983), p.252.

6.   John Foxe, The Acts and Monuments, ed. G. Townsend (London, 1843–1849), vol. 4, p.228. Barrett had died in the year of the magna abjurata. His benefactions and charitable bequests to the Goldsmiths' Company were still remembered in the eighteenth century. See William Herbert, The History of The Twelve Great Livery Companies of London (London, 1836), vol. 2, p.273.

7.   Foxe, vol. 4, pp.229–30, 234, 236, 237, 239.

8.   The Certificate of Musters for Buckinghamshire in 1522, ed. A.C. Chibnall, Historical Manuscripts Commission Joint Publications Series, 18 and Buckinghamshire Record Society 17. (H.M.S.O., London, 1973). Subsidy Roll for the County of Buckingham anno 1524, ed. A.C. Chibnall and A. Vere Woodman, Bucks. Rec. Soc., 8. (1950). The best introduction to this group based on records in Foxe is in Claire Cross, Church and People 1450–1660 (Fontana, N.p., 1976), pp.32–35. See also W.H. Summers, The Lollards of the Chiltern Hills (Francis Griffiths, London, 1906).

9.   Foxe, vol. 4, p.226. Feeling was fuelled by local pride and a resentment at external interference. Roger Squire said of Holmes 'This is one of them that make all this business in our town with the Bishop. I pray God tear all the bones of him.'

10.   Foxe, vol. 4, p.227.

11.   Foxe, vol. 4, pp.219–240. Cf. the similar figures for late seventeenth century dissent in, for example, Alan Everitt, 'Non-conformity in Country Parishes' in Joan Thirsk (ed.), Land, Church and People (British Agricultural Society, Reading, 1970), pp.180, 186–8.

12.   It can be shown however that there were Amersham Lollards who fell into this lowest category.

13.   Calculated from Amersham Lollards named in Foxe, Vol. 4, pp.219–40, correlated with sources cited in note 8.

14.   John Fines, 'Heresy Trials in the Diocese of Coventry and Lichfield, 1511–12' in Journal of Ecclesiastical History, vol. 14 (1963), pp.164–74; and Imogen Luxton, 'The Lichfield Court Book: a Postscript' in Bulletin of the Institute of Historical Research, vol. 44 (1971), pp.120–5.

15.   J. Strype, Ecclesiastical Memorials (Oxford, 1822), 2, no. 22; Jennifer C. Ward, 'The Reformation in Colchester, 1528–1558', in Essex Archaeology and History: Transactions of the Essex Archaeological Society 3rd ser., vol. 15 (1983),

p.85.
16. Foxe, vol. 5, pp.251-3; A.G. Dickens, Lollards and Protestants in the Diocese of York 1509-1558, pp.145-6 (OUP for University of Hull, London, 1959); J.F. Mozley, John Foxe and his Book (SPCK, London, 1940), p.21; Oath Book or Red Parchment Book of Colchester, (ed.) W.G. Benham (Colchester Essex County Standard 1907), pp.143, 145.
17. J.J. Scarisbrick, The Reformation and the English People (Blackwell, Oxford, 1984), pp.6, 46.
18. David Zaret, The Heavenly Contract: Ideology and Organization in Pre-Revolutionary Puritanism (University of Chicago Press, Chicago, 1985), p.49.
19. K.B. McFarlane, John Wyclif and the Beginnings of English Nonconformity (London, 1952) chapter 6; 'Lollardy and Sedition, 1381-1431' in M. Aston, Lollards and Reformers; Images and literacy in late medieval England (Hambledon, London, 1984), pp.1-47.
20. See for example, Heresy Trials in the Diocese of Norwich 1428-31, ed. Norman P. Tanner, Camden Soc., 4th ser., vol. 20 (Royal Historical Society, London, 1977), pp.90, 99.
21. K.B. McFarlane, Lancastrian Kings and Lollard Knights (Oxford University Press, Oxford, 1972), pp.162, 167-8, 175.
22. Ibid., part 2, chapter 6; Public Record Office, P.C.C. (Prerogative Court of Canterbury) 14 Rous.
23. J.S. Roskell, Parliament and Politics in Late Medieval England (Hambledon, London 1983), pp.383-96. Margery died in 1502 (Calendar of Inquisitions Post Mortem, Henry VII., (2 vols., HMSO, London, 1878 8. 19/5) ll., 629,) not 1526 (Roskell, vol. 3, p.396).
24. Foxe, vol. 4, pp.180, 214-15; Cal. Inq. P.M. Hen. VII, vol. 1, 278; S.A.A. Majendie, Some Account of the Family of De Vere (Tindall, Chelmsford, 1907), p.34.
25. John Bale, Scriptorium Maioris Brytanniae Catalogus, vol. 1, p.715 (Basle, 1557). But cf. E.G. Rupp, Studies in the Making of the English Protestant Tradition (CUP, Cambridge 1966), p.68, n.1, where it is suggested that Bale's assertion was made without evidence.
26. Great Chronicle, p.331.
27. Victoria County History of the Counties of England, 'Essex' (9 vols, Institute of Historical Research, London, 1903-83). vol. 2, pp.184-5.
28. Foxe, vol. 4, pp.180, 214-15. Arrested at

the same time were Lewis John and his wife Joan, Lewis being a recurrent personal name in the John alias FitzLewis family.

29. Brass in Stadhampton Church. Both The Genealogist, n.s., vol. 29, p.186 quoting B.L. Stowe MS 714 and Harl. MS. 1, 357, and Publications of the Harleian Society (117 vols, privately printed, London, 1869-1977: new series, 4 vols, London 1977-85), vol. 5, pp.195-6, 301-2, incorrectly give her maiden name as Barentine, or Hall. By this marriage she was an ancestor of the Wilmot earls of Rochester. See Oswald Baron, 'The Wild Wilmots', in The Ancestor, no.11, pp.1-25.

30. At her subsequent examination views on the sacrament of the altar were not sought, or if sought not recorded, or if recorded not transcribed by Foxe.

31. Sir William Barentine and probably his second wife Anne Eaton, widow of Richard Grey, sheriff of London (Notes and Queries, vol. 183, pp.190-192, 350). She died in late 1522 (Frederick George Lee, History and Antiquities of the Church ... of Thame (London, 1883), p.66). He remarried a great niece of Margery Wood (Sussex Archaeological Collections, vol. 3 (1850), pp.96-7). Thomas Doyly, nephew and namesake of her third husband, was to marry a daughter of the house, Alice Barentine. This Alice has sometimes been confused with the Lollard, as in the Grant of Arms cited in note 37.

32. Foxe, vol. 4, pp.239-40.

33. Public Record Office, C1/516/42.

34. The Dictionary of National Biography, Leslie Stephen and Sidney Lee (eds.) (21 vols, Smith, Elder and Co., London, 1908-9), Art. John London. London was installed as a prebendary of Lincoln in 1522, probably the year of Alice's examination.

35. Public Record Office, C1/516/42; S.P. 1/157-158 = Letters and papers ... of the reign of Henry VIII (ed.) J.S. Brewer and R.H. Brodie (HMSO, London, 1920-), vol. 4, 3486.

36. The Gates copy is J.Forshall and F. Madden, The Holy Bible ... in the earliest English versions (Oxford University Press, Oxford, 1850), no. 151 (Dubl. A.1.10). See Collectanea Topographica et Genealogica (8 vols, John Bowyer Nichols and Son, London, 1834-43), vol. 1, p.396; Margaret Deanesly, The Lollard Bible and other Medieval Biblical Versions (CUP, Cambridge 1920), pp.366-7. Sven L. Fristedt argues strongly against Purvey's ownership in The Wycliffite Bible, Part I (Stockholm Studies in English 4, Stockholm, Almquist 1953), pp.119-22, and plates 5 and 14. The De Vere copy is in Forshall and

Madden, <u>Holy Bible</u>, no. 176 and subsequently belonged
to the Doyly family.
37. Foxe, vol. 4, p.226.
38. Foxe, vol. 4, p.236.
39. Alice was wife of the future martyr William
Harding.
40. Foxe, vol. 4, p.227-8.
41. Foxe, vol. 4, p.237; Sir Robert Atkyns, <u>The
Ancient   and   Present   State   of   Gloucestershire</u>
(Bowyer, London, 1712), p.840.
42. In   contrast   to   accusations   of   occult
practices, middle aged or elderly women seem to have
been   least   at   risk   from   heresy   proceedings,
especially in this period. This contrasts with their
undoubted importance. See Aston, p.50 n.3; and Claire
Cross   '"Great   reasoners   in   scripture":   the
activities of women Lollards 1380-1530' in Derek
Baker   (ed.),   <u>Medieval Women</u>   (Blackwell,   Oxford,
1978), pp.359-80.
43. L.P., vol. 4, 4029, 4128, 4175, 4850.
44. J.A.F. Thompson, <u>The Later Lollards, 1414-
1520</u> (OUP, London, 1965), pp.90-1. His wife's cousin,
James Morden, was martyred in 1522.
45. Thompson, <u>Later Lollards</u>, p.137.
46. John Strype, <u>Ecclesiastical Memorials</u> (3
vols, Clarendon Press, Oxford, 1820-40), vol. 1, 2,
p.17 (Letters and Papers, vol. 4, no. 4218).
47. Foxe, vol. 4, pp.210-11.
48. Foxe, vol. 4, p.222.
49. Foxe, vol. 4, p.233.
50. They were an English version of Luther's <u>De
Libertate   Christiana</u>   which   masqueraded   as   by
Augustine, and an <u>Exposition upon the Pater Noster</u> as
by Hilary. Monmouth was accused of having had the
latter translated from an original by Luther, but
elsewhere he describes it as 'an old book', and it
does seem more likely to have been one of the Lollard
works of that name. John Strype, <u>Ecclesiastical
Memorials</u> (Oxford, 1822), i, 1, p.489; i, 2. p.364.
51. Foxe, vol. 4, p.222.
52. Cf. Agnes Squire: 'Men do say, I was
abjured; it may well be a napkin for my nose, but I
will never be ashamed of it.' Foxe, vol. 4, p.227.
The Squires were an outspoken family, see note 9.
53. The relaxation may have been routine,
occurring as it did with others (<u>An Episcopal Court
Book   for   the   Diocese   of   Lincoln 1514-1520</u>,   ed.
Margaret Bowker, Lincoln Record Society, no. 61,
pp.15-17).   There   is   however   the   intriguing
possibility that the object of his pilgrimage was
changed to Great Missenden by those who did not want

to see him back in Lincoln.

54.   Foxe, vol. 4, p.232.

55.   Foxe, vol. 4, pp.225-6.

56.   J. Fines, 'Heresy trials', p.167.

57.   E.g. Thomas Clerk 'it is a holy thing' (Foxe, vol. 4, p.233); and Richard Collins 'a certain figurative thing of Christ in bread' (Foxe, vol. 4, p.235).

58.   Foxe, vol. 4, p.224.

59.   In 1540 when Barwick curate Thomas Mettingham was discussing the repair of the church, James Hardcastell told him 'that there was no thing in the church that would do him good, but God above'. Quoted in A.G. Dickens, Lollards and Protestants, in the Diocese of York, 1509-1558, p.46.

60.   Selections from English Wycliffite Writings, ed. Anne Hudson (CUP, Cambridge, 1978), p.116.

61.   Foxe, vol. 4, p.224.

62.   Foxe, vol. 4, p.228.

63.   For example by Richard Fox (Letters and Papers, vol. 4, 4545) and John Pykas (Letters and Papers, vol. 4, 4029).

64.   Hudson, Selections, p.116.

65.   Foxe, vol. 4, p.224-5. For the very different treatment accorded the same subject by an orthodox writer, Nicholas Love, appealing to much the same constituency of the literate layman, see Janel M. Mueller, The Native Tongue and the Word: Developments in English Prose Style 1380-1580 (University of Chicago Press, Chicago, 1984), pp.77-8.

66.   "Friar Daw's Reply" 1.33, in Jack Upland, Friar Daw's Reply, and Upland's Rejoinder, ed. P.L. Heyworth (OUP, London, 1968), p.74.

67.   For an analysis of an earlier Lollard group see 'William White's Lollard Followers' in Aston M., Lollards and reformers: images of literacy in late medieval England (Hambledon Press, London, 1984), pp.71-100. The principles behind this discussion are drawn from the General Prologue to the Wycliffite Bible, providing evidence of the continuing vitality of the literary tradition, Forshall and Madden, vol. 1, p.3.

68.   L.P. vol. 4, 4029, 4175.

69.   The intellectual compromises behind the notion of different Christian denominations came only with the recognition of an apparently irreparable breach in unity. The most interesting perspective is gained perhaps by viewing Lollardy as a special type of the late medieval fraternity.

70.   J.F. Davis has recently argued that

Lollardy did have such an organisation, and cites three examples: the London Christian Brethren, Mendlesham in Suffolk in 1531, and Salisbury in 1541. In each case the evidence is not conclusive. It is not clear that the London Brethren were not a response to the problems of the dissemination of reformation literature. The Mendlesham evidence suggests a political initiative springing from social discontent, although there is an heretical dimension. There is no evidence for the L.P. date of 1531. The Salisbury association to finance reforming literature is too late not to have been influenced in one way or another by the reformation. See J.F. Davis, 'Lollardy and the Reformation', in <u>Archiv für Reformationsgeschichte</u>, vol. 73 (1982), pp.217-36.

71. Cf. the hierarchic table of Lollards in the Diocese of Norwich in 1428 in Aston, <u>Lollards</u>, p.83 and 'tiers of importance' p.99.

72. Foxe, vol. 4, p.226.

73. See for example the divergent views on images analysed in 'Lollards and Images' in Aston, <u>Lollards</u>, pp.135-92, and the assessment of the impact of William White on the transmission of Lollard ideas in 'William White's Lollard Followers', ibid., pp.71-100.

74. The Lollard was the physician John Phip. On the importance of books see 'Lollardy and Literacy', in Aston, <u>Lollards</u>, pp.193-217, esp. pp.200-1.

75. See 'The Debate on Bible Translation, Oxford 1401', in Hudson, <u>Lollards and their books</u> (Hambledon, London, 1985), pp.67-84 esp. pp.77-80, 83.

76. Forshall and Madden, no. 168. The inscription must post-date 1443 when Eborall was a Doctor of Theology. He took a leading part in the prosecution of Pecock (V.H.H. Green, <u>Bishops Reginald Pecock: A Study in Ecclesiastical History and Thought</u> (Cambridge University Press, Cambridge, 1945), p.38), and was commissioned to investigate the heresies of Andrew Tey or Tye (Calendar of Patent Rolls, Henry VI (6 vols, HMSO, London, 1901-8), Vol. 5, 1446-1452, p.584).

77. Anne Hudson ed. <u>English Wycliffite Sermons</u> (OUP, Oxford 1983), pp.191, 195 and n.19.

78. Foxe, vol. 4, p.175.

79. Thomas Arnold, <u>Select English Works of John Wyclif</u> (OUP, Oxford, 1871), vol. 3, p.83.

80. A.L. Kellog and Ernest W. Talbert, 'The Wycliffite "Pater Noster" and "Ten Commandments", with special reference to English MSS. 85 and 90 in the John Rylands Library', in <u>Bulletin of the John</u>

Rylands Library, vol. 42, no. 2 (March 1960), pp.345-58, 367-77; The Lay Folks Catechism, ed. T.F. Simmons and H.E. Nolloth (EETS, orig. ser., 118); but see also Aston, Lollards, p.217, n.81 and Hudson, Lollards, p.162, n.81.

81. See Aston, Lollards, pp.208-12. Hudson, Lollards, p.21 lists the authorities cited in the Lollard Floretum: Augustine, Ambrose, Jerome, Gregory, Basil, Chrysostom, Gregory Nazianzen, Origen, Cyprian, Leo, Bede, Cassian, Cassiodorus, Peter Lombard, Lyra, Bernard, Hugh and Richard of St. Victor, Peter Comestor, William of St Amour, Hugh of St Cher, Peter of Blois, Holcot, Aquinas, FitzRalph, Grosseteste, Higden, Aristotle, Seneca, and Boethius, as well as writers on the Canon Law. For a similar list cited in the 'Opus Arduum' see ibid., pp.48-9.

82. Cf. 'A Lollard Sect Vocabulary?' in Hudson, Lollards, pp.165-80, esp. p.166-7.

83. Foxe, Vol. 4, pp.229-30. The idea of the poor as the images of God was an old one. See Aston, Lollards, pp.155-61.

84. Henley has been underestimated as a centre of heresy. Longland also came from the town, so that his animosity to Lollardy may have roots in his past.

85. Foxe, vol. 4, p.205. Similar views were expressed in 1499 by John Whitehorne, rector of Letcombe Bassett. See Claude Jenkins, 'Cardinal Morton's Register' in R.W. Seton-Watson (ed.), Tudor Studies (Longmans Green, London, 1924), p.48.

86. A common assertion deriving from Thomson, Later Lollards, p.239 where however the statement is much qualified. Cf. Aston, Lollards, pp.9, 13, 212-13. There is virtually no evidence for the contention (J.J. Scarisbrick, The Reformation and the English People (Blackwell, Oxford, 1984)), that Chiltern Lollardy was 'deep rooted upland semi-paganism' (p.6) and not many would share the difficulty of distinguishing the words of Thomas Beele or Agnes Ashford 'from pre-Christian survivals' (p.46).

87. Foxe, vol. 4, p.208.

88. This argument persisted and was felt by some still to need refutation even after the Reformation. See Peter Brooks, Thomas Cranmer's Doctrine of the Eucharist (Macmillan, London, 1965), pp.119-20. On the importance of visual interpretation of these gestures see 'Devotional Literacy' in Aston, pp.101-33, esp. pp.121-22. According to Langforde's 'Meditations in the time of the Mass' (J. Wickham Legg, ed., Tracts on the Mass (Henry Bradshaw Soc. London, 1904), vol. 27, p.28), thoughts of the

Ascension should be provoked at the conclusion of the
mass with the words 'Ite missa est', when the priest
stands in the midst of the altar and blesses the
people, who, Langforde recommends, should 'call to
... remembrance ... how our saviour standing in the
midst of his disciplines at the Mount of Olives,
blessing them did ascend to heaven, where he is now
resident, and ever more shall be, sitting on the
right hand of his father'. This was composed probably
a few years before these proceedings.

89. Foxe, vol. 4, pp.228, 237.
90. Foxe, vol. 4, p.239.
91. See 'A Lollard Mass' in Hudson, Lollards,
pp.111-23; Aston, Lollards, pp.49-70 (celebration by
women) and p.87; John Fines, 'Heresy trials', p.166.
92. Roland H. Bainton, Here I Stand: A Life of
Martin Luther (Hodder and Stoughton, London, 1951),
p.203.
93. Ibid., p.173.
94. Ibid., p.185.
95. Vaclav Mudroch, The Wyclif Tradition, ed.
Albert Compton Reeves (Ohio University Press,
Athens, Ohio, 1979), p.7.
96. Aston, Lollards, p.244. On the Opus Arduum
see Anne Hudson, 'A Neglected Wycliffite Text', in
Hudson, Lollards pp.43-65, esp. p.46; and Aston,
Lollards, pp.226-7.
97. Thomas More, A Dialogue Concerning
Heresies, vol. 1, pp.268-9 ed. Thomas M. C. Lawler,
Germain Marchadour and Richard C. Marius (The Yale
Edition of the Complete Works of St Thomas More, vol.
6, New Haven and Yale University Press, London,
1981). More does not name Hacker but there can be
little doubt he is the heretic concerned.
98. L.P., vol. 4, 4029.
99. Aston, Lollards, p.229.
100. In the 1540s Coverdale produced two
editions of 'Wyclif's Wicket', a work which he would
have encountered on his visit to Steeple Bumpstead in
1528 if he had not done so before.
101. This is the subject of 'Lollardy and the
Reformation: Survival or Revival?' in Aston,
Lollards, pp.119-242; and '"No Newe Thynge": The
Printing of Medieval Texts in the Early Reformation
Period', in Hudson, Lollards, pp.227-48.
102. Foxe, vol. 4, p.584.
103. Foxe, vol. 4, p.583.
104. Gwendolen E. Wharhirst, 'The Reformation
in the Diocese of Lincoln as illustrated by the Life
and Work of Bishop Longland (1521-1547)' in
Lincolnshire Architectural and Archaeological

Society Reports and Papers, new ser., vol. 1, part 2,
pp.169-70 (1939 for 1937). It is both harsh and
improbable to suggest that Foxe suppressed Harding's
possession of works by Tyndale in order to blacken
Longland's name.
    105. Thomas More, The Apology, ed. J.B. Trapp,
The Yale Edition of the Complete Works of St Thomas
More, vol. 9 (Yale University Press, New Haven and
London, 1979), pp.372-3 and refs.
    106. Thomas Russell, ed. The Works of the
English Reformers William Tyndale and John Frith
(Palmer, London, 1831), vol. 3, pp.321-2.
    107. Public Record Office, London, Prerogative
Court of Canterbury (P.C.C.), Alenger 33.
    108. John Strype, Ecclesiastical Memorials, i,
nos. 17, 20, 21; L.P. vol. 4, 4545, 4850; Foxe, vol.
5, pp.17,41.
    109. S.R. Maitland, 'The Lollards', in Eight
Essays on Various Subjects (Rivington, London,
1852), pp.203-30, 244-51.
    110. There is perhaps an echo in the epitaph in
St Peter's Church, Colchester, of George Sayer
(d.1577), who may have been associated with the
Lollard group in the town. It recites his
achievements and then continues:

O happy Sayer, not for these things alone, Which
were but mundane, vain, and vile, and fade, and
fail each one; But happier thousand-fold to live
and love those days wherein God's gospel
brightly shines to his eternal praise. Thy oft
desired wish thou doubtless didst obtain, with
Simeon to depart in peace, and life by death to
gain.

As a magistrate he had, however, sat in judgement on
heretics in Mary's reign.
    111. Discussing the Old Testament prophets,
Bullinger wrote:

But even as in those times the true prophets of
God were not acknowledged for the true prophets
of (by) the priests of Baal, but were condemned
for schismatics and heretics; even so in certain
ages past the bishops of Rome with their
conspirators did excommunicate and persecuted
godly and learned men, who preached the word of
God and called for the reformation of the
church, and many of them did they put to death
with fire and sword.

The Decades of Henry Bullinger, ed. Thomas Harding (Parker Society, Cambridge, 1852), vol. 4, p.73.
    112. The Letters of Sir John Hackett 1526-1534, ed. Elizabeth Frances Rogers (Morgantown, West Virginia University Library, West Virginia, 1971) p.176; Stadsarchief Antwerpen PK93, fo. 116r (P. Genard 'Personen te Antwerpen in de xvie eeuw, voor het "feit van religie" gerechtelijk vervolgd' in Antwerpsch Achievenblad, vol. 7, p.176) L.P., iii. (1) 492 places Harman and Davy in Cranbrook just after the persecution and both were of settled Cranbrook families. Thomas Lawney, later to preach reform through Kent and East Sussex under the patronage of Cromwell and Cranmer, was a curate there at the same time. See Jules de Launay, 'Abstracts of Cranbrook Wills ... 1396-1640' (Kent Record Collections, Canterbury, 1984), no.134.
    113. This is the theme of J.F. Davis, Heresy and Reformation in the South East of England 1520-1559 (Royal Historical Society, London, 1983); 'Joan of Kent, Lollardy, and the English Reformation' in Journal of Ecclesiastical History, vol. 32 (1982), pp.225-33, and 'Lollardy and the Reformation in England' in 'Archiv für Reformationsgeschichte, vol. 73 (1982), pp.217-36.

Chapter Two

THE GOSPEL AND THE COURT: REFORMATION UNDER HENRY VIII*

Maria Dowling

The difficulties involved in the study of
protestantism under Henry VIII are largely the fault
of the protestants themselves. The religious climate
was far from propitious for radicals, and the dangers
of the times meant that protestants rarely voiced
their beliefs. Rather, they blended into the
established church and the political system. Thus
little is known about the beliefs of individuals,
apart from martyrs and exiles. These can be said to
have opted out of the national church, choosing
either to sacrifice themselves in order to inspire
the godly or to practise and propagate their faith
independently of the faithful in England.
Accordingly they are not the subject of this study,
which is concerned with the comparatively small
number of radicals who considered themselves the
Lord's elect and worked within the visible church of
England for its conversion.

The protestants' reticence about their beliefs
certainly obscures the religious history of the
reign. Where there are indications of radical thought
- with Anne Boleyn, for example - it is hard to
discern any logical system of doctrine. The word
'protestant' is in fact anachronistic for the major
part of the reign, and as it implies acceptance of a
formulated system of belief it will not be used in
this essay. 'Evangelical' is a much more appropriate
term; it was used at the time by such people of
themselves, along with the phrase 'upholder of the
gospel'. These will be used as blanket terms to
describe men and women who give evidence of some
inclination towards radical doctrine.

Besides the difficulties caused by the
Henrician evangelicals themselves, there are two
notable confusions brought about by later
historians. Firstly, there is a tendency to assume

36

that all evangelicals were Erasmian humanists, and that all humanists were evangelicals. Secondly, the relation of religion to court politics and to the patronage system has been inaccurately assessed. (1) This study will attempt to distinguish evangelical humanists from Erasmians; discuss the evangelicals' conception of the church and of their role within it; and examine the relationship between the 'cause of the gospel' and political events and circumstances.

The term 'humanism' has always been hard to define, and the anachronistic assumption that from the beginning it had some doctrinal bias has led to false conclusions about the nature of the new learning. Humanism (as it existed in early Tudor England) may be defined as the reappraisal of religion and morality through a return to the literary sources of Christianity; that is, scripture and the Fathers, supplemented by the salutary pagan classics. These would be known through new, authoritative editions of the basic texts, for which a knowledge of the Hebrew, Greek and Latin tongues was essential. Re-examination of the Bible and patristic writings, stripped of the commentaries and glosses of the medieval schoolmen, would lead to reform of clerical and lay morality and to the end of those abuses in devotional practice which verged on superstition.

It cannot be stressed too strongly that Erasmian humanism originally anticipated no reassessment of traditional doctrine. The new learning was established as the dominant intellectual trend in England during the first decade of Henry VIII, and until the exigencies of the royal divorce obliged the King to look more kindly on his evangelical subjects, 'establishment' humanism was uniformly anti-Lutheran. From 1521 onwards heresy was prosecuted with vigour, and English scholars led by Henry himself waged polemical war on Luther and his colleagues.

Even after the divorce and breach with Rome many humanists remained conservative in doctrine. However, fear of both doctrinal innovation and the King's wrath prompted them to avoid involvement in public affairs and discussion. Sir Thomas Elyot and the Bridgettine Richard Whitford both counselled their readers to an unquestioning faith; scripture was to be treated reverently, not debated in theological terms. Thomas Lupset advised a pupil to accept traditional interpretation of the Bible for the good of both soul and body: 'Your obedience to the universal faith shall excuse you before God,

37

although it might be in a false belief; and the same
obedience shall also keep you out of trouble in this
world'. Lupset prescribed meekness and resignation:

> Leave, therefore, my good Edmund, all manner of
> meddling, and pray to God to accept your
> obedience. Pray also bitterly, that his will may
> be fulfilled in this world among us, as the
> angels fulfil it in heaven. Thus pray, and
> meddle no further. (2)

Thus nascent protestantism was by no means
identical with the Erasmianism of the early years of
Henry VIII. At the same time, however, the linguistic
skills and biblical studies of the new learning
provided evangelicals with the instruments of a new
exegesis, and even before the divorce some scholars
were drawing new doctrinal conclusions from their
examination of scripture and the Fathers. Thomas
Coventree, a monk of Evesham, gained a pension at the
dissolution so that he could continue to study the
tongues, which he had commenced, he said, to 'wipe
away the colours of all those which have painted a
papistical and sophistical divinity and mired the
clean vein of God's word with man's dreams and
fantasies'. Robert Huycke, principal of St Alban's
Hall, Oxford, was deprived by the commissary there in
1535 because, his students claimed, he had 'laboured
with all his endeavour to restore to us the old
eloquence and commendable learning, inveighing ...
against Duns ... and such other barbarous authors'.
Huycke's humanism was under fire on this occasion but
later, as a royal physician, he was suspected of
heresy. Indeed, in 1537 he told Richard Morison that
the veil of Moses had been lifted from his eyes when
he had realised that justification did not come from
the law; that is, the tradition and authority of the
church. (3)

Thus although not all humanists were
evangelical, a significant number of evangelicals
might with justice be termed humanists. The
difference between Erasmian humanism and evangelicalism is that the former was concerned to reform
abuses, the latter to refashion dogma. A humanist
might attack the clergy for pluralism, non-
residence, immorality, simony and greed; an
evangelical would condemn all these things, but also
challenge the sacramental powers of the priesthood.
The case of Robert Barnes graphically illustrates the
difference between the two ideologies. On his return
from Louvain University in the early 1520s Barnes

taught Roman literature in the Augustinian priory at Cambridge, and 'then did he read openly in the house Paul's epistles, and put by Duns and Dorbel'. These humanistic innovations brought no trouble to Barnes; he was arrested for heresy because on Christmas Eve 1525 he preached at St Edward's church on Luther's postil for the day. (4)

The paucity of knowledge about the specific beliefs of individuals is in large measure the result of the evangelicals' discretion. They had to be cautious even during the divorce, when they were most useful to the King, and after that event, when they were helping to formulate a religious settlement, because of Henry's innate doctrinal conservatism. Thus there is very little information about evangelical belief. What there is comes occasionally from unguarded passages in private letters, though these are extremely rare. The best instance of this is a letter of about 1539 from Simon Heynes, Dean of Exeter, to his patron Dr Butts. Heynes declared, 'I shall write to you as I am wont freely to speak unto you', and went on to argue at length against the desirability of the King's reaffirming transubstantiation by statute. (5) Such boldness is seldom met with.

Most of the evidence about belief comes from recantations and examinations for heresy. It should be borne in mind that these sources only show what an individual believed at a particular point in his or her life; they cannot be taken as a measure of fixed opinion. Equally, hindsight is no reliable guide. Affirmations or denials made under Edward or Mary are no indication at all of a man's position under Henry. Furthermore, there is no reason to assume that all abjurations were insincere, mere matters of expediency. Nicholas Shaxton saved himself from the flames by a timely recantation in 1546, but thereafter he never changed his attitude and died a law-abiding papist under Mary.

Absolutely nothing concrete is known about the faith of some of the key figures of the Henrician reformation. Neither Anne Boleyn, William Butts, Sir Edward Bainton nor Sir Anthony Denny left any record of what they believed during Henry's reign. Katherine Parr's book The Lamentation of a Sinner is explicitly Lutheran, but it was not published until after her death in 1548 and there is no way of knowing when it was composed. As for Thomas Cromwell, the only direct evidence he left of personal religious belief was a conventional will of 1529 in which he ordered masses to be said for his soul. (6)

The issue is also obfuscated by John Foxe, whose great work was designed to show the continuity of the true English church throughout history. Thus he was anxious to show the unity and corporate spirit of the godly under Henry VIII in order to provide a respectable ancestry for Elizabethan protestantism. Consequently he is deliberately vague about the doctrine of many individuals, leading the reader to assume that they were all <u>devotees</u> of the same sort of reformed religion.

How real was this corporate spirit, and how did evangelicals recognise and address each other? Radicals considered themselves as an elite within the visible, established church. Other Henrician Christians were derided as superstitious, deluded or hypocritical, but evangelicals were the true, real or very upholders of the gospel, favourers of God's word or followers of Christ's doctrine. In evangelical writings certain words are used almost as ciphers. 'Christ's religion' and 'true learning' mean the evangelical cause, and only evangelicals are genuine 'setters forth of the word of God'.

Naturally enough, this use of language is found most strikingly in exile writings. John Bale, for example, said that Anne Askew was 'martyred in Smithfield by the wicked synagogue of Antichrist'. John Hooper in a letter to Bullinger showed his consciousness of belonging to the chosen few within a corrupt church: 'I had begun to blaspheme God by impious worship and all manner of idolatry, following the evil ways of my forefathers, before I rightly understood what God was'; 'my father ... is so opposed to me on account of Christ's religion'; 'I am in fear, and not without reason, of those perfidious bishops, to whom nothing is more acceptable than the spilling of the blood of the godly'. He also mourned the deaths of several prominent people - including Butts, Bainton and Sir Thomas Wyatt - whom he called 'the chief upholders of the gospel':

> all these were of the privy council, and real favourers of the gospel, and promoted the glory of God to the utmost of their power. They all died of the plague and fever; so that the country is now left altogether to the bishops, and those who despise God and all true religion. (7)

Evangelicals who remained in England were equally clear about the difference between the godly leaven and the unclean lump. Thus Matthew Parker

40

upbraided a friar named Stokes:

> Peradventure some there be that will be glad and
> desire to hear you allow their old trade, and
> superstition, and papistical dregs, whereby in
> very deed ye should do some great pleasure; but
> then again ye should dishonour God.

At the same time, evangelicals praised each other for
purity of religion. Cranmer in 1534 called Latimer 'a
man of singular learning, virtuous example of living,
and sincere preaching the word of God'. Tristram
Revell in 1536 lavished praise on Anne Boleyn for her
advancement of the gospel:

> Grace and peace from God the Father and the Lord
> Jesus Christ be with you, most gracious Queen,
> most humbly and with all reverence giving lauds
> and praisings unto almighty God for your grace,
> even after the mind of Saint Paul, always in all
> my prayers for your grace, with gladness,
> because of the fellowship which your grace hath
> in the gospel, from the first day until now; and
> am surely certified, that he which hath begun a
> good work in you will also go forth with it,
> until the day of Jesus Christ, with the increase
> and establishment of his gospel, as yet but
> young and hath many enemies, to whom the Lord
> send the day of his visitation, to his honour
> and glory, and your grace to persevere with all
> diligence, as your grace have begun to promote,
> further and set forth God's word, upon the
> selfsame zeal that Saint John cried in desert,
> 'Make ready the way of the Lord'.

Similarly, though in less extravagant terms, Cranmer
thanked Cromwell for persuading the King to authorise
the reading of scripture in English:

> These shall be to give you most hearty thanks
> that any heart can think, and that in the name
> of them all which favoureth God's word, for your
> diligence at this time in procuring the King's
> highness to set forth the said God's word and
> his gospel by his grace's authority. For the
> which act, not only the King's majesty, but also
> you shall have a perpetual laud and memory of
> all them that be now, or hereafter shall be,
> God's faithful people and the favourers of his
> word.

On the other hand, Stephen Vaughan upbraided Cromwell for neglecting his evangelical duty when he promoted an unworthy man to a bishopric:

> You have lately holpen an earthly beast, a mole, and an enemy to all godly learning, into the office of his damnation, a papist, an idolater, and a fleshly priest, unto a Bishop of Chester. Remember God in all your facts. Let none affections of persons lead you to condescend or work so evil a deed. You cannot undo that you have done. Such oppress innocents when they be lift up into the dignities of the world, and sit therein as tyrants to destroy realms, people, and kingdoms. Who knoweth more of the bishops' iniquity than you? Who knoweth more of their tyranny, falsehood, and untruth against God, prince, and man than you? And should you help – in this time specially – to increase the number of wicked men where there is a lack and so great a need of good and virtuous men? Be you sorry for it. (8)

All these passages reveal the evangelicals' awareness of being a minority within the established church, whose officers might be ungodly and might persecute them. None the less, they also expressed a certain missionary zeal, a desire to convert the common people. Thus Cranmer, seeking a licence for one of the brethren to preach in Norwich diocese, declared, 'it were great pity that the diocese of Norwich should not be continued in the right knowledge of God, which is begun amongst them'. In 1538 he wrote to Cromwell in favour of John Wakefelde, his comptroller of household, who had suffered material loss by declaring for the King during the Pilgrimage of Grace and refusing to join the rebels. Cranmer praised him as

> a man of good judgment and affection towards God's word, which I have known him for the space of these twelve years always ready to promote in his country, not rashly nor seditiously, but gently and soberly, so that his own country could neither greatly hate him or love him; they could not hate him for his kindness and gentleness ... and yet they could not heartily love him, because he ever commended the knowledge of God's word, studied in himself diligently, and exhorted them unto the same ...

The missionary spirit is clearly shown in Cranmer's attitude to Calais, which he considered an outpost of popery and idolatry. The King's deputy and his wife, Lord and Lady Lisle, were suspected of being papists, and Cranmer sent Lisle a denunciation of the papacy which, in his view, had distorted true religion and thus corrupted simple souls:

> it is not the person of the Bishop of Rome, which usurpeth the name of the Pope, that is so much to be detested, but the very papacy and the see of Rome, which hath by their laws suppressed Christ, and set up the Bishop of that see as a god of this world. And where the word of God was adversary and against his authority, pomp, covetousness, idolatry and superstitious doctrine, he spying this became adversary unto the word of God, falsifying it, extorting it out of the true sense ... And this is the chief thing to be detested in that see, that it hath brought the professors of Christ into such an ignorance of Christ.

A letter from Cranmer to Cromwell reveals the Archbishop's plan for evangelising Calais:

> And whereas among other of the King's dominions within this his realm there is no part (in my opinion) that more needeth good instruction of the word of God, or aid of learned curates to be resident, than doth the town and marches of Calais: considering specially, not alonely the great ignorance and blindness as well of the heads now resident there as of the common and vulgar people, in the doctrine and knowledge of scripture, but also having respect unto the universal concourse of aliens and strangers, which daily diverteth and resorteth thither: I think that it will be no less a charitable and godly deed than a singular commodity for this realm, to have in those parties at the least two learned persons planted and settled there by the King's authority in some honest living, whose sincerity in conversation of living and teaching shall shortly (no doubt) clearly extinct and extirpate all manner of hypocrisy, false faith, and blindness of God and his word, wherein now the inhabitants there be altogether wrapt.

Cranmer wanted the help of Cromwell and Anne Boleyn

43

in bringing this about, and his own candidate for a benefice in Calais was Thomas Garrett, the future martyr. Some three years later, when the town clerkship of Calais was vacant, Cranmer recommended Nicholas Bacon, who was 'of so good judgement touching Christ's religion, that in that stead he shall be able to do God and the King right acceptable service'. (9)

This coupling of God and the King was common among evangelicals; John Wakefelde, for instance, was said to have suffered 'partly for his sincere mind which he beareth towards God's word, partly for his true and faithful heart which he hath borne towards his prince'. How did radicals relate to the idea of a national church, and in particular, how did they cope with the problem of a conservative and suspicious Supreme Head? Firstly, they explicitly linked Henry's legalistic reformation - separation from Rome, attempts to regulate his church - with the cause of the gospel. Thus Cranmer exclaimed to Cromwell, 'Almighty God long preserve you to his gospel, and the wealth of our prince and his realm!' Parker in reproving Stokes spoke of the 'diligence our sovereign lord the King's grace bestoweth daily to reduce his people committed to his charge from their manifold blindness and superstitions they were in to the truth and right worship of God'. Most striking of all, Latimer conceived of God as blessing the English reformation by providing Henry with a male heir. He told Cromwell:

> Sir, here is no less joying and rejoicing in these parts for the birth of our prince, whom we hungered so long, than there was, I trow, <u>inter vicinos</u>, at the birth of Saint John Baptist ... God give us all grace to yield due thanks to our Lord God, God of England! for verily he hath showed himself God of England, or rather an English God, if we consider and ponder well all his proceedings with us from time to time. He hath overcome all our illness (ie, evil nature) with his exceeding goodness; so that we are now more than compelled to serve him, seek his glory, promote his word, if the devil of all devils be not in us ... And thus the God of England be ever with you in all your proceedings! (10)

The fact that Henry VIII was not himself an evangelical did, of course, cause problems. Evangelicals sometimes expressed the idea that it was not the King who got in the way of reformation, but interfering underlings. Stephen Vaughan, writing to Cromwell from Antwerp and mentioning the Confession of Augsburg, declared:

> I would gladly send such things to his highness, but I am informed he looketh not upon them himself, but committeth them to other. I am sorry he so doth, because I know his high judgment in learning to be such as might safely, without danger, approve men's opinions by reading thereof. And trusting to other men may haply be deceived.

Similarly, Latimer praised Barnes to Cromwell: 'Surely he is alone in handling a piece of scripture, and in setting forth of Christ he hath no fellow. I would wish that the King's grace might once hear him.' (11)

Cromwell's letter to Henry himself from the Tower in 1540 was in part a lengthy attempt to convince the King that the crown and the gospel were bound up together and that his own loyalties were to both. Cromwell made an astonishing twenty-four references to God or Christ, calling on him to witness that he was innocent of treason though, like all men, guilty of sin:

> Yet our Lord, if it be his will, can do with me as he did with Susan who was falsely accused; unto the which God I have only committed my soul; my body and goods at your majesty's pleasure, in whose mercy and pity I do wholly repose me; for other hope than in God and your majesty I have not ... Sir I do knowledge myself to have been a most miserable and wretched sinner, and that I have not towards God and your highness behaved myself as I ought and should have done: for the which mine offences to God, whiles I live, I shall continually ask for his mercy. (12)

Evangelicals largely managed to avoid antagonising Henry by refraining from incriminating remarks about doctrine. However, their writings allude to two points: the facts that the tyrannical papal supremacy had been overthrown and that the scriptures had been liberated from the jealous keeping of the Romish clergy and made freely available to the people.

The first reference was quite acceptable - in fact, inevitable - in terms of ecclesiastical politics, though it is noteworthy that when religious conservatives sought to clear themselves from suspicion of loyalty to the Pope they merely spoke of 'the Bishop of Rome' without any pejorative adjectives. The second assertion was, of course, wishful thinking; evangelicals pressed throughout the reign for an authorised version of scripture to which all might have access. The Great Bible was eventually published in 1539, but restrictions were put upon its use by the laity. These were not to 'read the said bibles with loud and high voices, in time of the celebration of the holy mass', nor to 'presume to take upon them any common disputation, argument, or exposition of the mysteries therein contained', while a statute of 1543 forbade women and the lower orders to read scripture. A good example of the expression of evangelical hopes on this point occurs in a prayer book which is said to have been given by Anne Boleyn to one of her ladies:

> Grant us most merciful father ... the knowledge of thy holy will and glad tidings of our salvation, this great while oppressed with the tyranny of thy adversary of Rome and his fautors and kept close under his Latin letters, and now at length promulgate, published and set at liberty by the grace poured into the heart of thy supreme power our prince ... as he hath graciously begun and ... had prosperous success in setting forth thy holy word ... he may virtuously prosper in the same and victoriously to achieve this his high and godly enterprise, to the utter abolishment of Antichrist and all his sects, and after this temporal crown here he may have an everlasting crown. (13)

The absence of allusion to dogma and Foxe's deliberate delineation of a united protestant community should not disguise the antagonisms which existed between evangelicals and the fact that the mainstream would take care to disassociate itself from conspicuous extremists. Partly, of course, this was for reasons of safety, but partly, too, there was a real fear of fringe elements who might try to bring about a too-rapid reformation and thus jeopardise the whole movement.

The story of John Lambert, a sacramentarian burned in 1538, is told by Foxe, though with some obvious glosses. The martyrologist as usual tries to depict the protestant community as a unified whole, and shows Cranmer as prosecuting Lambert because he did not yet share his views on the eucharist. In addition, Foxe recounts how Lambert was carried into Cromwell's house on the morning of his execution, where the minister begged his pardon for what he had done to him and where the condemned man ate a hearty breakfast before going cheerfully to the stake. There may well be truth in the story, but the full episode shows the caution of the more moderate evangelicals.

Lambert attended a sermon given in London by John Taylor, Master of St John's, Cambridge and a protégé of Dr. Butts, who would himself be prosecuted in 1546. Lambert began to argue about the sacrament with him, and Taylor wisely told him to write down his opinion. According to Foxe, Taylor

> willing and desiring, as is supposed, of a good mind to satisfy Lambert in this matter, amongst others whom he took to counsel, he also conferred with Dr Barnes; which Barnes, although he did otherwise favour the gospel, and was an earnest preacher, notwithstanding seemed not greatly to favour this cause; fearing, peradventure, that it would breed among the people some let or hinderance to the preaching of the gospel (which was now in a good forwardness), if such sacramentaries should be suffered. (14)

When Edward Crome was prosecuted in 1546 after a sermon he gave at Paul's Cross, Richard Coxe and Simon Heynes were among those who publicly took him to task during his examination. In 1546 the gospel was not 'in a good forwardness' but was suffering a barrage of attacks from conservatives. Consequently, though Crome had received patronage from Anne Boleyn, and had been recommended by Cranmer for first Dean of Canterbury because of his 'sincere learning, godly conversation and good example of living, with his great soberness', other evangelicals could not afford to identify with him. (15)

Tristram Revell, former scholar of Christ's was as unfortunate in his sense of timing as Crome. Early in 1536 he tried to present Anne Boleyn with an English translation of an extremely radical work, Francis Lambertus' <u>Farrago Rerum Theologicarum</u>. At this time Anne Boleyn was in serious danger herself. The death of Katherine of Aragon had made a new marriage by the King more feasible; she herself had miscarried of a son on the very day of her rival's funeral; and Henry was courting Jane Seymour. Accordingly she would have nothing to do with either

47

book or translator, and both were committed for examination. (16)
Similarly, though evangelical patrons could provide a measure of protection for their clients, this could not extend to those who, like John Lambert, were convicted of heresy and refused to abjure. Sympathetic courtiers might attend the executions of martyrs, but there was no attempt to speak for the victims lest more people should be incriminated. At the same time, many radicals felt that it was legitimate to dissemble one's beliefs in order to ensure the survival of the true church, and so they would exhort the obdurate to recant.
All these points are demonstrated by the case of Anne Askew. Her examinations in 1545 and 1546 were not concerned solely with the reclamation or destruction of a single heretic; they were an attempt to convict radical courtiers and politicians of heresy. Thus evangelicals from the court were sent to persuade Askew to be reasonable, but she was scornful of their efforts:

> Then came Master Paget to me with many glorious words, and desired me to speak my mind to him. I might (he said) deny it again, if need were. I said that I would not deny the truth.

John Dudley and William Parr were sent to her with their conservative enemy Gardiner, to persuade her to affirm belief in transubstantiation:

> Then said I to my Lord Parr and my Lord Lisle, that it was great shame for them to counsel contrary to their knowledge. Whereunto in few words they did say that they would gladly all things were well.

Shaxton tried to persuade her to make a recantation like his own but, echoing Christ's words about Judas, she told him 'it had been good for him never to have been born'. Anne Askew could not be saved because she would not compromise her conscience, and it was in the interests of her sympathisers at court to distance themselves from her. (17)
The activities of evangelicals were limited and to some extent controlled by the nature of the patronage system. This can best be described as a pyramid, with the King - the fount from whence flowed all preferment and protection - at its apex and the suitors for favour at its base. Access to the King's person was strictly limited; only those who held

office in the privy chamber (Henry's most private
apartment) were allowed in there, apart from a
favoured few like George Blage who had special
permission to enter. Consequently those at the bottom
of the 'pyramid' were dependent on intermediary
sponsors and middlemen who would bring them to the
attention of the King or of those immediately below
him in the patronage system.

These greater patrons not only had the ear of
the King, but themselves disposed of considerable
preferment. For evangelicals, the chief figures
under Henry VIII were Anne Boleyn, Thomas Cromwell
and Sir Anthony Denny. All these became influential
for different reasons. Anne was firstly the King's
Lady, then the official Queen Consort. During her
tenure of power she worked often with Cromwell, and
on her fall he succeeded to her mantle as chief
patron of the gospel. As a bureaucrat Cromwell
possessed a thorough knowledge of the workings of the
machinery of patronage, and his experience as an
intermediary sponsor left him with a multitude of
contacts at the different levels of the 'pyramid'.
On his fall in 1540 the torch passed to his associate
Denny, who had been a member of the privy chamber
from at least 1532 and one of the two chief gentlemen
since 1538; later he would become groom of the stool.
His frequent and intimate proximity to the King
ensured his influence.

Obviously, the great patrons of reform were
subject to the fluctuations of political fortune, and
both Anne and Cromwell were destroyed by factional
strife. Much, therefore, depended on the continued
existence and sustained activity of intermediary
sponsors such as Sir Edward Bainton and Dr William
Butts; without them, the cause of the gospel would
have been in doubt.

Bainton became Anne Boleyn's vice-chamberlain
in 1533 and served her four successors until his
death some ten years later. Thus, although he always
belonged to the Queen's household rather than the
King's, he was constantly at court. Moreover, he was
usually in favour with Henry. The King would stay at
his house in Wiltshire while on progress in the West
Country and Thomas Starkey described him to Reginald
Pole as 'one to whom the King's pleasure is not
unknown'. Bainton's flexibility and adroitness were
important factors both in his own career and in the
continuance of the cause of reform. He managed to
disassociate himself from Anne Boleyn and show
himself favourable to Jane Seymour before the events
of spring 1536, and when the evangelicals suffered a

temporary eclipse because of the King's marriage to a Howard he contributed to the unfortunate Queen's downfall.

Bainton occurs frequently as an intermediary between suitors for patronage and Anne, Cromwell and Henry VIII. He was a magnate of Wiltshire and a power in Salisbury diocese, where Shaxton was Bishop from 1535 to 1539. Hugh Latimer's benefice of West Kington, which he held from 1531, adjoined Bainton's property, and Latimer wrote to him about charges of heresy arising from his preaching. He also approached Bainton on behalf of two of his godly parishioners who had endured the loss of their cattle and the taunts of their conservative neighbours; Bainton showed the letter to Anne, who recompensed the couple for their loss and rewarded them for their religious sufferings. John Smith, a canon of St Paul's, implored Bainton's intercession with Anne, and John Barlow wrote to him about the troubles of his brother William, a client of Anne's whom she had promoted to be prior of Haverfordwest. (18)

Butts had a somewhat different career from Bainton's. He was one of the royal physicians, drawing bouche of court from at least 1526 and active in office until his death in 1545. Henry VIII combined an interest in medicine with a terror of disease, and thus Butts' appointment was potentially extremely important. Furthermore, the duties of a royal doctor – particularly one as urbane as Butts – meant that he could often be on hand during the King's more relaxed moments to ask favour or protection for suitors. Foxe gives a good instance of this in his story of Butts' mediation on behalf of Richard Turner, one of Cranmer's diocesan clergy who was prosecuted for heresy:

> spying his time, when the King was in trimming and in washing (as his manner was at certain times to call for his barber), Dr Butts (whose manner was at such times ever to be present, and with some pleasant conceits to refresh and solace the King's mind) brought with him in his hand this letter (from Cranmer's secretary). The King asking what news, Dr Butts pleasantly and merrily beginneth to insinuate unto the King the effect of the matter, and so, at the King's commandment, read out the letter ... the hearing and consideration whereof so altered the King's mind, that whereas before he commanded the said Turner whipped out of the country, he now commanded him to be retained as a faithful

subject.

Besides his office at court, Butts had numerous contacts at Cambridge, where he himself had been a student of Gonville Hall. This institution was reputedly so heretical by the early 1530s that, as Bishop Nix of Norwich remarked to Archbishop Warham, 'I hear no clerk that hath comen out lately of that college but savoureth of the frying pan, though he speak never so holily'. Butts looked after the interests of the university in general and, as will be seen, also drew off evangelical talent from Cambridge for royal patronage and court service. His influence, discreet but crucial, can be discerned throughout the course of the Henrician reformation. (19)

Having discussed the nature of evangelicalism and the machinery and personnel of the patronage system, it remains to relate patronage to religious politics in order to see its effect on the cause of the gospel. In the first half of the 1520s, following the papal and imperial condemnation of Luther, heresy was vigorously prosecuted in England. Suspect books were gathered in and burned in public bonfires; the universities were visited by Wolsey's agents; and evangelical writers and translators, failing to obtain preferment or even toleration in England, went into exile. The King, proud of the papal title <u>Fidei Defensor</u> which he had long coveted and finally won by his written defence of the seven sacraments against Luther, was completely hostile to the reformers abroad and their followers in England. (20)

With the advent of the royal divorce, however, and despite Henry's unflinching adherence to traditional dogma, the official attitude to evangelical religion changed. This came about through two factors: Henry's frantic need for some authority other than Rome for his proceedings; and the active evangelical interest of Anne Boleyn. Thus the 'King's great matter' provided both the opportunity of advancing the cause of the gospel and — because of the existence of an influential promoter and protector — the means of forwarding it.

It has been seen that little can be known of Anne Boleyn's specific religious beliefs; all that is evident is a predilection for vernacular scripture and a preoccupation with poor relief. In terms of policy, however, she showed her hand early. She was responsible for bringing two illicit books to the King's attention: Simon Fish's <u>Supplication for the Beggars</u> printed in Antwerp in 1528; and William

Tyndale's <u>Obedience of a Christian Man</u>, published at the same place in the following year. Both were bitterly anticlerical and critical of Wolsey, denouncing the clergy for financial exploitation of the laity and - more crucially - for usurping the King's authority. (21) In 1528 a heresy scandal occurred at Oxford which largely involved Wolsey's college there, and Anne's interest in several of the culprits is evident. Within a few years William Betts, formerly of Gonville, Cambridge, became her chaplain, and Nicholas Udall was employed to write verses for her coronation pageants. In addition, she interceded immediately with Wolsey for one of those most gravely implicated: 'I beseech your grace with all my heart to remember the parson of Honey Lane for my sake shortly'. This was either the curate, Thomas Garrett, whose activities as a seller of forbidden books in Oxford had started the whole affair; or his rector, Thomas Foreman. The latter, as President of Queens', Cambridge, had warned owners of forbidden books in 1524 that Wolsey's agents were about to descend on the university. He is noted by Foxe among those 'troubled and abjured' in 1527 and 1528, and he died in the latter year. (22)

It seems certain that Anne Boleyn was determined not only to replace Katherine of Aragon as queen, but to oust Wolsey as the King's chief adviser and to direct Henry's religious policy into more radical channels. The failure of the legatine court at Blackfriars to deliver the desired judgement on the marriage put Henry in a quandary and directly opened the way for the promotion of evangelicals.

It was Thomas Cranmer of Jesus, Cambridge who suggested that the universities of England and Europe be canvassed for a verdict on the King's marriage. Cranmer himself immediately entered the household of Anne's father, and a number of evangelicals at Cambridge distinguished themselves during the referendum there, so that they caught the eye of Dr Butts and earned themselves preferment. Hugh Latimer, already noted as an evangelical preacher, was taken to court by Butts, preached before the King when the university's verdict was presented, and 'remained a certain time in the said Dr Butts' chamber, preaching then in London very often'. Butts and Cromwell between them got him the royal benefice of West Kington, Anne Boleyn made him her chaplain, and in 1535 he became Bishop of Worcester. Nicholas Shaxton, who had graduated BA from Gonville in the same year as Butts, became Anne's chaplain and almoner, received a benefice from the King, and in

1535 was promoted to the see of Salisbury. It is interesting that both these evangelical bishops borrowed money from Anne in order to pay Henry their first-fruits. (23)

Two other members of Gonville attracted Anne's patronage. Edward Crome was proposed as a member of the university committee which would debate the divorce but was rejected because he had already approved Cranmer's book in the King's favour. Despite an examination for heresy in May 1530, Anne nominated him to the London living of St Mary Aldermary (a benefice in Cranmer's gift) in 1534. John Skip, fellow of Gonville and habitué of the White Horse Tavern, became Anne's chaplain and her almoner after Shaxton, and would become Bishop of Hereford in 1539. In 1534 he was sent to Cambridge to preach the royal supremacy with Simon Heynes. The latter had been one of the university delegates who had voted against the Aragon marriage. He received the living of Stepney – the richest parochial benefice in England – from the sinecure rector, Cromwell's client Richard Leighton. He was also rector of Fulham (where his confidant Butts is buried) and dean of Exeter. (24)

Other Cambridge scholars commenced successful careers either as a result of their support for the divorce or because of Anne's patronage. Cranmer succeeded Warham as Archbishop of Canterbury, while from Corpus Christi – William Betts' last college – Anne recruited two more chaplains, Matthew Parker and William Latymer.

Until her destruction in spring 1536 Anne Boleyn was active in two areas which particularly concerned evangelicals; dissemination of the vernacular Bible, and the protection of transgressors against the religious laws. Scripture was one of her paramount concerns. She herself owned a number of scriptural works in English and French, employing the mercer William Locke and her servants William Latymer and Jane Wilkinson to see that such books were fetched from abroad. She owned a copy of Tyndale's New Testament of 1534, which may have been the 'English Bible' which Latymer says she kept open on a desk in her chamber for the edification of her household. She also owned a French psalter and a volume in French and English of the epistles and gospels for the Sundays in the year, compiled for her by a kinsman. She is also said to have given her maids books of devotion in English, and the two extant volumes which are thought to be examples of this are largely scriptural. A French visitor described her reading Paul's epistles in Lent 1530, and praised her taste for 'approved translations from holy scripture, filled with all good doctrines; or equally, other good books by erudite men, giving salutary remedies for this mortal life and consolation to the immortal soul'. Besides Revell's translation of Lambertus' <u>Farrago Rerum Theologicarum</u>, she received the dedication to a manuscript version of Clément Marot's <u>Sermon du bon pasteur et du mauvais</u>. She encouraged her household people to read and debate scripture, especially when the King was present. (25)

Anne's effectiveness in promoting vernacular scripture was severely limited by Henry VIII's conservatism and suspicion of unauthorised versions. She was able to help Richard Herman, who had been arrested by the imperial authorities in the Netherlands and expelled from the house of the English merchants in Antwerp. Ordering Cromwell to bring about his reinstatement there, she declared that he had suffered simply because 'he did both with his goods and policy, to his great hurt and hindrance in this world, help to the setting forth of the new testament in English'. Less fortunate than Herman was George Joye, who in 1533 printed sample pages from the book of Genesis 'and sent one copy to the King, and another to the new Queen ... to purchase licence that he might so go through all the bible'. Henry was not yet ready to sanction an official English Bible, and nothing came of the project. (26)

A petition to Anne from Thomas Alwaye, who was prosecuted by the bishops in the time of Wolsey for buying 'English new testaments and ... certain other books prohibited', reveals her reputation as a refuge for religious offenders:

> I remembered how many deeds of pity your goodness had done within these few years, and that without respect of any persons, as well to strangers and aliens as to many of this land, as well to poor as to rich: whereof some looking for no redemption were by your gracious means not only freely delivered out of costly and very long imprisoning, but also by your charity largely rewarded and all thing restored to the uttermost, so that every man may perceive that your gracious and Christian mind is everywhere ready to help, succour and comfort them that be afflicted, troubled and vexed, and that not only in word and tongue, but even after the saying of St John. (27)

Alwaye's eulogy, which is doubtless exaggerated for

the sake of flattery and rhetorical effect, can none the less be supported by a number of proven instances. There is Anne's promotion of known Lutherans like Hugh Latimer, Shaxton and Crome, who were repeatedly in trouble with the ecclesiastical authorities. In addition, her mediation with the King assisted Thomas Patmore, parson of Hadham, Herts and a former member of Gonville. In 1530 Patmore was accused of uttering heresy at Cambridge and of condoning the marriage of his curate Simon Smith, another old Gonville man, along with other charges. He was confined by Stokesley in the Lollards' Tower for two years. Thanks to Anne's intervention with Henry he was released, and able to have the bishop and his vicar-general investigated for alleged mistreatment. (28)

Among the 'strangers and aliens' to whom Alwaye alluded was Nicholas Bourbon of Vandoeuvre, a French poet. Imprisoned in France 'for that he had uttered certain talk in the derogation of the Bishop of Rome and his usurped authority', Bourbon appealed to Dr Butts for assistance. Butts informed Anne of his plight, and 'did not only obtain by her grace's means the King's letters for his delivery but also, after he was come into England, his whole maintenance at the Queen's only charges in the house of the said Mr Butts'. Anne's chaplain William Latymer also says that she offered shelter to a Frenchwoman named Marye and to the reformer Sturmius, but neither of these cases can be confirmed. (29)

What was the sum of Anne Boleyn's achievement for the gospel? She was unable to persuade Henry to a more evangelical policy, except when the requirements of his 'great matter' forced him to be tolerant of radicalism. She was unable to promote an authorised English Bible, or to save obdurate heretics; among those burned during her ascendancy were Bilney, Bainham and Frith. However, on the other side she was the direct cause of the breach with Rome, and because of the divorce, fear of doctrinal change among conservatives and the fact that she was the dominant influence on the King in a crucial period, it came about that the radicals took the initiative in religious matters, leaving their opponents to acquiescence or mute opposition.

Why was the cause of the gospel able to survive Anne's fall? Quite simply, because her clients and the lessor sponsors were able to distance themselves from her and her alleged guilt. Cromwell entered into an unlikely alliance with the supporters of Princess Mary, and it was this odd coalition which brought about the destruction of Anne and her replacement by Jane Seymour. The new wife was little more than a cipher, whose religious opinions are unknown and whose influence on Henry was in any case minimal. Thus when Cromwell helped annihilate Anne, and later outmanoeuvred his strange Marian bedfellows, he was able to take over the complete patronage of the gospel.

Equally important, while Anne and her political supporters were executed, the evangelicals she had promoted were able to disown the fallen favourite and transfer their allegiance to Cromwell. Two extant letters show how Anne was repudiated when her case was no longer tenable, and how evangelicals of necessity placed the survival of the cause over loyalty to a personality. Shaxton expressed shock at Anne's crimes, and implored Cromwell 'in visceribus Jesu Christi' to continue to uphold the gospel as she had encouraged him to do, though the cause had been slandered by her misconduct. Cranmer, in a rather rambling letter to the King, declared his incredulity at her guilt, said that if she were indeed guilty she was the lowest of the low, and disingenuously told Henry:

> I trust that your grace will bear no less entire favour unto the truth of the gospel, than you did before; forsomuch as your grace's favour to the gospel was not led by affection unto her, but by zeal unto the truth.

Cranmer was far from optimistic about Henry's loyalty to reform, however. He told Cromwell:

> I was ever hitherto cold, but now I am in a heat with the cause of religion, which goeth all contrary to mine expectation, if it be as the fame goeth; wherein I would wonder fain break my mind unto you. (30)

In the event, the change of chief patron was effected relatively smoothly. Having disposed of Anne to the King's satisfaction, Cromwell gathered up all the threads of evangelical patronage. Many of those who formerly relied on Anne - Hugh Latimer, Shaxton, Parker, Barlow, William Latymer - now looked to him for promotion and protection. (31) However, in terms of religious policy Cromwell, like Anne before him, was hampered by the King's yearning for orthodoxy. It was this difference of temperament as much as the blunder of supplying Henry with an

56

unwanted bride which probably brought about his own
downfall in 1540.

After the breach with Rome it was necessary to
find a formulary of faith which would satisfy most
shades of opinion in the Henrician church and which
would not outrage potential enemies abroad. On the
one hand, either Charles V or Francis I might use
schism as a pretext for invading England; on the
other, alliance with a protestant power was always a
possibility. Thus the English church settlement had
to be broad enough to accommodate both the fearful
conservatives and the hopeful evangelicals, to avoid
rebellion at home and isolation abroad.

The first attempt to define the faith of the
English church must be understood against the
background of diplomatic negotiations with the
German Lutherans. The latter demanded that Henry
accept the Confession of Augsburg as a condition of
entry into the Schmalkaldic League, and Cromwell
encouraged the King to do this by employing Richard
Taverner to translate the Augsburg declaration and
Melanchthon's defence of it and getting Robert Redman
to print it. This publication was not meant to
'elaborate the religious settlement', it was merely
Cromwell's attempt to influence policy; and it
failed. (32)

The first Henrician formulary of faith, the Ten
Articles approved by convocation in July 1536, was
far from being an overtly 'protestant' document.
While it followed Luther in omitting four of the
seven sacraments, it did not so much reject them as
pass them over in silence. The remaining three –
baptism, confession and the eucharist – were defined
in an orthodox sense, and though there was no direct
definition of purgatory, prayers for the dead were
said to be efficacious and desirable. (33)

The Ten Articles were too ambiguous to please
either wing of the English church, and by the
following February the bishops were employed on a new
formulary of faith. Cromwell supervised their
debates closely, but there was much heated argument.
In July an exasperated Hugh Latimer declared:

I had lever be poor parson of poor Kington again
than to continue thus Bishop of Worcester ...
forsooth, it is a troublous thing to agree upon
a doctrine, in things of such controversy, with
judgements of such diversity, every man (I
trust) meaning well, and yet not all meaning one
way.

Edward Foxe told Cromwell of a day when 'we wanted much your presence', but it was not merely the minister's inability to cajole the opposition in person that prevented the radicals winning the day. The bishops' letters frequently mention the King's pleasure and intentions, and it was his watchful monitoring of the discussions which prevented either side from being too assertive. (34)

Consequently the new formulary of faith was as equivocal as the first. All seven sacraments were maintained, though transubstantiation was not explicitly asserted and the authority of scripture over tradition was accepted. The King himself would not adopt such a vague statement, and so The Godly and Pious Institution of a Christian Man was known merely as the 'Bishops' Book'; it was recommended to the parish clergy for private study, but was never put before parliament or convocation. Clearly, another attempt at defining faith would have to be made.

When Parliament met in April 1539 a committee was set up at the King's command which was composed of three evangelical bishops and three conservative, with Cromwell presiding as viceregent. Agreement naturally proved impossible for this divided body, and in May Henry went over its head. He allowed the conservative Duke of Norfolk to present six questions for debate in the House of Lords which were framed so as to admit of only one answer. These answers were converted into six articles, and passed into law as the Act for Abolishing Diversity of Opinion. The title alone reveals Henry's determination. Transubstantiation, communion in one kind, auricular confession, private masses, clerical celibacy and vows of chastity were all unequivocally affirmed. The statute was confirmed by The Necessary Doctrine and Erudition of a Christian Man, composed by the bishops and printed in 1543, and known as the 'King's Book' because Henry gave it authorisation. He was closely involved in the production of both book and statute, as manuscript corrections in his hand on a number of relevant documents bear witness. Thus it was the King who prevented further doctrinal innovation. (35)

With the 'Act of Six Articles', the Cleves divorce, the Howard marriage and the fall of Cromwell, the future looked bleak for the evangelical cause. Cromwell's life as chief upholder of the gospel had in any case been uneasy, as a supportive letter from Cranmer of 1537 shows:

> if you continue to take such pains for the
> setting forth of God's word, as you do, although
> in the mean season you suffer some snubs, and
> many slanders, lies, and reproaches for the
> same, yet one day he will requite altogether.
> And the same word (as St John saith) which shall
> judge every man at the last day, must needs show
> favour to them that now do favour it.

The evangelical John Lassells went to court after
Cromwell's demise and asked two brethren how matters
stood for the cause, 'seeing we have lost so noble a
man which did love and favour it so well'. Hearing
that Norfolk was somewhat vocally in the ascendant,
he advised a friend to keep a low profile until the
enemies of the gospel had betrayed themselves. The
evangelicals' fears about the immediate future are
implicitly expressed in Cranmer's letter to the King
about Cromwell which, like his earlier letter
concerning the fallen Anne Boleyn, voiced his doubt
about the minister's guilt, affirmed his own
allegiance to Henry, and sought to keep him faithful
to the gospel:

> I heard yesterday in your grace's council, that
> he is a traitor: yet who cannot be sorrowful and
> amazed that he should be a traitor against your
> majesty; he that was so advanced by your
> majesty; he whose surety was only by your
> majesty; he who loved your majesty (as I ever
> thought) no less than God ... I loved him as my
> friend, for so I took him to be ... But now, if
> he be a traitor, I am sorry that ever I loved
> him or trusted him, and I am very glad that his
> treason is discoverd in time: but yet again I am
> very sorrowful; for who shall your grace trust
> hereafter, if you might not trust him? ... But I
> pray God continually night and day, to send such
> a counsellor in his place whom your grace may
> trust. (36)

In the event, the Act of Six Articles created
comparatively few martyrs, though a number of
radicals like Coverdale and Bale went into exile and
Shaxton and Latimer felt obliged to resign their
sees. Clearly, evangelicals could continue to hope
for protection from influential quarters. The final
part of this study is concerned with the identity and
activities of these guardians of the gospel.

Modern historians have focussed on Katherine
Parr as the head of reform during Henry's final

years; this is inaccurate, and distorts the true picture of power and influence at court. In 1890 Agnes Strickland praised Katherine as

> the first protestant Queen of England. She was the only one among the consorts of Henry VIII who, in the sincerity of an honest heart, embraced the doctrine of the reformation, and imperilled her crown and life in support of her principles ... the learned and virtuous matron who directed the studies of Lady Jane Grey, Edward VI and Queen Elizabeth, and who may, with truth, be called the nursing-mother of the reformation.

Strickland's eulogy has been echoed and amplified in the two twentieth century biographies of the Queen, while a modern study of humanism and politics depicts Katherine as the head of the reform faction at court and describes her organisation of a 'royal nursery' where the King's three children, with aristocratic companions, imbibed heretically-tinged Erasmian piety under the Queen's benevolent eye. This thesis has been reiterated by many recent historians. (37)

The question of who directed the education of the King's heirs is a crucial one because it points to the real influence at work on Henry VIII himself. (In addition, of course, those about Edward could presumably hope for continued influence in the following reign.) It is indisputable that Edward's education was in the hands of evangelicals rather than conservatives, but if the disposal of religious and cultural patronage in Henry's closing years is to be assessed accurately the existence of the putative 'royal nursery' must be questioned. Whatever her private virtues, Katherine Parr was not the head of the reform party at court, and it is both physically and politically impossible that a royal nursery existed in her household. Katherine's true role can be demonstrated by considering her own character and learning, the extent of her influence with the King, and the movements of the royal children. Moreover, by looking at faction and patronage at court, and in particular at the backgrounds of the men who taught Henry's children, it is possible to discern a more potent evangelical influence at work than that of the Queen.

Katherine's encomiasts depict her as a woman of unusual learning, but it seems that her erudition was both limited and acquired late in life; that she began to be learned, not in young girlhood, but after her marriage to the King. In 1546 Prince Edward congratulated her on her progress in Latin and literature, praised her Roman handwriting and relayed his tutor's flattering amazement at its fineness; these compliments surely imply that Katherine was rather a neophyte in humanist studies than a seasoned scholar. Edward wrote to her in Latin as to all his correspondents (this being his main academic exercise in composition), but the only reply of hers which is extant, a corrected draft written on the cover of her stepson's letter, is not in her hand. (38) When Cambridge university wrote to her in Latin begging her intercession with the King she replied graciously in English, gently chiding them for addressing her in Latin. There is no reason to think that this was false modesty.

Katherine's letter to Cambridge is also instructive for revealing a certain anti-intellectual tendency. She warned the scholars:

> as I do well understand all kind of learning doth flourish amongst you in this age as it did amongst the Greeks at Athens long ago, I require and desire you all, not so to hunger for the exquisite knowledge of profane learning that it may be thought the Greeks' university was but transposed or now again in England revived, forgetting our Christianity ... That it may not be laid against you in evidence at the tribunal seat of God, how ye were ashamed of Christ's doctrine.

Again, in The Lamentation of a Sinner she condemned 'dead, humane, historical faith and knowledge (which they have learned in their scholastical books),' and proudly asserted, 'I have certainly no curious learning to defend this matter withal, but a simple zeal and earnest love to the truth, inspired of God'. (39)

Thus it seems fair to say that Katherine Parr was not fitted intellectually to supervise the studies of the royal children in the way that Katherine of Aragon had organised and participated in the instruction of Princess Mary in the earlier years of the reign. Katherine Parr was interested in culture and very pious; her chaplain Francis Goldsmith said that she made every day like a Sunday, and besides the Lamentation of a Sinner she produced a creditable little volume of Prayers or Meditations, wherein the mind is stirred patiently to suffer all afflictions. She also sponsored the translation into

English of Erasmus' paraphrases of the new testament. The general editor of the work, Nicholas Udall, told the Queen of his hope that Henry VIII

> will not suffer it to lie buried in silence, but will one day, when his godly wisdom shall so think expedient, cause the same paraphrase to be published and set abroad in print to the same use that your highness hath meant it ... to the public commodity and benefit of good English people now a long time sore thirsting and hungering the sincere and plain knowledge of God's word.

However, it is a pointer to the extent of Katherine's influence with the King that neither the paraphrases nor the Lutheran <u>Lamentation of a Sinner</u> was published until the following reign. (40) The Queen's interest in humanist and evangelical literature may have stimulated Henry's children, but none the less she was not qualified to direct a royal nursery.

Moreover, it was both physically impossible and - in terms of current educational theory - highly unlikely that the King's children shared a schoolroom. Two of them might reside together for a time (Edward and Elizabeth at Hatfield, for example, or Elizabeth and Mary at Havering), and one or two might be present at court, but there is no evidence of shared lessons. Katherine Parr is credited with bringing all three together at court (where, it is presumed, they studied together) on two definite occasions, Christmas 1543 and July 1544. A letter of Elizabeth to the Queen written at the latter date flatly contradicts this. The unfortunate girl complained that she had not seen Katherine for a year (that is, since her wedding, which both princesses attended), and that she was still - for some tantalisingly unknown reason - in disgrace with her father. She thanked the Queen, however, for mentioning her in her letters to Henry, 'For heretofore I have not dared to write to him'. Possibly, indeed Katherine's references to all the King's children in letters to him have misled historians into thinking that they were all living together. The imperial ambassador Chapuys revealed with some malice that Elizabeth was sent from court within a month of the Parr marriage to live with Edward, but her usual residence in these years was at Cheshunt in a house of Sir Anthony Denny. Thus the royal school lacks one of its pupils for a major part of its alleged existence. Edward's letters to his stepmother, moreover, show that he was generally away from her, and Mary, too, had her own establishment. (41)

Even if the King's children had been together it is improbable that they would have been educated in a common 'nursery'. Mary, born 1516, was rather too old for lessons with her sister, born 1533, and brother, born 1537. In any case she had already received a first class humanist education organised by Katherine of Aragon and the Spanish scholar Juan Luis Vives. Much has been made of the fact that Katherine Parr persuaded the conservative Mary to translate Erasmus' paraphrase of the gospel of John; but Mary had been directed by Vives to read the paraphrases some twenty years before, and Katherine of Aragon had ensured that she read scripture, the Fathers and the works of Erasmus and other contemporary scholars. (42)

Thus Mary would not have been a student in Katherine Parr's nursery. Nor would Edward. Contemporary humanist educational theory usually stipulated that boys be taken from female company (mothers, nurses and other attendants) since these would incline them to wantonness, effeminacy and frivolity. Instead, they should be given over to male governors and tutors. That this occurred in Edward's case is shown by his own recollections in his <u>Journal</u>:

> was brought up, till he came to six years old, among the women. At the sixth year of his age, he was brought up in learning by Master Doctor Coxe, who was after his almoner, and John Cheke, Master of Art, two well learned men. (43)

This change took place in July 1544, when Edward's household was reorganised and the tutors appointed. As the Prince was residing at Hampton Court with Katherine Parr during the King's absence at the war in France, it has been thought that she was responsible for this reorganisation and was able to supervise Edward at first hand. In reality, Katherine had nothing to do with the selection of the tutors. Furthermore, it would have been odd by current standards if Edward had been educated under the eye of his stepmother. Similarly, very few of even the most advanced humanist theorists advocated equality of education for boys and girls, and thus it is impossible that Elizabeth should have taken lessons with her brother; she had her own tutors and, as a later letter of Ascham's shows, her own programme of studies.

Moving from educational theory to patronage, there is no evidence that Katherine had any influence in the appointment of her stepchildren's tutors. On the contrary, when she tried in 1548 to place her chaplain Goldsmith as tutor to Elizabeth he was rejected in favour of Ascham. (44) Though this incident took place in the following reign it is a significant indication of the real influence behind educational appointments - and religious patronage - at Henry VIII's court; Ascham was the last link in a very interesting chain of sponsorship.

All the royal tutors in the mid-1540s were Cambridge men, as were Butts and Sir Anthony Denny. Butts' activities in relation to patronage need no further description here, and Denny's credentials as a patron of scholarship and reform are indisputable. Denny was educated at Colet's School of Jesus at St Paul's, London and Fisher's college of St John's, Cambridge, two institutions which pioneered humanist studies in England. He is often found helping scholars and their suits at court. He was one of the courtiers to whom Ascham, a St John's man, sent copies of his Toxophilus in 1545 in the hope of patronage. There are other links with St John's. Denny settled the affairs of Sedburgh School, originally a chantry founded by Roger Lupton but converted by him into a preparatory school for St John's. Thomas Chaloner, a scholar of St John's, dedicated his Homily of Saint John Chrysostom to Denny in 1544.

Other scholars presented works to Denny with effusive dedications. Thomas Paynell in the preface to his Sermon of Saint Cyprian made on the Lord's Prayer praised

> your sincere affection to God and his holy word, your great fidelity and diligence toward our most gracious sovereign lord the King ... your faithful, wise and friendly counsels, your continual exhortations and persuasions to virtue, your liberal and most gentle nature.

Thomas Langley in his Abridgment of the Notable Work of Polydore Vergil lauded Denny in the necessarily veiled language of evangelicals as both a humanist and an upholder of the gospel, calling him 'not only inflamed with desire of knowledge of antiquities, but also a favourable supporter of all good learning and a very Maecenas of all toward wits'; the present work was to be

> a continual monument of the special love and
> mind that you have to further the knowledge of
> the truth and abolish ignorance, hypocrisy and
> all other like painted holiness ... your
> alacrity and readiness in preferring the
> blessed word of God and the sincere setters-
> forth of the same.

An anonymous epitaph similarly praised Denny for both
his humanism and his commitment to the evangelical
cause:

> Farewell, most worthy knight laid up in quiet
> rest, Maecenas to the learned, an author to
> religion, To those an open haven that were for
> Christ oppressed, An enemy to the Pope and his
> superstition.

Denny's wife Jane, who figured in the prosecution of
Anne Askew as an intended victim, received the
dedication to <u>A sweet consolation, and the second
book of the troubled man's medicine</u> from her servant
William Hugh in 1546. He praised her as

> A wife not unworthy of him whom God, the maker
> of all honest marriages, hath given you for your
> husband. What commendation is comprised herein,
> judge they that know the goodly and godly
> qualities, the authority and wisdom, the
> virtues and singular gifts, which God hath moved
> him withal. (45)

Denny worked with Cromwell on at least one
occasion. In 1538 Sir Thomas Elyot reminded the King
in the preface to his <u>Dictionary</u> of how Henry had
promised to assist him in his labours on the work
after hearing good reports of it from Cromwell, the
royal librarian William Tildisley, and 'gentle
Master Anthony Denny, for his wisdom and diligence
worthily called by your highness into your privy
chamber'. It seems unlikely, given their community of
interest, that this was an isolated incidence of
joint-patronage. There is also an instance of his
relation to Katherine Parr in the field of
educational patronage. Matthew Parker's college of
Stoke-by-Clare (where he had founded a humanist
school) was threatened by the Chantries Act of 1545.
He wrote to Katherine and her council appealing for
the intercession with the King, as the college was in
the queen consort's gift. However, Stoke owed its
preservation not to Katherine, but to Denny. (46)

65

Indeed it was Denny and Butts, who both maintained numerous contacts with Cambridge, who influenced the selection of the royal tutors. The careers of those scholars display a number of links with these two eminent members of the King's privy chamber.

Richard Coxe, Edward's first preceptor, had been one of the Cambridge men imported by Wolsey into Cardinal College, Oxford who had been implicated in the heresy scandal there in 1528. He managed to evade the consequences of the affair, returned to Cambridge and became chaplain successively to Bishop Goodrich of Ely (formerly one of Anne Boleyn's Cambridge clients) and to Cranmer. The Archbishop was the Prince's godfather, and it was possibly he who secured Coxe's appointment with Edward. As will be shown, Cranmer was heavily indebted to Butts and Denny for the protection of his interests, and it is possible that this piece of promotion was manipulated between the three of them. (47)

Edward's other chief tutor, who increasingly took over the teaching duties as Coxe's health declined and his other duties multiplied, was John Cheke. He was not only a member of Denny's old college, but a protégé of Butts, who had introduced him and Thomas Smith to the King in 1534. Henry gave them both exhibitions for study abroad; later he made Cheke first Regius Professor of Greek at Cambridge, while Smith was given the chair of Civil Law. Cheke's high regard for his initial sponsor is shown by a letter of consolation written to Butts during his last illness and by the epitaph composed for his tomb. (48)

The Cambridge connection also held good in the household of Princess Elizabeth, which normally resided in Denny's house at Cheshunt. Ascham praised Elizabeth's progress in study under William Grindal and Lady Champernoun. The latter was Lady Denny's mother, who was widowed in 1544 and may have gone to live at Cheshunt. Elizabeth's governess was Lady Denny's sister, Katherine Astley. Grindal was Ascham's own pupil at St John's and was appointed tutor to the Princess in 1544 after being sent to Cheke at court with a letter from his master. That Ascham succeeded his pupil in the post was no matter of random chance. He was already giving Elizabeth writing lessons, mending her pens, sending her books, and advising her governess as to how she should be taught. He also later told Cecil that 'Many times by mine especial good master Master Cheke's means I have been called to teach the King (Edward) to write in his privy chamber', though it is uncertain whether this also happened in Henry VIII's lifetime. (49) Thus there was a line of patronage extending from Cambridge to the court, a line with which Katherine Parr could have no business; it is well to remember her one letter to the university in 1546 which sought to admonish rather than to praise those learned men.

Moving out of the royal schoolroom and into the wider arena of court politics, the picture of Katherine Parr as a minor member of the reform faction rather than its leader is confirmed. The well-known story in Foxe of Katherine's 'trouble on account of the gospel' has obscured her role in the closing years of Henry's reign, and has been used by more recent writers to show her as the dangerous head of reform whom the conservative party had to eliminate at all costs. (50) Closer examination of Foxe's account, however, shows that the Queen's influence with Henry was tenuous in the extreme.

According to Foxe, Katherine rashly began arguing theology with her autocratic and ill-tempered husband. This naturally irritated Henry, and when he gave vent to his feelings before Bishop Gardiner this seemed like a heaven-sent opportunity for the conservatives to get rid of the Queen by implying that she was guilty of heresy. Katherine, be it noted, was blissfully unaware of her peril until warned by certain 'godly persons', among them Thomas Wendy, the royal physician lauded by Ascham as Butts' successor in the patronage of learning and, like Butts, a former member of Gonville Hall. Thanks to Dr Wendy she made a prudent submission to Henry and was saved by a hair's breadth from arrest by Wriothesley. Had Katherine really been the head of reformation she would surely have been more certain of her hold on the King, and would not have needed to be rescued by other evangelicals.

Furthermore, the attack on Katherine Parr was only one of a number of attempts against prominent evangelicals at court which were staged by the conservative faction between 1543 (the year of her marriage) and 1546. The first target was Cranmer, who was apparently saved from destruction through the 'Prebendaries' Plot' by the intervention of Butts and Denny.

Contrary to legend, Cranmer was not the only man Henry VIII ever loved or trusted, but an extremely vulnerable figure. In the 1530s he was constantly indebted to Cromwell for mediation with the King about numerous matters. One of the last services the minister rendered him was the interception of Cranmer's own book against the Six Articles,

carelessly dropped into the Thames by his secretary
Morice and acquired by a 'popish priest', who
intended to send it to Gardiner or Sir Anthony Brown.
After Cromwell's fall Cranmer became dependent on
Denny and Butts. The latter had already done him one
favour; Cranmer was apparently left behind in the
scramble for monastic lands, but was granted an abbey
in Nottinghamshire through the unsolicited
intervention of Butts. (51) In the 1540s he was
indebted to both his patrons for services of a more
urgent nature.

Accusations of heresy from his own canons at
Canterbury in 1543 gave Cranmer's enemies on the
council a handle against him, and they suggested to
the King that if he were put under lock and key his
accusers would not be afraid to testify against him.
Henry agreed to have him arrested in the council
chamber the following morning, but that night he sent
Denny to bring the Archbishop to court, warned him of
his danger and promised him favour. Morice and Foxe
both recount how Butts found Cranmer kept waiting
outside the council chamber and informed the King of
his primate's humiliation, and how Henry unleashed
his anger on the hapless conspirators. However, the
familiar story is full of hidden obscurities. Was
Henry's reaffirmation of faith in his Archbishop
stagemanaged by himself with the assistance of Denny
and Butts, in which case the latter's intervention on
the fateful morning seems like an unnecessary touch
of malice against the plotters; or did Denny persuade
the King to summon Cranmer, in which case Butts'
talebearing reads like a genuine attempt to assist
the victim? The latter seems more likely, but
whatever the case, Cranmer was saved from arrest.

His troubles were not over, however. A
commission of the peace for Kent appointed to
investigate the charges against him was so heavily
biased against him that Morice wrote to Denny and
Butts asking them to use their influence in the
matter. His suit was successful, but there was a
further attempt to discredit Cranmer through the
prosecution of one of his diocesan clergy, Richard
Turner, who was accused of several varieties of
heresy; among them turning the mass into English and
using this new form of service in his church. Morice
again wrote to Denny and Butts asking their interest
with the King and explaining that Cranmer was
powerless to do anything: 'his grace hath told me
plainly, that it is put into the King's head that he
is the maintainer and supporter of all the heretics
within the realm'. It has already been recounted how

Butts' urbane mediation with the King saved Turner. (52)

Though Cranmer was preserved through the influence of sympathetic members of the privy chamber, the reform faction within that institution was itself involved in a heresy-hunt among the canons of St George's, Windsor. The prime mover was Gardiner, then in a mood of grim determination. According to Foxe, 'the gospellers were so quailed, that the best of them looked every hour to be clapped in the neck; for the saying went abroad, that the Bishop had bent his bow to shoot at some of the head deer'. At Windsor the organist John Marbeck was questioned with particular rigour about Sir Philip Hoby and Simon Heynes. Hoby was a diplomatist and gentleman of the privy chamber, and Heynes, of course, was Butts' confidant. The attack failed when the chief accuser, John London, over-reached himself and was found guilty of perjury, and on 31 August pardons for involvement in the affair were granted to a number of persons associated with the privy chamber, including Hoby, Sir Thomas Cawarden and Thomas Sternhold the psalmist. (53)

Butts died in November 1545, and perhaps it is not entirely coincidence that the following year saw a number of attempts against evangelicals at court. The attack on the preacher Edward Crome, who in palmier days had enjoyed the favour of Cranmer and Anne Boleyn, resulted in the prosecution of many members or clients of the privy chamber; Hugh Latimer was imprisoned, the royal doctor Huycke was questioned, and John Lassells was burned. There were other near-casualties. Nicholas Shaxton and John Taylor were found guilty of sacramentarian heresy, but made timely recantations. George Blage, an habitué of the privy chamber, was condemned to death for heresy against the eucharist, but members of that department of household (in particular, Bedford) successfully interceded for him with the King. Henry reacted as he had done after his reconciliation with Katherine Parr, and was 'sore offended' with the conservative persecutors 'that they would come so near him, and even into his privy chamber'. (54)

Finally, with the examination of Anne Askew, it was hoped to incriminate several evangelical women of the court. Anne, burned after gruelling questioning and the application of torture, was asked whether she had received any money while in prison from Ladies Sussex, Hertford, Fitzwilliam and Denny. The matter was of such importance that Anne's inquisitors resorted to force: 'Then they did put me on the rack, because I confessed no ladies nor gentlewomen to be of my opinion, and thereon they kept me a long time.' (55) The intended victims were not merely the ladies themselves but their eminent husbands, who would have been compromised if their wives had been convicted of heresy. Similarly, the condemnation of Katherine Parr would have brought down bigger prey than her own immediate feminine circle, since many of the ladies of the Queen's privy chamber were married to gentlemen of Henry's privy chamber.

In this context the attack on Katherine Parr must be read, not as a plot against the head of reform, but as one of a series of attempts against the evangelical faction, and as an effort to undermine that faction through one of the most vulnerable of their number. Curiously enough, an accurate impression of the disposal of power and patronage at court in the 1530s and 1540s may be gained from two books of poetry. Nicholas Bourbon's Nugae, published at Lyons in 1538, gives pride of place to his protector and deliverer, Anne Boleyn. Anne receives six poems, and there are also verses to evangelical clerics and courtiers: Cranmer, Latimer, Cromwell, Butts, Bainton and Dudley, to name the most prominent. John Parkhurst's Ludicra sive Epigrammata, composed in the last years of Henry VIII and in the reign of Edward, contains verses to a variety of upholders of the gospel, but here Katherine Parr is but one among many. There are poems to the King, Queen and Edward; the Brandon, Dudley and Grey families; Bainton and Butts, Coxe, Cheke and Sir Anthony Cooke; Cranmer, Coverdale, Becon and Aylmer; Walter Haddon and Thomas Wilson; Sir Anthony Cope and Anne Carew from the Queen's household; Robert Dymmock, David Whitehead and Nicholas Udall. It is noteworthy that though Parkhurst was Katherine Parr's chaplain, his work gives no particular emphasis to her reforming activities. (56)

Thus it appears that Katherine's role in the Henrician reformation has been gravely exaggerated, just as Anne Boleyn's has been seriously overlooked. While Katherine's interest in literature probably gave an impetus to the studies of the King's children, she was incapable of organising and directing a 'royal nursery'. While her evangelical piety cannot be doubted, her political influence was minimal, and it is notable that Henry VIII bequeathed her no part in the upbringing or government of his successor.

If Katherine is dismissed as a political and educative factor, it can be seen that the instruction

of Edward and Elizabeth was in the hands of the group
which controlled the machinery of religious
protection and scholarly patronage at court: the
reform faction within the King's privy chamber, led
by Denny. It was this group which warned and tried to
protect potential victims of conservative enmity
like Cranmer and Katherine Parr, and it was with
them, rather than with the Queen, that influence over
Henry lay. That Denny was the direct successor to
Anne Boleyn and Cromwell in the patronage of the
gospel was understood by Foxe, who declared in his
summary of Henry's religious achievement:

> If princes have always their council about them,
> that is but a common thing. If sometimes they
> have evil counsel ministered, that I take to be
> the fault rather of such as are about them, than
> of princes themselves. So long as Queen Anne
> (Boleyn), Thomas Cromwell, Archbishop Cranmer,
> Master Denny, Dr Butts, with such like were
> about him, and could prevail with him, what
> organ of Christ's glory did more good in the
> church than he? (57)

Notes

1. Cf. in particular J.K. McConica, English
Humanists and Reformation Politics Under Henry VIII
and Edward VI (Clarendon Press, Oxford, 1968),
passim. This work, which is extremely influential,
fails to distinguish humanists from either
protestants or medieval Catholics, but assumes that
all intellectual activity in England was 'Erasmian'.
In terms of patronage it ignores the role of both
Anne Boleyn and Sir Anthony Denny and the privy
chamber group, and grossly exaggerates the
importance of Katherine Parr. There is no documentary
basis for any of these conclusions.

2. Thomas Lupset, Exhortation to Young Men,
reprinted in J.A. Gee, Life and Works of Thomas
Lupset (Yale University Press, New Haven, 1928),
pp.233-62. The quotations are on pp.244, 257. Cf. Sir
Thomas Elyot, The Book Named the Governor, H.H.S.
Croft (ed.) (2 vols., Kegan Paul, Trench & Co.,
London, 1883), vol. 1, p.72.

3. Public Record Office, SP1/154, fo. 99,
Coventree to Cromwell; SP1/96, fo. 160, St Alban's
Hall to Cromwell. Both calendared in Letters and
Papers, Foreign and Domestic, of the Reign of Henry
VIII, J.S. Brewer, J. Gairdner, R.H. Brodie (eds.)
(21 vols., HMSO, London, 1862-1932), vol. 14 ii no.

437, vol. 9 no. 361 (hereafter cited as L&P). Cf. L&P
vol. 12 i no. 212, Huycke to Morison.
    4.   John   Foxe,   Acts   and   Monuments,   S.R.
Cattley (ed.) (8 vols., Seeley & Burnside, 1837),
vol. 5 pp.414-415. Cp. William A. Clebsch, England's
Earliest Protestants, 1520-1535 (Yale University
Press, New Haven and London, 1964), pp.43-6, who
denies that Barnes was a humanist.
    5.   British Library, Cotton MS Cleop. E V fos
60ff (L&P vol. 14 i no. 1035), Heynes to Butts (28
May?) 1539.
    6.   Cromwell's   will   is   printed   in   R.B.
Merriman (ed.), Life and Letters of Thomas Cromwell
(2 vols, Clarendon Press, Oxford, 1902), vol. 1.
pp.56-63.
    7.   Hastings Robinson (ed.), Original Letters
Relative to the English Reformation, Volume One
(Parker   Society,   Cambridge   University   Press,
Cambridge, 1846), pp.33-8, Hooper to Bullinger, 27
Jan. 1546.
    8.   John Bruce and Thomas Perowne (eds.),
Correspondence of Matthew Parker (Parker Society,
Cambridge University Press, Cambridge, 1853), pp.10-
14, Parker to Stokes; J.E. Cox (ed.), Miscellaneous
Writings and Letters of Thomas Cranmer (Parker
Society, Cambridge University Press, Cambridge
1846), p.309, Cranmer to the Dean of the Chapel
Royal; Tristram Revell, The sum of Christianity,
gathered out almost of all places of scripture by
that noble and famous clerk, Francis Lambert of
Avignon (Redman? London, 1536) preface; Cranmer,
Letters, pp.346-347; Sir Henry Ellis (ed.), Original
Letters Illustrative of English History (11 vols., 3
series, Harding, Triphook & Lepard, London, 1824,
1827, 1846), 3 series, vol. 2 p.285, Vaughan to
Cromwell.
    9.   Cranmer, Letters, pp.336, 362-3, 322, 310-
11, 384.
    10.   Ibid.,   p.315;   Parker,   Correspondence,
pp.10-14; G.E. Corrie (ed.), Sermons and Remains of
Hugh Latimer (Parker Society, Cambridge University
Press, Cambridge, 1845), p.385; cf. pp.410-11.
    11.   Ellis, Original Letters, 3 series, vol. 2,
p.207, Vaughan to Cromwell; Latimer, Remains,
pp.388-9, Latimer to Cromwell.
    12.   Ellis, Original Letters, series 2, vol. 2,
pp.162-9, Cromwell to Henry VIII, 1540.
    13.   Paul L. Hughes and James F. Larkin (eds.),
Tudor Royal Proclamations (3 vols., Yale University
Press, New Haven and London, 1964-9), vol. 1 pp.296-
8; A.G. Dickens, The English Reformation (Fontana,

72

London, 1973), p.264; G.R. Elton, <u>Reform and Reformation</u> (Edward Arnold, London, 1979), p.300; Robert Marsham, 'On a Manuscript Book of Prayers ... said to have been given by Queen Anne Boleyn to a Lady of the Wyatt Family,' <u>Archaeologia</u>, vol. 44, part 2 (Society of Antiquaries, London, 1873), pp.259ff.

14. Foxe, <u>Acts and Monuments</u>, vol. 5 pp.181-236.

15. <u>State Papers Published Under the Authority of His Majesty's Commission, Volume One, King Henry the Eighth</u> (HMSO, London, 1830), pp.842-5, the Council to Petre, 11 May 1546; Cranmer, <u>Letters</u>, pp.396-7.

16. Public Record Office, SP1/102, fo. 125 (<u>L&P</u> vol. 10 no. 371), confession to Tristram Revell.

17. John Bale, <u>The latter examination of Anne Askew, martyred in Smithfield by the wicked synagogue of Antichrist</u> (1547), pp.20b, 17b-18, 38b. The reference to Judas is Mark 14:22.

18. For Bainton's services to Anne Boleyn, <u>L&P</u> vol. 6 no. 1412, 7 nos 27, 89, 8 nos 209, 466, 702, 801. For his dealings with Hugh Latimer, <u>Remains</u>, pp.322-51 and William Latymer, 'A Brief Treatise or Chronicle of ... Anne Boleyn', Bodleian MS C Don 42 fos 27b-28. For letters from Smith and Barlow, <u>L&P</u> vol. 8 nos 466, 722.

19. For Butts as patron of Cambridge and of the evangelical cause, Maria Dowling, 'Anne Boleyn and Reform', <u>Journal of Ecclesiastical History</u>, vol. 35, no. 1 (January 1984), pp.35, 38, 39, 42. For the story of Turner, Foxe, <u>Acts and Monuments</u>, vol. 8. p.34.

20. For the King's attitude to Luther, Erwin Doernberg, <u>Henry VIII and Luther, An Account of their Personal Relations</u> (Barrie & Rockliff, London, 1961), passim.

21. For a fuller discussion of Anne's promotion of these two works, Dowling, 'Anne Boleyn and Reform', p.35-6.

22. Foxe, <u>Acts and Monuments</u>, vol. 5 pp.421-8; British Library, Cotton MS Vesp. FIII art. 32 (<u>L&P</u> vol. 4 app. 197), Anne to Wolsey; British Library, Royal MS 18 A LXIV, verses for Anne Boleyn's coronation; Nicholas Udall, <u>Dramatic Writings</u>, John S. Farmer (ed.) (privately printed, London, 1906), p.131.

23. Foxe, <u>Acts and Monuments</u>, vol. 7 p.454; William Gilpin, <u>Lives of Hugh Latimer and Bernard Gilpin</u> (R. Blamire, London, 1780), pp.32-5; John Venn, <u>Biographical History of Gonville and Caius</u>

College, 1349-1713 (7 vols., Cambridge University
Press, Cambridge, 1897), vol. 1, pp.17, 19; L&P vol.
9 nos 203, 252, 272-3, vol. 10 nos 1257 (lx), 117.
Cf. Allan G. Chester, Hugh Latimer, Apostle to the
English (University of Pennsylvania Press,
Philadelphia, 1954), pp.104, 230.
   24. M.A.E. Wood, Letters of Royal and
Illustrious Ladies (3 vols., Henry Colbourn, London,
1846), vol. 1, p.188, Anne Boleyn to Crome; W.G.
Searle, History of the Queen's College (2 vols.,
Cambridge University Press, Cambridge, 1867, 1871),
vol. 1, pp.178-82.
   25. PRO, SP1/103, fos. 262-3 (L&P vol. 10 no.
827), Mayor and Jurates of Sandwich to Henry VIII;
British Library, Additional MS 43, 827 fo.2,
narrative of Rose Hickman; Latymer, Brief Treatise,
fos. 31b-32; British Library, Harleian MS 6561,
epistles and gospels for the 52 Sundays in the year;
Stowe MS 956, 'Anne Boleyn's prayer book'; Royal MS
20 B XVII, treatise on letter-writing by Loys de
Brun; Royal MS 16 E XIII, 'Le Pasteur Evangélique' by
Marot. Anne's copy of Tyndale's new testament is in
the British Library; a French psalter she owned was
sold at Sotheby's in December 1982.
   26. Ellis, Original Letters, 1 series, vol. 2,
p.45, Anne to Cromwell about Herman; Foxe, Acts and
Monuments, vol. 5, p.132, Tyndale to Frith about
Joye.
   27. British Library, Sloane MS 1207, petition
of Thomas Alwaye. Not calendared in L&P.
   28. Foxe, Acts and Monuments, vol. 5, pp.35,
37; John Strype, Memorials of Thomas Cranmer (2
vols., Oxford University Press, Oxford 1840), vol. 1,
pp.643-4.
   29. Latymer, Brief Treatise, fo.28; Bourbon,
Nugae (Dolet, Lyons, 1538), passim. In November 1535
Simon Heynes reported that Sturmius had sent letters
to Cromwell through Shaxton or Skip; L&P vol. 9, no.
765.
   30. British Library, Cotton MS Otho C X fo.
260b (L&P, vol. 10, no. 942), Shaxton to Cromwell;
Cranmer, Letters, pp.322, 323-5.
   31. Cf. the printed correspondence of Cranmer,
Latimer and Parker for the later 1530s. For William
Latymer, C.H. and Thomas Cooper, Athenae
Cantabrigienses (2 vols., Deighton, Bell & Co.,
Cambridge, 1858, 1861), vol. 1, p.481; John and J.A.
Venn, Alumni Cantabrigienses, Part One, From the
Earliest Times to 1751 (4 vols., Cambridge University
Press, Cambridge, 1922-7), vol. 3, p.50.
   32. McConica, English Humanists, p.170 sees

74

Cromwell's publication of the Confession of Augsburg as government policy, but Elton maintains that only statements issued by the royal printer may be regarded as 'official'. Doernberg, <u>Henry VIII and Luther</u>, p.110 calls the Ten Articles 'a masterpiece of evasion'; thus it is very different in nature to the Augsburg declaration.

33. For the Ten Articles, Dickens, <u>English Reformation</u>, pp.243-5; Elton, <u>Reform and Reformation</u>, pp.256-60.

34. <u>State Papers of Henry VIII</u>, pp.563-4 (<u>L&P</u>, vol. 12, ii, no. 295), Latimer to Cromwell; ibid pp.555-7 (<u>L&P</u>, vol. 12, ii, no. 289), Foxe to Cromwell.

35. For the Acts of Six Articles, Dickens, <u>English Reformation</u>, pp.246-7; Elton, <u>Reform and Reformation</u>, pp.284, 286-8.

36. PRO, SP1/163, fo. 46 (<u>L&P</u>, vol. 16, no. 101), deposition of Lassells; Cranmer, <u>Letters</u>, p.401 to Henry VIII.

37. Agnes Strickland, <u>Lives of the Queens of England</u> (6 vols., G. Bell & Sons, London, 1890), vol. 2, p.390; Marian A. Gordon, <u>Life of Queen Katharine Parr</u> (Titus Wilson & Sons, Kendal, 1951) and Anthony Martienssen, <u>Queen Katherine Parr</u> (Secker & Warburg, London, 1973). McConica, <u>English Humanists</u>, Chapter 7 passim, was the first to elaborate the myth of the 'royal nursery'. It has recently been repeated in John N. King, <u>English Reformation Literature</u> (Princeton University Press, Princeton, 1982), p.23, and by Mortimer Levine, 'The Place of Women in Tudor Government', in <u>Tudor Rule and Revolution: Essays for G.R. Elton from his American Friends</u>, Delloyd J. Guth and John W. McKenna (eds.) (Cambridge University Press, Cambridge, 1982), pp.116-17.

38. <u>Literary Remains of King Edward VI</u>, J.G. Nichols (ed.) (2 vols., Roxburghe Club, Burt Franklin, New York, 1857), vol. 1 ep.17 (<u>L&P</u> vol. 21 i no. 1036), Edward to Katherine; British Library, Cotton MS Nero C X fo. 6 (<u>L&P</u> vol. 21 ii no. 685(2)), Katherine to Edward.

39. John Strype, <u>Ecclesiastical Memorials</u> (3 vols., Clarendon Press, Oxford, 1820-40), vol. 2, ii, p.337 (<u>L&P</u> vol. 21, i, no. 279), Katherine to Cambridge; Katherine Parr, <u>Lamentation of a Sinner</u> (Whitchurch, London, 1548), sig. B viii and B viiib.

40. <u>The first tome or volume of the Paraphrase of Erasmus upon the New Testament</u>, Nicholas Udall (ed.) (Whitechurch, London, 1548), sig. C. iiib, preface to Luke. As a comment on Katherine Parr's ability it may be noted that she did not translate

any part of the work herself; as a comment on her importance, it is interesting that there is no mention at all of her activities in the second volume, published in 1549.

41. British Library, Cotton MS Otho C X fo. 231 (L&P, vol. 19, i, no. 1021), Elizabeth to Katherine; L&P, vol. 18, ii, no. 39, Chapuys to Charles V. See also ibid vol. 19, i, nos 979, 1019, letters of Katherine to Henry.

42. For Princess Mary's education, Foster Watson, Vives and the Renascence Education of Women (Edward Arnold, London, 1912), passim, Maria Dowling, Humanism in the Age of Henry VIII (Croom Helm, London, 1986), pp.219-29.

43. Literary Remains, vol. 2, p.209. For humanist educational theory and practice, Dowling, Humanism, chapter 6 passim.

44. Whole Works of Roger Ascham, Giles (ed.) (3 vols, J.R. Smith, London, 1864-5), ep. 99 to Sturm on Elizabeth, ep. 85 to Cheke on his appointment as tutor.

45. Ibid., ep. 36 to Denny; Sermon of St Cyprian made on the Lord's Prayer, Thomas Paynell (trans.) (Berthelet, London, 1539), sig. A ib; Thomas Langley, Abridgement of the Notable Work of Polydore Vergil (Grafton, London, 1546), sig. A vib, A vii-viib; William Hugh, A Sweet Consolation (Hertford, London, 1546), sig. A iiib; British Library, Harleian MS 78, fos. 25b-26, epitaph on Denny. Chaloner's translation of Chrysostom was taken from Cheke's new Greek text.

46. The Dictionary of Sir Thomas Elyot (in aed. Berthelet, London, 1538), sig. A iib; Parker, Correspondence, p.33.

47. For Coxe as Edward's tutor, Dowling, Humanism, pp.212-14.

48. For Cheke's relations with Butts, John Cheke, D. Ioannis Chrysostomi Homiliae Duae (Reyner Wolfe, London 1543), preface to Henry VIII; John Strype, Life of the Learned Sir John Cheke (Clarendon Press; Oxford, 1821), pp.27-30. The link between Cambridge and the Court is examined in Winthrop S. Hudson, The Cambridge Connection and the Elizabethan Settlement (Duke University Press, Durham, North Carolina, 1980).

49. Ascham, Whole Works, eps 31 to Elizabeth, 23 to Cheke. Cheke and Coxe also tried to assist Walter Haddon of King's, Cambridge when he visited Edward at Hertford. Coxe gave him a (no doubt commendatory) letter for the Prince which he delivered to Cheke unwillingly, since he did not wish

for a courtier's life; <u>Literary Remains</u>, vol. 1, p.lxxvii. For Ascham's lessons with Edward, ibid. p.lii.

50. Foxe, <u>Acts and Monuments</u>, vol. 5, pp.553-61.

51. Ibid., p.388 for Cranmer's book; for the abbey land, J.G. Nichols, <u>Narratives of the Days of the Reformation</u> (Camden Society, J.B. Nichols & Sons, London, 1859), p.263. For the 'Prebendaries' Plot', Foxe, <u>Acts and Monuments</u>, vol. 8, pp.24-9.

52. Ibid., vol. 8 pp.29, 31-4.

53. Ibid., vol. 5 pp.464-95; cf. McConica, <u>English Humanists</u>, pp.220-2. For Hoby and his wife, who was also implicated in the affair, <u>Holbein and the Court of Henry VIII</u> (catalogue of an exhibition at the Queen's Gallery, Buckingham Palace, 1978-9) (Lund Humphries, London and Bradford, 1978), pp.105-8.

54. <u>State Papers of Henry VIII</u>, pp.842-51, proceedings against Crome; Foxe, <u>Acts and Monuments</u>, vol. 5, p.564.

55. Bale, <u>Latter Examination of Askew</u>, pp.40-40b, 43-43b, 44b-45. Cf. Foxe, <u>Acts and Monuments</u>, vol. 5, pp.537-47.

56. John Parkhurst, <u>Ludicra sive Epigrammata Juvenilia</u> (Daye, London, 1573), passim. For Bourbon's <u>Nugae</u>, see note 29 above.

57. Foxe, <u>Acts and Monuments</u>, vol. 5, p.605.

* I would like to thank Ms Catharine Davies and Professor A.G. Dickens for reading and commenting on this essay.

Chapter Three

'POOR PERSECUTED LITTLE FLOCK' OR 'COMMONWEALTH OF CHRISTIANS'; EDWARDIAN PROTESTANT CONCEPTS OF THE CHURCH

Catharine Davies

What do you mean when you talk about the church? This may appear rather an impertinent question to put to Edwardian protestants. Was this not the period which produced two prayer books, two Acts of Uniformity, the first book of Homilies and the Forty Two articles? These documents certainly signalled the direction in which the reform of the doctrine and liturgy of the church were going. But although these were the documents to which the population at large was most exposed, they were left largely to speak for themselves. In the contemporary surge (it was too disorganised to call it a campaign) of protestant propaganda and polemic (1) the defence of the prayer books, or even of the idea of corporate worship itself (apart from the discrete question of the Lord's Supper), was notable by its absence. The defence of the English church was not so much a question of defending its visible institutions and observances as of attacking popery in all its manifestations. (2)

This priority placed certain limitations on the ways in which the positive protestant image of the church as a visible institution could develop. Obviously under Henry VII the case against popery had been organised around the royal supremacy. As we shall see the godly prince continued to matter enormously to Edwardian protestants, but the supremacy as such did not bulk large in Edwardian polemic. (3) Certainly their acceptance of the supremacy did not prevent Edwardian protestants from regarding Henry VIII's work as a godly prince as incomplete; he may have cast out the pope from his dominion but he had been deceived by conservative elements in the church into retaining popish doctrines and ceremonies and even into persecuting the upholders of the gospel. (4) By explaining these

78

undesirable aspects of late Henrician religious policy as popish tyranny protestants maintained their self image as a 'persecuted little flock of Christ'. Such a vision of the true church proved surprisingly influential throughout Edward's reign and it is the basic contention of this paper that there remained a tension within Edwardian protestantism between that vision of the church as a persecuted minority and a rather grander image of the church as a commonwealth of Christians, a whole nation enjoying a covenanted relationship with God under the rule of a Christian prince. By the reign's end, it will be argued, the tension between those two views of the church had produced a renewed concern with excommunication and the question of whether the reformed church could exercise spiritual discipline over its own members.

In dealing with the first view of the church the key text is John Bale's Image of both churches. This was written and published during Bale's exile in the mid 1540s and was republished three times during Edward's reign, (5) when its central themes recur (albeit in less coherent form) in protestant writing.

There is no need now to discuss the Image as either a work of apocalyptic thought or of history, (6) but only to sketch out the central antithesis between the true and false churches around which its argument is organised.

Bale declared that the purpose of his commentary was to draw attention to the key importance of the book of Revelation for the godly reader, for

> herein is the true Christian church which is the meek spouse of the lamb without spot in her right-fashioned colours described. So is the proud church of hypocrites, the rose coloured whore, the paramour of Antichrist and the sinful synagogue of Satan in her just proportion depainted, to the merciful forewarning of the Lord's elect. And that is the cause why I have entitled the book the Image of Both Churches. (7)

By developing the idea of the struggle between the two churches Bale was able, as his Lutheran predecessors had been, to turn Catholic accusations of schism upside down. (8) Thus the claim of the papacy to head the universal church was denounced as the deception and domination of the world by Antichrist, while the universality of the true church was a function of the recurrence, scattered in place

79

and time, of the witness of true believers.
Reformation would occur where true preachers were
allowed by providence to operate without hindrance
and thus call the people out of popery. (9) The need
to maintain a sharp contrast between the two churches
rather than any great intellectual subtlety or
theological creativity lay at the centre of Bale's
account. The true church was based on an inward,
justifying faith in Christ, while the false church
put its trust in the merits of those outward works
that it had itself devised and enjoined. As the faith
of the true church was based on the word of God, it
could act only as a unifying force. The false church,
however, was built on the shaky foundations of human
tradition and was thus always prone to dissension and
internal division. (10)

This doctrinal polarisation - between faith and
works - was made manifest by the self-images of the
two churches:

> for whereas the wicked do seem to themselves to
> be witful, strong, learned, rich righteous and
> holy spiritual fathers; thou esteemeth thyself
> but an abject of the world, wretched, weak,
> poor, sinful and a miserable doer, as concerning
> the flesh. (11)

The vainglory and price of the false church was
reflected in its powerful, wealthy and tyrannical
organisation; the humility of the true church in
refusal of its members ot be spiritually governed by
anything but the gospel. (12) The false church was
not just a false hierarchy, topped by the extravagant
claims of the papacy, it was the majority of the
people in the world. (13) The historical actuality of
the domination of Christendom by the Roman Church was
conflated with the fact that the majority of the
people were ungodly. Thus the true church was always
a godly minority, what John Bossy has recently
described (referring to Lollardy) as the 'ghostly
diaspora of the predestined'. (14) In this context
there was little room for the development of the idea
that the true church could be identified with
national reformations.

Bale celebrated the achievement of the
reformers but retained an ambiguous attitude to
princes, regarding them as just as likely to act as
the agents of Antichrist, as the patrons of reform.
(15) He was thus able to remain unspecific about the
precise nature of true visible churches and this
enabled him to avoid identifying the English church

with the true church. The distinguishing marks of the true church were government by the word (which involved reception of the gospel preached), unity in faith and charity and vindication through suffering (which meant persecution). (16) Such a vision drew on the spiritual qualities of the godly minority, rather than on the claims of a nascent national church. This was natural since for Bale the government of the Church of England under Gardiner's influence was a case of popery surviving under the supremacy and subverting it from within. (17) To an extent, therefore, the English church in the 1540s had more in common with the false church than the true. However, the true church retained its individual witnesses in the person of Henrician martyrs like Bilney, Frith and Barnes. (18)

The experience of the Marian persecution, placed so memorably by Foxe within a vision of the struggle between the true and false churches taken ultimately from Bale, ensured that in the long term the vision of the church as a persecuted minority achieved a central place in the consciousness of English protestants. (19) What perhaps requires more explanation was the persistence of the theme of persecution and suffering in the literature of the Edwardian period, when English protestants had undergone no tests or trials remotely comparable to the traumas of Mary's reign and when the government was increasingly well affected towards the gospel. (20) This was less a tribute to Bale's 'influence' than to the continuing relevance of persecution and the attitudes towards the church that went with it to the polemical needs and practical situation of English protestants. It is to those attitudes and the needs which they met that we must now turn.

The fact that the period of the Act of Six Articles was not marked by intense or large scale persecution did not prevent both the Henrician exiles and authors of the period 1547 to 1549 from presenting it as a time of struggle under the cross of persecution for the true church. 'If this book, therefore, seem too sharp toothed,' wrote George Joye in 1546, 'consider in how sharp a time it was written and by whose counsel and labour then most tyrannously and ungodly so many good books, holy bibles and testaments yea and the innocent Christian holy members of Christ were burned.' (21) Moreover, as both Joye and Anthony Gilby pointed out, the Act of Six Articles was backed up by 'false preaching' and 'false doctrine craftily handled and painted' which together won over the 'simple unlearned folk' and encouraged those who 'more favoured the Romish religion than Christ's'. (22) Gilby's answer to Gardiner's persistent reference to 'the doctrine of the Church' was (with Bale) to redefine the church; the church that defended transubstantiation was that of Rome and Antichrist, whereas the true church was the church of the risen Christ which possessed spiritual, scriptural knowledge. This was, of necessity, a 'little flock' but from the time of Abel it had never lacked true witnesses. (23) Of late this witness had consisted of resistance not merely to the world or the enemies of Israel but to popery.

> This thousand years that this enemy hath troubled the world with popish pomp and pride, keeping and locking up the word of God from us; God hath not destituted and forsaken, but hath always, from time to time, stirred up witnesses of his truth, whom partly the popish have slain, but some God hath reserved and always the good simple people have had their eyes unto the living God in heaven, whatsoever the priest did babble of his own handiwork. (24)

Gilby compared the 'gloriousness' of the school doctors, some of whom had been canonised, with the faithful simplicity, obscurity and patient suffering of the godly, who were kept immune from Gardiner's propaganda by contemplation of the true church.

> But unto the godly (whose desire is to be like their master Christ in suffering with him in this world, that they may reign with him in the world to come) having before their eyes all the prophets (who suffered for the truth) and all other martyrs and witnesses (whom the world hated and was unworthy to have still among them) considering that the scriptures cannot lie which sayeth that whosoever shall live godly in Christ shall suffer persecution all your persuasions are vain and of no effect. (25)

For Hooper too the way of Christ was by definition the way of a minority. In all the treatises he wrote from exile in Zurich he stressed that the Christian conscience only believed the word of God and that which was consonant with it; without scripture no purely human authority based on either numbers or worldly power could command the assent of the believer (26). Of course, there must always be a visible church, existing in the midst of the world, but it was a 'commonwealth' defended not by 'carnal weapons' but by the Holy Spirit and nourished in Isaiah's words 'by the bread of adversity and the water of affliction'. (27) He compared it 'unto Daniel sitting among the lions, destitute of all human aid and defence. Deliver it out of the cave yet shall it wander upon the earth as a contemptible thing of no estimation, not knowing where to rest her head.' (28) Hooper's references to the affliction of the church were some of the more restrained and generalised comments passed by the Henrician exiles, in large part because they were modified with expressions of hope concerning the new King's patronage of the gospel. Yet even Hooper in his letters to Bullinger of 1546-7 revealed a deep anxiety that the upholders of the gospel (himself included) were being sorely tried by persecution. (29)

Unsurprisingly, in the doggerel verses and scurrilous prose pamphlets that flooded from the presses between 1547 and 1551 no such restraint was observed. According to Peter Moone, 'This whip (the Six Articles) was very meet for their pestilent complexion. For through such tyranny the people's hearts were raw.' (30) An important part of William Punt's Inditement of the mass was that it 'crucifies Christ every day anew and not only in her doctrine but also she persecuteth him afresh in his faithful members, if they would not believe her false doctrine.' Punt based this claim on a list of Henrician martyrs. (31) William Samuel's Warning to London began with the theme of the persecution of true preachers, with three verses on Anne Askew, fixing his attention on 1546 as the high point of London's hostility to the gospel. (32) Through Bale's hagiography Anne had become the classic example of persecution; in her powerlessness in the world (as a woman) her faithful strength in torment and her refusal to budge from a literal interpretation of scripture she represented a type of the true church. (33)

In part the persistence of persecution as a subject under Edward is attributable to the fact that Somerset's relaxation of the censorship of Henry's reign allowed many Henrician manuscripts to be rushed to the press. (34) Such an explanation obviously applies to the earlier part of Edward's reign, but the continued prevalence of the theme of the little flock of Christ after the first surge of anti-Catholic propaganda surely shows that the capacity to identify themselves against a persecuting power had become an integral part of the self image of English protestants, and one which they were unwilling to give up even when it no longer really fitted with their objective situation. Moreover, such a self image allowed protestants to distance themselves from a regime whose intentions toward the church and the gospel they might not entirely trust and thus to maintain a crucial pocket of ideological independence in what were otherwise dourly erastian times. Here the political and social instability of the reign, together with the inability of the church to finance a proper preaching ministry (35), came to the protestants' rescue, enabling them to continue to present themselves as the poor persecuted flock of Christ.

Persecution of the godly began with slander of the preachers. In Latimer's Court sermons he revelled in the title 'a seditious fellow' because his self conscious 'unpopularity' with the powerful allowed him to identify his own ministry with that of other prophets like Isaiah, Paul and even Christ himself, who had been reviled and persecuted for preaching the gospel. (36) For Latimer preaching was an inherently difficult and dangerous task. In his sermons on the parable of the wedding feast he claimed

> the bidders of his guests are preachers; but here are so many lets and hindrances; covetousness is a let; ambition is a let; cruelty is the greatest let. For they beat his servants, brake their heads, yea murdered them which bade them to his bridal. 'The highest promotion that God can bring his unto in this life is, to suffer for his truth. And it is the greatest setting forth of his word; it is God's seed. And one suffering for the truth turneth more than a thousand sermons.' (37)

These passages were neither a dismissal of the efficacy of preaching nor a prophecy of his own fate, but a dramatisation of the evangelical predicament of the true preacher. Latimer followed it with a vivid account of one of his own interrogations for heresy, when, he claimed, only the presence of the Holy Spirit saved him from the 'Many snares and traps' laid for him by the bishops. (38) The incident to which he was referring had taken place under Henry but it was recent enough to maintain a sense that testimony to the truth was an arduous task that was likely to attract the hostile attention of the powers that be. (39)

Using an Old Testament example Hooper presented the dilemma of Jonah as a paradigm for the situation with which all outspoken contemporary preachers were confronted. Theirs was a choice between 'obloquy and contempt'; contempt if the condign punishments for the sins of the nation which they foretold failed to occur; obloquy and a reputation as a 'cruel tyrant and seeker after blood' if they did. Hooper's perception of the 'displeasure and great emnity' which greeted his pulpit performances was sharpened by his identification of his own ministry with that of earlier persecuted prophets. (40) Gilby made the same point, albeit more positively.

> For it is not Jeremiah, nor Latimer, nor Lever, nor Hooper, nor Becon, nor Horne that speaketh unto them but the Spirit of God which always by such weak vessels doth so utter itself that when these are gone others cometh of their ashes. And if these should not speak the very stones should cry out against our wickedness ... The shame you would lay upon the true preachers lasteth but an hour; no it is no shame but the greatest honour you can do them. But your shame is everlasting. (41)

Richard Finch, whose <u>Epiphany of the church</u> was written in 1550 in the wake of Ridley's visitation of London, (42) followed the Baleian antithesis between the true and the false church, so that for him the unpopularity of the reformation, (43) made manifest by the 1549 rebellions was further evidence of Antichrist's persecution of the true church.

> O what murmurings and complainings have they made since their mass decayed? What lies have their idle brains invented, what slanders have they imagined and what false rumours have they sprinkled abroad in the world against them that have sincerely preached the gospel? How conspire they against good Christian ministers which according to their vocation attend their flocks? What tumults, uproars and rebellions have they raised against their superiors, to the great hindrance of God's holy word? May not a man manifestly behold in them the monstrous beast that fighteth against the lamb and word of God. (44)

Particularly in the light of recent writings on the progress of the English reformation it might be

argued that all we have here is the internalisation
by the ministers of the inherent unpopularity of
protestantism. (45) Yet their own rather more subtle
reading of their predicament saw the social disorder
and covetousness of the time as a natural product of
the enmity between Satan, Antichrist and the world on
the one hand and the true church on the other. As
such the heightened activity of these enemies of the
gospel served both to validate the status of the
godly minority as the true church and to show that
the preacher's message was in some sense striking
home. Lever spoke of the godly fleeing to safety from
the hordes of the 'superstitious papists, carnal
gospellers and seditious rebels' who surrounded them
on every side. (46) Attacking the combination of lay
greed and clerical pluralism which resulted in a
chronic shortage of preaching Lever denounced 'a
miserable mart of merchandise ... and yet now so
commonly used that thereby shepherds be turned to
thieves, dogs into wolves and the poor flock of
Christ, redeemed with his previous blood, most
miserably pilled and spoiled, yea cruelly devoured.'
(47) Hutchinson in his (unpublished) sermons On
oppression, affliction and patience spoke of those
oppressed by enclosers, forestallers and regraters
as 'God's martyrs' - so long as they bore their
grievances patiently. (48) In his Commentary on Micah
Gilby wrote cryptically of 'the church and faithful
congregation of Christ scattered abroad with popish
boar, devoured with covetous and greedy wolves, bears
and lions and trodden under the foot with stinking
goats.' (49)

On the one hand the flock of Christ was still
endangered by the activities of the papists (50) and
on the other by a new breed of 'carnal gospellers'
who, enriched with the sacrilegious spoils of the
church, were busy undermining the purity of the
protestant message. (51) Some writers went so far as
to see these threats as but different aspects of the
same evil force. The description of covetousness as
the 'new idolatry' which was common to Gilby, Lever
and Hutchinson (52) should not just be dismissed 'as
the type of futile lamentation which had been heard
for centuries'. (53) It was a conscious adaptation of
the language of anti-popery to the description and
criticism of a supposedly reformed commonwealth, so
that what was indeed an age-old theme was
successfully invested with a fresh contemporary
resonance. While it is no doubt true enough, as
Professor Elton has observed, that the denunciations
of the preachers did not constitute 'a novel or

practical blueprint for social or economic reform, (54) it is far from clear that they were ever attempting to produce such a programme. Rather, the sympathy shown by men like Lever and Crowley for the poor was more a function of their evangelical protestantism than of any adherence to a 'commonwealth' ideology. (55) Thus traditional themes were given new impetus and relevance by the anti-hierarchical thrust of the Edwardian rejection of all things popish. As Crowley told Shaxton, Christ had by his grace made poor fishermen apostles when there had been no reason why he could not have chosen the emperor himself if he had wanted to. (56) Christ, according to Latimer, was to be found among the poor, but among those who were poor by providential circumstance not through their own hypocritical vows. (57)

Finding the church amongst those who were oppressed and suffering in the world allowed free rein to a spirituality that enjoined passivity, obedience and glorified suffering under the cross of affliction. (58) In a period which lacked a developed casuistry of personal assurance (of the sort later perfected by the puritans) affliction was often seen not only as a test of faith but also as a sign of election. As Phillip Nicholls wrote in his Godly new story of twelve men sent ... to spy out the land of Canaan of 1548: 'thus doth the Lord try his elect with trouble and adversity, that faith may shine and appear in his right kind. And unless it be tried how shall it be known.' (59)

This insistence on adversity as a test of the presence of the true church was not merely a useful device in appealing to a flock of 'simple people'; it also shaped protestant appeals to the Christian prince and thus provided a much needed link between the vision of the church as a little flock and as a Christian commonwealth. Thus in his Declaration of Christ Hooper described the troubles of rebellion at home and foreign war that had afflicted Henry VIII when he 'took God's cause in hand' as the direct consequence of Henry's disturbing the security of that 'leopard and dragon of Rome'. (60) The King should not, therefore, be disturbed to find that he was championing the religion of a minority for the religion of the majority was by definition that of the rebellious 'church of Korah'. (61) Thus by aligning himself with the cause of the true church the prince became part of that little flock of Christ against which the forces of Satan, the world and Antichrist were ranged.

Of course, the role of a Christian prince thus recruited to the cause of the gospel was not restricted to offering a space within his dominions for the 'afflicted church' to 'rest in'. (62) On the contrary, a truly Christian prince could provide conditions in which the church could become synonymous with the nation. (63) The significance of the comparison between Edward and the young Josiah, which was so dear to Edwardian protestants, was not merely that both kings were young, it lay rather in the fact that Josiah had presided over the providential rediscovery of the law by the priests and its reinstatement as the governing principle according to which Judah was ruled. (64) Latimer set the King's office in the conditional terms of Deuteronomy 17, demanding that Edward should set his face against politic counsel in the crucial areas of defence, finance and marriage and instead follow the promptings of the word. (65) Government according to the law of God, based on a set of examples taken from the Old Testament, clearly implied that England, like Israel, was a covenanted nation; Josiah had completed his reforms by symbolically renewing the covenant. To fulfil the nation's covenant with God it was necessary that the prince enforce properly godly standards of behaviour on his subjects. It was this which produced Latimer's obsession with official corruption and negligence in the dispensation of justice. (66) Just as in the secular sphere the maintenance of justice was the responsibility of the prince, so in the church it was up to the prince to provide a properly trained and financed preaching ministry. (67) Failure in this would be particularly serious since it was ignorance of the word which caused sin and social disorder. Crucially, while the word was not preached the people perished in ignorance of the gospel. (68) As the reign wore on the performance of the regime seemed to the preachers to fall disastrously short of these exalted standards. The time was short and the corruption of the nation seemed to demand drastic action. Hooper, for instance, made an impassioned plea for the King to heed the 'prophets' who pointed out the sins of his people and led them in an act of mass repentance. (69)

To ignore such pleas was to risk the judgement of God visited upon the whole nation. Just as Edwardian protestant notions of the church oscillated between a little flock of Christ, cowering under the cross of persecution and a Christian commonwealth, enjoying the benefits of a covenant with God, so Edwardian England was conceived as existing in a twilight world between these two states. If the prince and the magistrates beneath him responded to the dictates of the word, laid before them by preachers like Latimer and Hooper, discharging their role as prophets at court, then the status of a godly commonwealth could be attained; if not, then the little flock of Christ would labour once more under the cross of persecution.

Thus far the thought of the Edwardian protestants has been presented as resting upon a strict distinction and division of labour between the secular and spiritual swords. The spiritual sword wielded by the clergy was equated almost exclusively with preaching and was taken to apply only to the internal spiritual realm of conscience. The realm of external action, the regulation and control of the outward behaviour of church members, through the application of external punishments and rewards, was left entirely to the magistrate. (70) This enabled protestants to equate all forms of clerical power, all claims to a jurisdiction over the laity (other than that exercised from the pulpit) with popery. It also assured the preachers of a considerable spiritual and moral autonomy in their chosen role as prophets, interpreting the law of God to the relevant human authorities. However, so exalted was the scriptural model of the Christian commonwealth being propagated from the pulpit and press and so dire the consequences of any failure to live up to that ideal, that, as the reign wore on, protestants found themselves impelled by the logic of their own rhetoric into a deepening moral crisis. As it became clearer and clearer that the English were not behaving as the members of a godly commonwealth should, some protestants turned again to the spiritual sanctions which the church, rather than the magistrate, could use to control the sins of its members. Thus in the official catechism written towards the end of the reign (probably by John Ponet) discipline featured for the first time in an Edwardian definition of the church. Even here Ponet's primary definition stated simply that the church consisted of the godly governed spiritually by Christ. (71) Bale would hardly have disagreed with that, but Ponet went on to talk of the church as a 'kingdom or commonwealth Christians' in terms which could scarcely apply to a Baleian concept of the true church as a persecuted minority. Ponet's definition is worth quoting in full:

> The marks ... of this church are first pure
> preaching of the gospel, then brotherly love out
> of which as members of all one body springeth
> good will of each other. Thirdly upright and
> uncorrupted use of the Lord's sacraments
> according to the ordinance of the gospel, last
> of all brotherly correction and excommunication
> or banishing those out of the church that will
> not amend their lives. This mark the holy
> fathers terms discipline. This is that same
> church that is grounded upon the assured rock
> Jesus Christ and upon trust in him. This is that
> same church which Paul calleth the pillar and
> upholding stay of truth ... whosoever believeth
> the Gospel preached in this church he shall be
> saved, but whosoever believeth not he shall be
> damned. (72)

While the first three marks of the church listed
by Ponet could apply just as well to Bale's vision of
the true church, Ponet included discipline as the
fourth mark and made no mention of suffering. At
first sight this might seem to be a slight shift of
emphasis within a unitary protestant view of the
church, a shift moreover entirely explicable in terms
of the different situations in which the two men were
writing; Bale in exile, with the true church
suffering under the Act of Six Articles, Ponet in a
formally protestant church, where, deprived of the
persecuting attentions of the false church to provide
a validating test of the constancy of the true church
and appalled by the sinfulness of even formal
protestants, he turned from suffering to discipline
as a mark of the church. (73) Be that as it may the
result was a view of the church with radically
different implications from that produced by Bale.
Having said that, it has to be admitted that the
topic of spiritual discipline and excommunication
was only addressed by a few writers. It was, for
instance, surely significant that John Foxe's De
censura (1551) (74), which was the only full length
treatment of the subject of excommunication, was
written in Latin and aimed at a learned, clerical
rather than a general lay audience. Discussion of the
issue of spiritual discipline was not necessarily a
product of continental influence; George Joye, an
exile, did not think it was worth restoring
excommunication, while John Foxe, who did, did not
draw on continental authorities or examples in
framing his case. (75) What precipitated the
discussion was the problem of the persistence of sin

in a supposedly reformed Christian commonwealth.
Considering that England had enjoyed the gospel for
years many protestants felt that things were getting
worse not better. The reputation of the gospel was
being besmirched by those who had used it as a 'cloak
for covetousness'. The 'carnal gospeller' had become
almost as big a problem as 'the privy papist'. (76)
Joye, who selected adultery as the most pressing
social outrage, treated popery and sin as equal
threats; he wanted 'all papistry clean swept out of
our churches and justly punish open obstinate
incurable sinners, lest for these two impediments the
gospel denied us as they shall be sharp thorns in our
eyes and spears in our sides.' (77) Ideally this
purge was to be led by the magistrate, the minister
and all good citizens acting together,

> which as they will suffer nothing to grow that
> may destroy the city and commonwealth, even so
> should the professor suffer no vice nor false
> doctrine nor sinner unpunished in the church
> whereby the congregation is corrupted and
> grievously slandered and turned from the fear of
> God who is to be feared and praised forever.
> (78)

Latimer in his <u>Ultimum Vale</u> to the court in 1550
asked for the restoration of Christ's discipline of
excommunication to be a means 'to pacify God's wrath
and indignation against us and also that less
abomination shall be used than in times past hath
been and is at this day'. (79) Joye and Latimer were
both troubled by what they saw as an increase in
sexual licence but Foxe pointed out that
excommunication could also be used against a wide
range of social evils, including exploitation of the
poor, lack of charity and (significantly) contempt
for the ministry. (80) A more Bucerian tone was
struck by Edmund Allen who argued that excommunication should be used against 'all such as will not
hear the Church and congregation, reproving and
admonishing them for their souls' health and they
also which have offended the church and congregation
with any manifest, grievous and notable crimes'. (81)
In a few writers it was not merely the moral
crisis that provoked their concern with the issue but
the question of the integrity of the Lord's Supper.
The author of <u>The song of the Lord's Supper</u> advocated
that 'all such as God's word slander, irk, slake or
detest, all wilful weak which in blind ceremonies
will rest are to be refused till they wish for God's

kingdom'. (82) Thomas Lancaster argued that the presence of manifest sinners at communion should not be tolerated by the congregation which was after all the body of Christ. God would judge the hypocrites who covered their sins with a 'shining mantle of holiness' as Judas had done. (83) But these demands were isolated instances in the great volume of material advocating a return to the 'primitive use of the Lord's Supper' since the issue of excommunication was still tainted with more than a hint of the excessive powers claimed by the popish clergy. Foxe made a particular point of distinguishing between the legitimate uses of excommunication and popish abuse such as its deployment for trivial offences in the course of political quarrels or to satisfy the whims of the clergy. (84) Not only had excommunication played a central role in the spiritual tyranny exercised by the popish clergy, as an external ceremony it was rejected by many protestants as inherently 'carnal', an outward form to be rejected in the search for an 'inward' and properly spiritual religion. (85) Indeed, having rejected transubstant-iation excommunication may well have come to seem almost irrelevant since most protestants agreed that only the godly truly communicated while the ungodly 'ate to their own damnation'. In short the issue of excommunication brought the matter of externals to the fore again, at a time when protestant anti-clericalism had made repentance a matter for the individual lay conscience. Thus in the wider debate about the sacrament far more was made by protestants of the spiritual reconciliation wrought by Christ's unique sacrifice on the cross than of the sacrament as an occasion for the exclusion of the ungodly. (86)

The need for excommunication highlighted the church's role as a visible institution, active in the world. Hooper, who had demanded it as early as 1547 in order to bring the church into line with the institutions of the apostles, recognised as much when he compared churches lacking discipline to 'an army without weapons'. (87) 'This act and discipline of the church is but an act politic and civil to such as hath professed to live in the commonwealth of Christ's church in an order lest that the vicious life of the person should be slander unto the word of God.' (88) Again, when Foxe asked for discipline to be restored on the grounds that England must set an example as 'another Israel' he was clearly referring to the outward reputation of the reformation in England. (89)

In discussing the practicalities of excommuni-

cation Foxe placed his emphasis on the authority of
the minister. Initially he presented excommunication
as one of a range of remedies to be applied to the
individual sinner by the minister acting as a
physician of the soul. (90) Subsequently he reverted
to an image of the minister as a surgeon, excising
the evil members from the body of the church. (91)
For Foxe the discretion and personal moral authority
of the minister were paramount because the
responsibility for disciplining the flock rested
solely with him. (92) However, Foxe's prime concern
remained the control of sin rather than the reform of
the church. If all pastors both could and should
enforce excommunication then that would surely knock
another nail into the coffin of episcopal power. (93)
Foxe, however, did not spell out the full
implications of such a radical step; his was a plea
for an improvement in the quality of the parish
clergy rather than for a basic restructuring of the
government of the church. The same moderate instincts
led him to draw back from involving the congregation
in the exercise of excommunication. In contrast to
the reformed churches of Switzerland (and even to the
Stranger Churches in London) Foxe accorded the
congregation only a passive role in the exercise of
spiritual discipline. Amongst Edwardian protestants
only Edmund Allen (who had been a late Henrician
exile and drew on Continental models) hinted at the
use of elders to help the minister enforce
discipline. Indeed, he stressed that discipline
should be administered by the minister on behalf of
the congregation, as a natural extension and
culmination of their normal exercises in mutual
encouragement and admonition. (94)

Nor was the internal structure of the church the
only question raised by Foxe's treatment of the
subject; once the minister claimed to exercise
external sanctions, was that not to trespass on the
magistrate's jurisdiction over the external actions
of his subjects? Foxe spent a whole chapter firmly
distinguishing between the two swords. While the
magistrate's job was to punish criminals with the
secular sword, the minister used the spiritual sword
of excommunication to tackle the problem of sin
itself. (95) Roger Hutchinson approached the same
problem from the opposite end of the ideological
spectrum, when he claimed that the restoration of
spiritual discipline would be a good thing, only if
it was not allowed to present an anabaptistical
threat to the power of the magistrate. (96) So
worried were many protestants by even the appearance

of a popish or anabaptistical encroachment on the powers of the prince that they limited the spiritual sword wielded by the clergy to the word preached. In normal circumstances that should be sufficient to meet the challenge of sin but as Joye admitted wilful and hardened sinners 'will neither hear nor believe but thrust it from them'. Joye's response to this was the more typical one amongst Edwardian protestants, he appealed to the secular magistrate to apply the law more effectively and in the case of adulterers to adopt the Mosaic law and execute them. (97) For Edwardian protestants in search of a godly commonwealth the power of the magistrate was far less problematic than the authority of the church in regulating the external conduct of the English.

The whole notion of discipline therefore raised more questions than it answered. It must be remembered that (Hooper apart) calls for discipline only started in the second half of the reign, when the wave of anti-papal polemic had begun to subside and the first prayer book had been established. It was moreover, to a large extent, limited by the essentially erastian framework set up by the Henrician reformation. With both the King and protestantism in their infancy the overwhelming need was for a church which defined itself in missionary terms: The position of protestantism under Edward was too precarious for the preachers to start thinking of the church as a temple built only of lively stones, as did many Elizabethan divines later in the century. (98) The image of the poor persecuted church spoke more directly to the experience and circumstances of Edwardian protestants. It certainly allowed the preachers to identify with earlier prophets who had likewise castigated a corrupt establishment. It allowed them both to praise and appeal to the godly prince and yet disassociate themselves from the more questionable activities of the regime. Theirs was not a settled church and they were free, therefore, largely to ignore difficult questions about the spiritual powers necessary to run such a church. The result was that despite their very close links with the governments of both Somerset and Northumberland, Edwardian protestants could see themselves as a sort of permanent opposition. They inhabited an Israel which they saw as riven with idolatry and corruption. The accession of Mary and the consequent dismantling of the Edwardian reforms came not so much as a bitter and unexpected disappointment to protestants, but rather as the culmination of earlier judgements and punishments sent from God and a vindication of their own unheeded warnings about the dangers of sin and ingratitude for the gospel. (99) The ideological tension between the images of the poor persecuted flock and the Christian commonwealth had of necessity been resolved, for a time at least, by political circumstances. 'It was an easy thing to hold with Christ whiles the prince and world held with him', wrote Hooper, 'but now the world hateth him, it is the true trial who be his'. (100) When all possibility of a godly commonwealth had been eliminated, only the little flock was left to face its 'true trial'.

Notes

1.   Discussion of the trends in printing in this period is most fully covered in P.M. Took, Government and the Printing Trade, 1540-1560, unpublished London Ph.D. thesis, 1979. For the view that Protector Somerset supported a protestant 'press campaign', see J.N. King, English Reformation Literature (Princeton, UP, 1982), chapter 2.

2.   The main focus of attack was the Mass and consequently the 'sacrificing priesthood', e.g. Edmund Guest, Treatise against the Privy Mass, in the behalf and furtherance of the most holy Communion (London, 1548); Jean Vernon, The five abominable blasphemies that are in the Mass (London, 1548); William Turner, A new dialogue wherein is contained the examination of the Mass (London, 1548). Other issues included the celibacy of the clergy, e.g. John Ponet, A Defence of the Marriage of Priests, by scripture and ancient writers (London, 1549); fasting, e.g. Anon. The Recantation of Jack Lent, late Vicar-General to the most cruel Antichrist of Rome (London, 1548); and the primacy of scripture over tradition, e.g. Phillip Nicholls, The copy of a letter sent to one Master Chrispyn, canon of Exeter, for that he denied the Scripture to be the touchstone and trial of all other doctrines (London, 1548). Though the papacy is mentioned, it was no longer the subject of primary importance that it had been in the 1530s, for obvious reasons.

3.   This attitude is neatly summarised in the verse prologue to William Turner, The rescuing of the Romish Fox, otherwise called the examination of the Hunter devised by Stephen Gardiner (Bonn, 1545), pseudonymously published as 'William Wraghton, Winchester, by me Hans Hitprick'. Woodcut on title-page of a fox dressed as a pope, with clipped ears; below is the verse:

> The banished fox of Rome speaketh:
> My son Stephen Gardiner with weeping tears
> Hath cut away the tips of mine ears
> But the rest of my body remaineth whole still
> I trust mine ears shall grow again
> When all the gospellers are slain
> Which Stephen my son, both stark and stout
> Doth now right earnestly go about ...

4.   Opposition to the religious reforms of Edward's reign was on the disingenuous lines that the king was too young to be responsible and would reconsider when he came into his majority. Latimer attacked this attitude in his first sermon at Court, Lent 1549; in Sermons, ed. G.E. Corrie (Parker Society, Cambridge, 1844), pp.118-19, as did Hooper in his dedication to An oversight and deliberation upon the holy prophet Jonah (London 1550) (in Early Writings, ed. S. Carr (Parker Society, Cambridge 1843)), p. 437, and also John Bale, An expostulation or complaint against the blasphemies of a frantic papist of Hampshire (London, 1550?), sigs. B1-C7vo.

5.   Revised STC proofs, nos. 1296.5, 1297, 1298, 1299. I am grateful to the English Antiquarian Section of the British Library for letting me have this information.

6.   This has been done very fully by L.P. Fairfield, John Bale, Mythmaker for the English Reformation (Purdue University Press, 1976), passim, and K. Firth, The Apocalyptic Tradition in Reformation Britain (Oxford 1979), chapter 2.

7.   John Bale, The Image of Both Churches in Select Works (ed.) H. Christmas (Parker Society, Cambridge 1849), p.251.

8.   The theme of inversion in Lutheran propaganda has been discussed, with reference to woodcuts, by R. Scribner, For the sake of simple folk (Cambridge 1981), chapter 6.

9.   This began to take place in the sixth age (beginning with Wyclif) which Bale considered to be still happening. It was however an age of extreme difficulty for the true church, as its revival enraged Antichrist. Thus the primacy achieved by princes in their own realm was not necessarily an advantage to the true church; Bale, Image, 358-65; peace on earth for the true church will only be achieved in the 'silence' of the seventh age, ibid. p.341.

10.   E.g. Bale's description of the monastic orders as 'sects', ibid. p.352, and the references to the power struggles that characterised the rise of

the papacy, ibid. p.317.
    11. Ibid., p.290.
    12. These included such disparate elements as early medieval theologians and writers such as Bede and Alcuin, ibid.; 347, monastic reformers like St Bernard, ibid., p.327, and heretics like the Waldensians and Albigensians, ibid., p.327.
    13. The idea of the false church as the majority of the people or ungodly multitude is illustrated by the image of the Beast rising from the sea, ibid., p.420.
    14. J. Bossy, Christianity in the West, 1400-1700 (Oxford, 1985), p.80.
    15. Cf. note 9. Also Bale, Image, the wounded Beast is healed, p.427-8, which also referred to the events in England, 1540-5, pp.509-11.
    16. Government by the word, ibid., pp.274-5; persecution, ibid., passim, but n.b. comparison with Christ: 'For after none other sort reigneth his church here than he reigned afore them, whose triumph was greatest on the cross.' Ibid., p.567.
    17. Ibid., pp.440-3. Cf. also note 15.
    18. Ibid., p.394.
    19. John Foxe, Acts and Monuments, ed. S.R. Cattley, vols. 6-8. See also the essay by Jane Facey in this volume.
    20. The answers to Stephen Gardiner's A Detection of the Devil's Sophistry by Hooper (Zurich, 1547) and Gilby (London, 1547) were two of the most detailed works produced in this period: translations of the works of continental reformers and short tracts and ballads against the Mass make up the bulk of the rest. Examples of works supporting Somerset are rarer than those supporting the Lord's Supper (as introduced in the March 1548 order of Communion and more fully in the June 1549 Prayer Book); e.g. R.V. The old faith of Great Britain and the new learning of England, whereunto is added a simple instruction concerning the King's majesty's proceedings in the Communion, (London, 1549), and John Mardeley, A declaration of the power of God's Word, concerning the Holy Supper of the Lord, confuting all liars and false teachers, which maintain their masking Mass invented against the word of God and the King's majesties most godly proceedings (London, 1548). This last example was dedicated to Somerset. Cf. also note 1.
    21. George Joye, The refutation of the bishop of Winchester's dark declaration of his false articles, once more confuted by George Joye (London, 1546), 'To the Reader'.

22. Ibid. 'To the Reader'. Cf. Anthony Gilby, An answer to the devilish detection of Stephen Gardiner, Bishop of Winchester, published to the intent that such as be desirous of the truth should not be seduced by his errors, nor the blind and obstinate excused by ignorance (London, 1547), The Prologue, viii. v.

23. Gilby, An answer, sig. lv-K2.

24. Ibid., sig. H4v.

25. Ibid., sigs. X7vo-X8.

26. Hooper, Early Writings, pp.83-85, 213, 286-293.

27. Ibid., pp.79-80.

28. Ibid., pp.201.

29. Optimism for the advancement of the gospel, ibid., pp. xi-xiv, 203-4. Persecution of the gospel, 1546 in Hooper's letters, in Original Letters relative to the English Reformation, vol. 1, ed. H. Robinson (Parker Society, Cambridge, 1846), pp.35, 41.

30. Peter Moone, A short treatise of certain things abused (Ipswich, 1548), sig. A3v.

31. William Punt, A new dialogue called the inditement against mother Mass (London, 1548), sig. C4v. His list of 'martyrs' starts with Richard Hunne and gets as far as Barnes, Garrett, and Jerome, but does not include the 1546 group which included Anne Askew and John Lascelles. Could this indicate an earlier date of composition? Cf. note 34.

32. William Samuel, A warning for the city of London, that dwellers therein may repent their evil lives for fear of God's plagues (London, 1550), verses 15-17.

33. Bale, Select Works, pp. 136-248. See also L.P. Fairfield, 'John Bale and English protestant hagiography' in Journal of Ecclesiastical History, vol. 24 (1973).

34. e.g. Gilby, An answer (1547); Robert Crowley, A confutation of xiii articles to which Nicholas Shaxton, bishop of Salisbury subscribed ... refers to an Henrician event (1546) though it may have been written in 1547 - it refers to Gilby's Answer approvingly and was not itself published until 1548. Walter Lynne's edition of The beginning and ending of all popery (London, 1548) is an example of an earlier text published with a new dedication to Edward VI. Without additional evidence, however, it is difficult to tell whether a text was actually written in Henry's reign, or whether the author came to his conclusions under Henry and was not free to write and publish till Edward's reign. Richard Tracy,

A brief and short declaration made, whereby every man may know, what is a sacrament (London, 1548) is an example of these possibilities.

35. Robert Crowley, The way to wealth (London, 1550) and Thomas Lever, A sermon preached the third Sunday in Lent before the King's Majesty and his most honourable Council (London, 1550) are well-known examples of this type of anxiety. Note, however, the emphasis on more and better preaching as a remedy, which undue emphasis on social and economic criticism has tended to ignore.

36. Latimer, Sermons, pp.128-43.

37. Ibid. pp.284-5, 29.

38. Latimer's predicament is a personal gloss on the prophecy of Christ in Mark 13: 10-13.

39. According to H.S. Darby, Hugh Latimer (London, 1953), pp.72-3, this is a description of his examination before Stokesley in 1532.

40. Hooper, Early Writings, pp.548-9.

41. Anthony Gilby, A commentary upon the prophet Micah (London, 1551), sig. E3v-E4.

42. Richard Finch, The Epiphany of the Church, 1550, published London, 1590. Dedicated to Nicholas Ridley; the dedication recalled the hostility with which Ridley's visitation was received, sig. A2.

43. The Henrician and Edwardian Acts were, according to Finch, equally unacceptable to the ungodly; ibid. sigs. A2v-A4.

44. Ibid.; sig. D3vo. Cf. John Cheke, The Hunt of Sedition (London, 1549), sigs. A4-A6.

45. E.g. C. Haigh, 'The recent historiography of the English Reformation' in Historical Journal, 1982, vol. 1, pp.995-1007.

46. Lever, Sermon preached at Court, sig. A4.

47. Thomas Lever, A fruitful sermon preached at St. Paul's Church in the Shrouds, the second day of February 1550 (London, 1550), sig. B4v.

48. Roger Hutchinson, Works, ed. J. Bruce (Parker Society, Cambridge, 1842), pp.301-2.

49. Gilby, On Micah, sig. D2v.

50. E.g. Bale, Expostulation against a frantic papist, sigs. A3-A4v; Robert Crowley, The confutation of the misshapen answer to the misnamed, wicked ballad, called the Abuse of the Blessed Sacrament of the Altar (London, 1548). Crowley accused Miles Hoggard of being an enemy to the Sacrament, sig. A2, and also a persecutor who was involved in all the burnings at Smithfield from John Frith to Anne Askew, sigs. A3v-A4.

51. E.g. 'They have set forth the Bible that all men may see how far they do swerve in life from

God his holy word. They are called gospellers in
spite (as I do take it) of the holy gospel. For the
holy gospel of God is slandered and evil spoken of
both of our papists in England and in other nations,
so far as our English gospelling is known. Because in
the beginning thereof all things were compelled to
serve their covetousness and lascivious liberty, and
so it is still continued.' Gilby, <u>On Micah</u>, sigs. F5-
F5v.

52. E.g. Gilby, <u>On Micah</u>, sig. A6v; Thomas
Lever, <u>A Sermon preached at Paul's Cross, the 14th
day of December 1550</u> (London, 1551), sigs. A3v-A4;
Hutchinson, <u>Works</u>, p.338.
53. G.R. Elton, <u>Reform and Reformation</u>
(London, 1977), p.321.
54. G.R. Elton, 'Reform and the "commonwealth-
men" of Edward VI's reign', in <u>The English
Commonwealth</u>, ed. P. Clark A. Smith and N. Tyacke
(Leicester UP, 1979), pp.26-34.
55. E.g. Robert Crowley, <u>Pleasure and Pain,
Heaven and Hell</u> (London, 1551) esp. the plagues that
God will send to England for oppression of the poor,
sigs. A2-A3; Lever, <u>Sermon preached at Court</u>, remedy
for social disorder and poverty is provision of
preaching and organised charity, sigs. D5-E3.
56. Crowley, <u>Confutation of Shaxton's artic-
les</u>, sig. B8.
57. Hugh Latimer, <u>Remains</u>, ed. G.E. Corrie
(Parker Society, Cambridge, 1845), pp.126-8.
58. Best expressed in Miles Coverdale's
<u>Fruitful lessons upon the Passion, Burial,
Resurrection, Ascension and Sending of the Holy Ghost</u>
(?1540-7), in <u>Writings</u>, ed. G. Pearson (Parker
Society, Cambridge, 1844), esp. pp.199-321.
59. Phillip Nicholls, <u>Here beginneth a godly
new story of twelve men that Moses, by the
commandment of God sent to spy out the land of
Canaan, of which twelve only Joshua and Caleb were
found faithful messengers</u> (London, 1548), sigs. D3v-
D4.
60. Hooper, <u>Early Writings</u>, p.80.
61. Ibid., p.84.
62. Ibid., p.xiii.
63. Phillip Gerrard, <u>A godly invective in the
defence of the gospel</u> (London, 1547), sigs. D8v-E1.
64. 2 Chronicles 34: 14-33.
65. Latimer, <u>Sermons</u>, pp.87-103.
66. Ibid., pp.151-93; noted disparagingly by
M.L. Bush in <u>The government policy of Protector
Somerset</u> (London, 1975), pp.66-7.
67. E.g. Hooper, <u>Early Writings</u>, pp.480-1;

Lever, <u>Sermon preached at Court</u>, sig. D8; Latimer, <u>Sermons</u>, pp.122-3.

68. Proverbs, 29; 18. E.g. Thomas Becon, <u>The Fortress of the Faithful</u>, 1550, in <u>The Catechism of Thomas Becon ... with other pieces written by him in the reign of King Edward VI</u>, ed. J. Ayre (Parker Society, Cambridge, 1844), pp.595-6.

69. Hooper, <u>Early Writings</u>, pp.539-42.

70. Latimer, <u>Sermons</u>, pp.85-6.

71. ?John Ponet, <u>A short Catechism or plain instruction containing the sum of Christian learning</u> (London, 1553), sigs. F6-F6v.

72. Ibid. sig. Glvo-G3.

73. N.B. Ponet's definition of discipline is restricted to excommunication. It is not developed into a discussion of church polity.

74. For a detailed discussion of the significance of <u>De censura</u>, see C.M.F. Davies and J.M. Facey, 'A reformation dilemma; John Foxe and the problem of discipline', <u>Journal of Ecclesiastical History</u>, forthcoming.

75. Joye referred to Henry Bullinger's <u>The Christian state of matrimony</u> (tr. Coverdale, 1541) in documenting his assertion that adultery should be dealt with by the secular powers; George Joye, <u>A contrary to a certain man's consultation that adulterers ought to be punished with death. With the solution of his arguments for the contrary</u> (London, ?1549), sigs. A6-A7, B6-B7.

76. Cf. notes 56 and 57; also John Foxe, <u>De censura, sive excommunicatione ecclesiastica, rectoque eius usu</u> (London, 1551), sigs. B5v, C7, E6.

77. Joye, <u>A contrary</u>, sig. A7v.

78. Ibid., sig. Blv.

79. Latimer, <u>Sermons</u>, p.258.

80. Foxe, <u>De censura</u>, sigs. D6-D8.

81. Edmund Allen, <u>A catechism, that is to say a Christian instruction now newly corrected</u> (London, 1551) sig. L7v.

82. E.T., <u>Here beginneth a song of the Lord's Supper</u> (London, 1550?), sig. A2.

83. Thomas Lancaster, <u>The right and true understanding of the Supper of the Lord and the use thereof</u> ... (London, 1550), sig. D4.

84. Foxe, <u>De censura</u>, sigs. A2, D4-D5.

85. For excommunication as a form of clerical tyranny, see e.g. Ponet, <u>Defence of the marriage of priests</u>, sigs. C6-C6v. For the rejection of external ceremonial in the excommunication ritual, see Foxe, <u>De censura</u>, sigs. D3-D3v. General examples of the rejection of external ceremonies include Gilby, <u>An</u>

answer to the devilish detection, sig. T8; William
Turner, A new dialogue wherein is contained the
examination of the Mass (London, 1548), sigs. F6-F6v.
    86. E.g. Thomas Cranmer, Writings and
disputations ... relative to the sacrament of the
Lord's Supper, ed. J.E. Cox (Parker Society,
Cambridge, 1844), pp.347-8.
    87. Hooper, Early Writings, pp.90-1.
    88. Ibid., p.183.
    89. Foxe, De censura, sig. A5.
    90. John Foxe, De non plectendis morte
adulteris consultatio (London, 1548), sigs. B5-B5v.
    91. Foxe, De censura, sig. A7v.
    92. Ibid., sigs. C4-Dlv.
    93. Ibid., sigs. E7-E8.
    94. Cf. Doctrine de la pénitence publique,
London, 1552, sigs. *5vo, 8; Allen, Revised
catechism, sigs, L4v, Ml.
    95. Foxe, De Censura, chapter 7.
    96. Hutchinson, Works, pp.323-4.
    97. Joye, A contrary, sig. E6vo.
    98. J.S. Coolidge, The Pauline renaissance in
England: puritanism and the Bible (Oxford, 1970),
pp.58-60.
99. E.g. Nicholas Ridley, A piteous lamentation of
the miserable estate of the church in England
(London, 1566), reprinted in Works, ed. H. Christmas
(Parker Society, Cambridge, 1841), pp.49-80. See
also Joy Shakespeare's essay in this book.
    100. John Hooper, Later Writings, ed. C.
Nevinson (Parker Society, Cambridge, 1852), p.618.

Chapter Four

PLAGUE AND PUNISHMENT

Joy Shakespeare

When Edward VI died on July 6th 1553 the cause of protestantism in England was endangered. Northumberland's coup in favour of his daughter-in-law, Jane Grey, was abortive, in spite of his attempt to manipulate the forces of the reformation against Mary, and when Mary came to London she was greeted by a cheering crowd. It seemed to her, at least, that God had intervened on behalf of the rightful heir and the Catholic faith, and many observers must also have felt that there was indeed an element of the miraculous in her speedy success. Despite Mary's submission to the royal authority of her father, her belief in the tenets of the Church of Rome and the spiritual headship of the Pope had not wavered, and it was only a matter of time before England was legally returned to the Catholic and papal fold. Because of this, for many protestants Mary's accession was a disaster, and spelt the end for their dreams of England as a truly godly land. A substantial group of over 800, anticipating persecution for their religious beliefs, or punishment for their political involvement with Northumberland, decided in favour of discretion, and withdrew to the continent. From their comparative safety abroad these Marian exiles had to come to terms with the new status quo in England, and evolve an argument in theological terms to account for the victory of the forces of the ungodly over the godly, and the apparent rejection of the Edwardian church by God. Their dilemma in many ways was hardly unprecedented; it had been faced many times before by minority Christian groups out of sympathy with the prevailing religious authorities, but for the Marian exiles the situation was exacerbated by the fact that for a few years at least they had enjoyed the benefits of being able to control, to a considerable

103

extent, the religious development of their country. They needed to provide, for themselves and for their countrymen, an ideological framework within which they could account for the eclipse of English protestantism, while at the same time castigating their successors to power, the Catholics.

This paper is an attempt to give an account of that ideological framework evolved by the exiles and presented in their works which they intended for English consumption. In order to present a clearer picture I have necessarily concentrated on the similarities in exile writings, rather than on the undeniable differences and shades of meaning and expression within the works of individual writers. In other words, I have viewed the body of exile literature as a homogeneous mass and have not attempted to distinguish the contributions of particular individuals.

The exiles turned to the scriptures for inspiration and guidance, and indeed it was inevitable that they should do so, since the Bible represented for protestants the first and finest source of authority, that commodity so necessary for the proving of any early modern assertion, whether literary, political, practical, or theological. Within the pages of scripture then, the exiles found the schema they required in the doctrine of the causal relationship between the sin of man and divine punishment. In Genesis III the major elements of this cause and effect pattern were clearly to be seen: Adam and Eve had had specific limitations set on their actions, and when these limits were over-stepped, when Eve succumbed to the serpent's temptations to eat of the fruit of the tree of knowledge of good and evil, and prevailed upon Adam to follow her example, the judgement of God was swift and severe. The serpent was condemned to crawl on his belly; the woman to bear children in pain, and be in subjection to man; and the man to make his living only by the sweat of his brow. These sentences remain unrepealed.

The pattern of sin and subsequent divine judgement as set out in Genesis III is not unique within the pages of scripture. However there seem to be four major variations on the basic theme which can be demonstrated by reference to four biblical stories, all of which occur as illustrations of Marian exile theology in different contexts. The first concerns the Great Flood, wherein the whole race of mankind was destroyed by an act of vengeance pure and simple by a God who repented the fact that he had ever made man, and resolved to destroy his evil creation. The Great Flood was both unprecedented and unique; by the rainbow God promised that he would never again visit the earth in this totally destructive and vengeful manner. The second major variation of the basic pattern can be seen in the case of the destruction of the cities of Sodom and Gomorrah because of their wickedness. Here God again is vengeful and destructive, and again a tiny group of godly people, in this case Lot's family, is preserved. The difference lies in the prayers of Abraham for the cities, when he secures God's promise that if even ten righteous people are found within them, then Sodom and Gomorrah would escape the vengeance prepared for them. In other words, a godly minority would act as leaven in the lump and so preserve the whole.

The third variation can be seen in the plagues that were visited upon the Egyptians when Pharaoh failed to accede to Moses' demand to let the Israelites go free. The plagues of locusts, frogs, and eventually the deaths of the first born son of all Egyptian families were not intended by God to be merely punitive, that is, they were not simply evidence of God's wrath against the Egyptians and Pharaoh for the refusal to allow the children of Israel to leave, but rather the plagues were used as firstly a proof of the power of the God of the Israelites, and secondly as a message or warning to persuade Pharaoh to concede to the demands of Moses and Aaron. The fourth major variation has many examples, and concerns the use of plague (a general word in this context to describe any manifestations of the divine wrath) by God in a reformative, corrective fashion, as well as in a punitive one. The children of Israel were visited by God in this way many times throughout their long history; one excellent example is that described in Numbers XXI of the plague of fiery serpents sent by God after the people had grumbled against him for the hardships they were enduring in the wilderness. Those bitten by the serpents had one recourse - by looking on a serpent made of brass that Moses had set up on a pole they could be cured. In other words, the punishment for sin could be mitigated by an act of faith. A further element in the stories of the plagues endured by the Israelites for sin's sake was that they were almost invariably preceded by warnings issued through the mouths of the prophets. Only when the warnings and prophecies had no effect on the erring people did the wrath of God make itself felt.

105

The idea of the faithful remnant saved by God
from the consequences of his divine wrath, as
expressed in the prophecies of Isaiah, serves as a
bridge between the Old and New Testaments in that it
begins to make the distinction between the whole
Israelite nation and the elect minority within it. In
the New Testament the use of plagues by God as a
means of chastising the faithful for their ultimate
benefit is further elaborated, and as we shall see,
the exiles also made use of this doctrine in their
writings. As we look at the works of the Marian
exiles on the nature of plague, punishment and
persecution, we shall be returning to these variant
patterns of the causal relationship between sin and
divine punishment, but it is worth making the point
at this stage that the Marian exiles made little
attempt to categorise their examples and
illustrations, and used biblical reference and
precedent in a far less systematic fashion. They were
almost scriptural opportunists in the sense that they
fitted biblical examples to their ideology without
particular reference to the circumstances and
peculiarities of the events that they selected. Such
an opportunist use of authorities is, of course,
typical of all brands of sixteenth century
literature.

The Marian exiles were not by any means the
first Christians to trace this cause and effect
mechanism between sin and divine punishment. It was
no new idea even to sixteenth century English
protestants. For example, Miles Coverdale in 1538
argued that 'this horrible plague of the pestilence'
(he is referring to the late sweating sickness)
'cometh out of God's wrath, because of the despising
and transgressing of his godly commandments'. (1)
When the two Suffolk boys, sons of Charles Brandon,
Duke of Suffolk, and his wife Katherine, died
suddenly in 1551, Thomas Wilson wrote a funeral
oration for them, which he included in his Art of
rhetoric of 1553. Commenting on their deaths, he
argued that God 'thinking them meeter for heaven than
to live here upon earth took them from us in his
anger, for the bettering of our doings and amendment
of our evil living'. (2) There was no escaping the
judgement of God. Richard Morison in his Invective
against treason claimed that the plague that had hit
the north harder than the south had been specially
sent to punish these rebellious souls who had
participated in the Pilgrimage of Grace and yet
escaped secular justice. (3) Similarly, Henry VIII
did not take much persuading that his lack of a male

heir could be traced directly to his transgression of
divine law in marrying his brother's widow.

It was therefore relatively easy for the exiles
to discover a reason for the failure of English
protestantism and the return of popery. God must be
punishing the English for their sins. Once this stage
had been reached it was again not difficult for the
exiles to point the finger at the particular sins
that had resulted in such an overwhelming proof of
God's anger. On this issue the exiles wrote
copiously, and spoke with the martyrs with one voice.
The cause of the plagues of popery had to be
unthankfulness and ingratitude of the people for the
gospel whilst they had it, and their failure to seize
their God-given opportunity to follow the principles
of the gospel and lead godly lives. From exile,
Thomas Becon summed up his view of the situation in
these words: 'We abhorred the light of God's word
therefore are we now justly overwhelmed with the
darkness of men's trifling traditions and devilish
decrees.' (4) Again and again the exiles hammered at
the shortcomings of the nation in the days of Edward
VI. The anonymous author of the Humble Supplication
unto God of 1554 blamed 'our unthankfulness and
wicked living' (5) for the removal of the true
gospel, and the current plague of popery. This
unthankfulness and ingratitude for the benefits of
the gospel so generously and freely granted to the
English nation by God, and the failure to live in a
manner befitting such favoured people meant that God,
in sorrow and anger, very justly, had felt the need
to withdraw the marks of his especial grace. That
this punishment was well merited the exiles agreed,
as they also agreed that the consequences of these
sins were now manifested in the Marian regime having
been granted dominion over the people. Some writers
were more specific about which sections of society
were most to blame for the plague now being suffered;
the godly community was singled out by many exiles
for its signal failure to set the proper example of
righteous conduct. They were thus guilty of having
failed to provide sufficient leaven in the lump to
counteract the sins of the people at large, just as
in the case of Sodom and Gomorrah where insufficient
righteousness was found by God to prevent him from
pouring out his justifiable wrath. Other writers
placed special blame upon the Court and the governing
classes who had promoted the reformation of the
church, not out of true faith and piety, but out of
greed and avarice for church possessions, and because
they desired political power. But whoever was the

107

most guilty, the end result was the same. The whole
nation now had to suffer the penalties of sin, and
papistry had been permitted by God to subdue the
people because of the failure on a national level to
grasp at the chance of a godly commonwealth.

The exiles seldom cared to distinguish between
the English nation as a whole and the elect minority
or remnant within the nation. This meant that they
could adapt their message of plague as punishment or
chastisement to the particular audience they were
addressing at any one point, whether that audience
was the whole nation or more specifically the godly
elect. Thus the whole nation could be castigated for
failure to submit to godly standards in the same way
as Old Testament Israel had often similarly failed.
There is therefore an unresolved tension within exile
works between the theory of predestination which
entails the belief that the majority must be, and
must remain, unregenerate and incapable of
salvation, and the exiles' understandable desire to
make a large impact on English society as a whole, by
tacit acceptance of the idea that England had a
special contractual relationship with God, which had
been broken by the sins of the people. The exiles had
already gone some way, under Edward VI, towards
evolving a theory of England as a favoured or
covenanted nation, and though this theory remained
implicit rather than explicit, from exile English
protestants made this theory felt by their copious
usage of parallels between England and Old Testament
Israel. This tension within the works of the Marian
exiles ties in with more general protestant problems
concerning the whole question of the nature of
covenant theology. For to argue that man's
relationship with God is contractual, or based on a
covenant, requiring that man as well as God has a
certain part to play in his salvation, is to a
considerable extent in direct opposition to true
predestinarian theology in which man is unable to
influence the divine decision regarding his ultimate
election or damnation. The exiles naturally wished
to emphasise the contract or covenant idea, since it
was a vital ingredient of their explanation of why
the Marian plague had now come upon England, but they
still needed to retain the doctrine of the elect
remnant especially when discussing the use of plagues
as chastisement rather than just punishment. They
managed to incorporate both by their general
reluctance to make too careful a distinction between
the nation as a whole and the elect minority within
that nation. Their failure explicitly to recognise or

account for the tension that such a lack of
distinction must entail leaves them open to the
charge of opportunism - in this case theological
rather than scriptural - yet it is very hard to see
how else they could have argued in the particular
circumstances of their time, which forced them to
offer some explanation in theological and scriptural
terms for the apparent failure of protestantism in
England.

In the same way as the lack of true godliness
had led to the triumph of ungodliness, so the
ingratitude of the people for their king, Edward VI,
had caused God to remove him. If Edward had been
highly praised during his life, after his death he
became one of the wonders of the world. This godly
imp, the young Josiah, stood in sharp contrast to
Mary, especially in retrospect. Mary was a Catholic
idolator, a tyrant and a female to boot. These facts,
for the exiles, made her a plague per se, while her
seeming attempts to bring England into submission to
the foreign domination of the Spaniard and the Pope
were further punishments heaped up upon the English
by a vengeful deity. God's hand in the accession of
Mary and in the circumstances and events of her reign
was indeed self-evident to the exiles. (6)

As we have already seen, the plagues visited on
Israel by God were not solely punitive in character,
but also contained an element of chastisement
intended to reform rather than merely destroy. As for
Israel, so of England, and the exiles emphasised that
these plagues of popery and tyranny were intended to
make the English people as a whole recognise their
failings under Edward VI. Again, the parallel with
Old Testament Israel was reinforced by the role which
the Marian exiles carved out for themselves in their
schema of the causal relationship between sin and
divine punishment. They saw themselves as prophets
delivering the message of God to an erring nation.
In this role the exiles made use of the language of
prophecy hallowed by Old Testament usage, calling on
the people to recognise their sins and admit that the
plagues now come upon them were from the hand of God
and so justly deserved. In the Old Testament prophets
were sometimes successful in provoking the people to
a recognition of sin and a desire for mercy before
the plagues of God appeared, as when Jonah made his
successful appeal to Nineveh. At other times the
warnings went unheeded, as did those of Jeremiah, and
with the people remaining obdurate, the plagues duly
fell. The exiles recalled with barely concealed
delight that various Edwardian preachers had called

attention to the specific sins of ingratitude and
wicked living, and had warned that unless repentance
and amendment of life were speedily forthcoming,
God's plagues would surely fall upon England. John
Knox, for example, in his Marian writings refers many
times to his own prophetic utterances along these
lines in the days of Edward VI, and indeed some
Edwardian sermons do have a highly prophetic ring,
not least that of Hugh Latimer, who, preaching for
the first time in 1549 before the King and court,
urged his audience to leave sin and turn to the Lord,
threatening them with papal and foreign domination
should Edward die young and his successor, one of his
half-sisters, marry a foreign prince. (7) It was
obvious to the exiles that the godly preachers had
failed in their attempt to divert the anger of God by
successfully provoking the people to a general
repentance. But in their way they had followed the
time-honoured pattern of Israel: no one could claim
that the plagues of God had come unannounced. The
failure of the Edwardian prophets to avert the
plagues therefore did not mean that they and the
exiles should renounce their prophetic role.
Instead, their claims to such a role were enhanced,
since their prophecies had come to pass, albeit all
too soon and all too well. In their role as prophets
to the English, therefore, the exiles were able to
trace the reasons for the current plagues of Marian
tyranny and popery now hanging over England. However,
they did have more to say on the subject of the exact
nature of these current plagues.

The Marian exiles specified that the plagues
consisted of the death of Edward VI, the accession of
Mary, bringing in her wake popery and the threat of
Spanish domination, the cessation of the true
preaching of the gospel and the replacement of the
true shepherds by popish hirelings. Many writers
carried the simple argument that ingratitude for the
gospel had led to its removal one stage further, and
in so doing managed both to account for the general
apathy of the people to the reintroduction of
catholicism, and to categorise this apathy or
indifference as one more aspect of the nature of the
plague now suffered by England. They based this
argument on a text in II Thessalonians 2, which
reads: 'Because they received not the love of the
truth, that they might be saved ... for this cause
God shall send them strong delusion, that they should
believe a lie: that they all might be damned who
believed not the truth, but had pleasure in
unrighteousness.' (8) In several tracts, for example

in Thomas Cottisford's preface to his translation of
Zwingli's Account Reckoning and Confession of Faith,
this text is directly cited, whlie in many other
works writers argued the same point in slightly
different terms. Thomas Becon, for example tells how
God has been moved by the nation's sins 'to withdraw
the most pleasant and comfortable light of his loving
countenance from us and to suffer the prince of
darkness to shadow us with his wings of hellish
ignorance and devilish blindness unto our great
discomfort and sorrow'. (9) Similarly John Knox tells
his readers that God has given them over 'in to a
reprobate mind'. (10) The main thrust of the argument
is that because the true gospel had been spurned and
rejected by the people, God had removed from them the
very chance of belief - their eyes had in fact been
deliberately blinded by a vengeful God because they
did not recognise the truth when they saw it. Thus
belief in the lies of Catholic idolatry was in itself
a divine punishment; the just retribution for
unbelief in the truth was a God-sent delusion of
belief in falsehood. The people therefore were not
merely being subjected to the idolatry of the
papists; they were also being deluded into a false,
and, of course, ultimately damning, belief in that
idolatry. The hireling priests of the papists had
been given charge over the English flock and from the
exiles' point of view the blind were now more
certainly leading the blind, to their mutual
disadvantage. The usefulness of this mode of argument
as an explanation of general indifference to the
change of religion did not, and does not, need to be
spelt out.

So much for the general account of what had
caused God's anger, and what form that anger had
taken. The exiles could not be satisfied with this
account of punishment as the sole reason for the
current situation in Marian England, for it was an
undeniable fact that the godly seemed to be suffering
rather more than their fair share of the plagues on
offer, if these plagues were solely intended as a
punishment for the nation. As I have already said,
some exile writers blamed themselves and the godly
community in general for the anger of God first and
foremost - on the grounds that most would be expected
from those who had received most, but as a reason for
their near monopoly of suffering under the Marian
regime this could hardly suffice. The effects of
God's anger against sin were self-evident, and the
cause and effect mechanism of sin and divine
punishment was established to their own

111

satisfaction, but the problem of the extra-ordinary tribulation endured by the godly, as opposed to the more (or rather, less) deserving ungodly, remained. It should be noted that although this problem tended to exercise the minds and pens of those awaiting martyrdom rather than those of the exiles, neither the martyrs nor the exiles considered that any great gulf separated the two groups. The relative sufferings endured by the martyrs and exiles were in general placed on the same plane - exile was quite definitely not viewed as an easy option or as simple cowardice in the face of the enemy. Exile, imprisonment, and martyrdom are linked together in almost all accounts of the sufferings of the godly, both by those who participated in the exodus to the continent, and by those who remained behind, for the giving up of one's lands, goods, home and family for the faith was seen as a sacrifice along exactly the same lines as was the giving up of one's life. Thus the problem of godly suffering had to be faced by both groups, and indeed exile writers were far from silent in the matter.

Again they turned to the scriptures for their arguments - this time to the New Testament rather than to the Old, and found the answer in the doctrine of the chastisement of the faithful by a loving heavenly Father for their own ultimate benefit. Again the exiles were not the first to 'discover' this doctrine, nor did they have a monopoly of it, for the Catholic author, Roger Edgeworth, in his 1557 volume of sermons stated that 'Blessed is the man or woman that is correct and punished for our Lord God. And the reason is this, for if man's correction may be good and wholesome, then God's correction must needs be much more wholesome.' (11) The godly must needs suffer on earth, not only as punishment for sin (although that aspect is never excluded) but also, and indeed much more because the dross of the worldly or natural man needs to be burnt away in the fire of persecution and tribulation, leaving only the pure gold of the spiritual or regenerate man. Like gold tried in the fire, or wheat separated from the chaff by the wind, the elect suffer on earth that they might more nearly approximate to the example of the apostles, and particularly of Christ himself, and so might not suffer damnation with the world. The godly suffer also because, in the words of Acts 14 v 22, 'we must through much tribulation enter into the kingdom of God'. Or, as Paul wrote to Timothy, 'if we suffer, we shall reign also'. (12) The road to heaven lies only and solely through the narrow gate - and

112

the man who will not follow Christ's example in
enduring tribulation cannot hope to share Christ's
throne in heaven. Persecution is not the only road,
and sole means of suffering for these ends, but it is
a specially blessed route. Thus for the Marian exiles
and martyrs the present circumstances were far from
being merely a punishment for their past sins. Just
as a wise parent is exhorted not to 'spare the rod
and spoil the child', so God chastises his people on
earth for their ultimate benefit.

Chastisement or suffering also serves to
distinguish the true from the false believer, real
faith from pretence. The true believer is revealed by
his reaction to trials. The man whose faith is not
securely founded will be swift to blame God when
things go wrong, while the true believer will
maintain his faith in the wisdom, love and power of
the Almighty. The true believer is also revealed by
whether he sticks to his profession in time of
persecution, and it was a major, and well-founded
fear amongst the exiles that few professed gospellers
would be found to continue in their protestant
beliefs once popery had been restored. As John Knox
lamented to the English people as a whole, 'in you
alas is neither found gold, silver, nor precious
stone, but all is brent'. (13) For as the scriptures
teach, in the fires of persecution the dross is
consumed and only the gold of true faith and
godliness remains. In this context the exiles also
made use of the parable of the sower from, for
example, Matthew 13. The Marian persecution served to
demonstrate which of the people were the 'good
ground' bringing forth much fruit, and which were the
'stony ground' wherein the seed of the word of God
withered when the trials of persecution and
tribulation came.

For the godly, suffering is a gift of God and
proof of his love towards the elect 'for whom the
Lord loveth he chasteneth'. (14) Robert Pownoll in
his Epistle of 1556 sees the sufferings of the godly
as proof of their election: 'Then begin we (as it
were) partly to know and lively to feel, that we
cannot be damned, but that we shall be most certainly
saved.' (15) Thus suffering and especially
persecution must be seized upon with joy -
'Therefore, my brethren, let us ... not lament but
laud God, not be sorry but be merry, not weep but
rejoice and be glad, that God doth vouchsafe to offer
us his cross, thereby to come to him to endless joys
and comforts.' (16) The true church must always
suffer persecution, and persecution is one of the

113

marks of the true church, and some writers came
dangerously close to assuming that if a man or a
church underwent persecution, the truth of the faith
of that man or that church was thereby proven. But
generally the exiles saw the need to underline the
fact that persecution on its own was no guarantee of
true faith, although the possession of true faith
must still guarantee persecution in one form or
another. The exile writers, having expounded the
doctrine of chastisement, urged their readers to
exhibit patient resignation under the hand of God,
coupled with full repentance for past sins and
continued faith in the promise of God, given in I
Corinthians 10 v 13, that he would never permit them
to be tempted above their capacity for endurance.

The plague of Marian rule in England, therefore,
served a dual purpose at least. For the ungodly, it
served as a just punishment for sin, and for the
godly it was a benefit of grace from the hand of a
loving heavenly Father. The sufferings of the godly
were also intended, argued the exiles, to give a
warning and example to the ungodly, for if God
permits his chosen to suffer thus, how must worse
will be the fate of the unregenerate unless
repentance and amendment of life are forthcoming? In
other words, the Marian plague was in itself a
warning; as well as being a punishment for past sins,
it was also intended as a kind of half-way house
between god's favour and the full manifestation of
his wrath. Through the experience men should be
induced to call upon God in repentance before further
and much greater plagues overtook them. For the
Marian exiles were not content merely to use their
prophetic gifts to analyse the past and explain the
present; they also looked to the future, and sought
to forecast the fate of the nation, basing their
prophecies on their analyses of current events and
attitudes.

For the exiles and the rest of the godly
community the future was relatively clear in any
event, for once they had been sufficiently chastised
for their own benefit, God would either take them
into glory immediately through martyrdom, or else
reward them for their patience and constancy like
Job, and give them back again the worldly prosperity
which they had been forced to renounce, or which had
been taken from them. It is difficult to assess how
far the exiles felt that protestantism would one day
triumph again in England, and in any case they had
few grounds for supposing, at least until after the
failure of Mary's supposed pregnancy in July 1555,

that the reign of Mary would so quickly and easily give place to that of her half-sister Elizabeth in November 1558. In fact, rather than prophesy the return of the gospel to England in the comparatively near future, the exiles concentrated on a far different picture, mainly, one feels, for its propagandist effect on their audience. They continued to play out their self-imposed roles as Old Testament style prophets to the English nation, and repeatedly warned that the wrath of God was as yet unsatisfied. They based this assertion not only on the sins of omission under Edward VI, but increasingly throughout the reign on the sins of commission under Mary. Despite the fact that they had argued that the blindness of the people to the truth, and their current belief in, and submission to, idolatry were to a large extent God-induced as a punishment for their ingratitude for the gift of the gospel, they insisted that this did not, and could not, excuse for one minute the actual sin that was now being committed. According to Calvinist doctrine, the fact that God chose men for election or damnation from the beginning of the world without regard to their actual level of godliness did not, and could not, mean that the sinful man was therefore not completely responsible for his own shortcomings, for to argue otherwise would mean that God must be the first cause of sin, a theological impossibility. Those who participated in Catholic ceremonies and rites were bound to receive just retribution for their open disobedience to the express commandments of God against such idolatry. The same cause and effect mechanism of sin and divine punishment must necessarily operate in the present and future, just as it had in the exiles' schema of the past and present. Contemporary idolatry and the blood of the martyrs would surely join together in calling down upon England yet more severe, but justified divine retribution. The exact nature of the plagues still to come was usually unspecified, since even the Marian exile prophets could not foretell with complete accuracy where the axe of God would next fall, and so threats of famine and disease go hand in hand with threats and dire warnings of foreign domination and even conquest.

Just as with the religious doubletake – the plague of papistry to be followed by a plague incurred by papistry – so the political argument had a similar double edge. Mary's reign, as the exiles were fond of pointing out, was most certainly tyrannical as well as idolatrous. In the Old

Testament tyrants were a recognised and familiar
medium for the punishment of national shortcomings by
God. Thomas Lever sets out this general principle in
his <u>Treatise of the Right Way</u>: 'Take ye heed and be
warned as well princes as peoples ... for when as the
one is punished by the faults of the other, then
commonly the ungodliness of them that do suffer, is
the cause of the fault in the other.' (17) Lever
refers to such notable examples of tyrants being used
in this way as Saul, Jeroboam and Nebuchadnezzar.
Although at the beginning of her reign Mary herself
usually escaped the calumny heaped on her advisors
such as Stephen Gardiner, Bishop of Winchester, and
Bonner nicknamed 'Bloody', Bishop of London, by the
end she was being depicted in terms that were
flattering even to such notorious Old Testament anti-
heroines as Jezebel and Athaliah, with whom she was
frequently compared. Mary's wickedness as an
idolatrous tyrant remained as yet unpunished because
at the present she was being used as a scourge, a
stick to beat the sinful populace. She and her
advisors were said to be acting in accordance with
God's will in so doing, yet were still being held in
bondage to Satan, and they were attributed with the
unquiet consciences of those who perform acts of
tyranny and cruelty against God's people, while
recognising the ultimate futility of such behaviour
in the face of God's ever-present care for his own.
But despite being used in this manner as instruments
of God's wrath Mary and the others responsible for
persecution were duly warned that they could not hope
to escape God's anger, for they, like the people who
had submitted to belief in idolatry, were still held
to be personally responsible for their deeds. 'Though
the Lord hath called thee to be a scourge to other,
yet remember he commandeth you to do nothing
unrighteously.' (18) So the anonymous author of the
1553 tract in <u>An Admonition to the Bishops</u> advised
the Marian religious authorities. Mary and her co-
scourges could not hope to escape the wrath of God,
and their ultimate fate was described by another
anonymous exile writer in these terms: 'When he (that
is, God) hath used thee as a rod / to correct us / for
our unthankfullness / (he) will cast thee his scourge
and rod / into everlasting fire.' (19) So the
persecutors had no safety net, or escape route, for
while in one way they were denied freedom of action
by God, yet still they were to suffer the due
penalties for the crimes that they had committed
under such duress. They had been placed, to the
exiles' own evident satisfaction, in a theologically

perfect cleft stick.

There was a further reason, the exiles
explained, why Mary and her partners in crime had so
far been granted immunity from the wrath and
vengeance of God. The exiles hardly ever suggested,
and then in only the most perfunctory manner, that
this respite was intended in order that the Queen
might be brought to see the error of her ways and
repent. Mary, unlike the people of England, was not
granted the hope of repentance and ultimate pardon by
the exile writers. Instead they argued that her
wickedness would be permitted to continue until the
full measure of evil had been heaped up, thus
demonstrating to all observers the justice of God
when eventually she came by her just deserts. In some
ways Mary could be likened to the Pharaoh of Egypt,
whose heart was hardened by God, so that he would not
seize his chance, listen to the words of Moses and
Aaron, and let the Children of Israel go, before the
disaster of divine wrath overtook him.

The exiles had argued that subjection to belief
in idolatry could not excuse the participators in the
ungodly Catholic rites from the punishment that would
be bound to follow their sin in so doing, and using
the same logic, some exiles, if not all, insisted
that although the existence of the tyrannous Queen
Mary was in itself God's punishment for the people's
ingratitude for the godly Edward, as evidenced, for
example, by popular rebellions against him, yet still
this provided no easy excuse for merely submitting to
that tyranny. Those who supported Mary's tyrannous
regime, whether actively or passively, rendered
themselves partners in her guilt and therefore in her
subsequent punishment, and in any case the people's
acquiescence in the continuation of such an ungodly
ruler would be a major factor in calling down God's
heavy displeasure upon England. For those who argued
in this way (the names of John Knox, John Ponet, and
Christopher Goodman stand out) the people, or more
usually, the 'lesser magistrates', had the right, or
rather the God-endorsed duty, to rise in rebellion
against Mary and forcibly remove her from her usurped
throne. Such incitements to rebellion occur mainly in
the latter part of the reign, from 1556 onwards, and
their subsequent fame has slightly obscured the fact
that they represent only a part of Marian exile
viewpoints. (20) Yet such arguments are not greatly
out of step with the mainstream of exile theology,
for since the exiles saw themselves as prophet
figures, their duty, like that of Jonah to the city
of Nineveh, was not merely to prophesy of forthcoming

doom, but to warn against it, providing a means or remedy whereby such doom could be averted, and God's wrath appeased.

The recommendation of rebellion was indeed one of these remedies, but one theme above all else stands out in Marian exile litererature, and that is the pressing, dire need for repentance and amendment of life on the part of the nation as a whole, as well as on the part of particular groups, for example the godly elect, within the nation. The resistance writers, too, advocated repentance - their departure from other exiles lay in the fact that they espoused rebellion as the best means to demonstrate the necessary amendments of life following repentance. All the writers from exile, and in this once again they were in full agreement with the martyrs, insisted that only through repentance and amendment of life could the current plagues suffered by the English be brought to a happy conclusion, and further threatened plagues be averted. This repentance had to be genuine; the example of Nineveh was in common usage, as in this plea of an unknown exile for a 'general repentance with the Ninivites fasting and praying, most earnestly calling upon the true living God.' (21) For the exiles the bad harvests of the latter part of the reign, Mary's marriage to Philip of Spain, and particularly the fall of Calais were God-sends, literally as well as figuratively. These disasters acted as jumping-off points, from whence the exile writers could move with ease and authority to such warnings as that given in this last of a series of verses appended to John Bradford's 1556 Copy of a Letter:

> England repent whiles thou hast space,
> If thou couldst repent as Nineveh did,
> Then shouldst thou be sure of God's grace
> And so might thy enemies quite be rid.
> But if thou be blind and wilt not see,
> Then hasteth destruction for to destroy thee.
> (22)

Again, the full title of one of Bartholomew Traheron's tracts illustrates the particular value of the fall of Calais for the exiles as an 'awful warning'. It reads: A warning to England to repent, and to turn to God from idolatry and popery by the terrible example of Calais, given the 7. of March. Anno D. 1558. Such a spectacular proof of God's continuing wrath against England naturally further reinforced the exiles' self-imposed prophetic role, since they could claim with considerable justification to have issued many warnings that just such plagues would fall if the people continued obdurate in the face of the word of God.

Rebellion, or armed resistance, to the Marian regime was one method put forward as a means whereby true repentance could be demonstrated, but many exiles were unable to discard so easily the long-standing, and well-taught doctrine that the Christian owed obedience to the 'higher powers' whoever they might be. Therefore in many exile tracts rebellion was not seen as the best proof of sincere belief in the gospel. Rather, the preferred alternative is that of passive resistance, that is, obedience to the civil authorities in all things not directly contrary to the revealed will and word of God. It is better to serve God than man, as many writers indicated, and when the directives of the government would involve the subject in disobedience to the explicit word of God as set out in scripture, the repentant believer must not obey the authorities but rather endure all the penalties and sufferings imposed upon him. This is rather general, but the exiles were much more specific - on no account whatsoever must any one who hoped for salvation ever participate in the ungodly and idolatrous Catholic religious services. Attendance at mass was the real test for the would-be faithful, and the exiles devoted a great deal of time and paper to proving that not only was the mass in essence idolatrous and antichristian, but also that it was impossible for any true believer to conform outwardly while yet keeping inward faith, as many seemed to be doing. Outward conformity not only imperilled the conformist himself; it also gave encouragement to the papists, and weakened still further the wavering faith of the undecided or unlearned brethren. As such, outward conformity, sometimes termed Nicodemitism after Nicodemus the disciple who came to Jesus by night, was almost worse than simple belief in idolatry, and merited the severest possible rebuke, which the Marian exiles duly gave. With Elijah, the prophets of Marian England cried upon such people: 'How long halt ye between two opinions? if the Lord be God, follow him: but if Baal, then follow him.' (23) This text is cited in the treatise by Thomas Lever already referred to. The fate of the compromising brethren was clear - 'desperation the end of dissimulation' (24) and the suicidal despair of such as Judas Iscariot, the betrayer of Christ.

The exiles obviously recognised that such a

remedy as this refusal to attend mass that they so
enthusiastically recommended might well bring in its
wake some rather unpleasant consequences. For those
whose faith was insufficient to stand the ultimate
test of martyrdom, a gracious God had provided an
alternative, a means whereby they could forsake
idolatry, be witnesses to the gospel, and enjoy godly
fellowship in safety. They encouraged others to come
'out of Babylon' and the perils of idolatrous Marian
England to those cities abroad like Geneva, Basle,
Zurich and Strasbourg, where they themselves had
found refuge. The true believer should liken himself
to Abraham, called out of the ancient city of Ur, or
to the bride of Christ, and follow the picturesque
advice of Robert Pownoll in his 1556 <u>Epistle</u>:

> For what faithful honest woman is there that
> having her husband in a strange country and
> sending for her, doth not forthwith forsake
> father and mother, friend and acquaintance,
> goods and lands, nothing regarding neither
> peril, nor poverty that may happen unto her, so
> that she may be in the fellowship and company of
> her husband ... Wherefore now if your celestial
> husband Jesus Christ for your salvation and
> commodity and because he would make you like
> unto himself, doth now call you out of your own
> country do ye refuse to follow him ... whereas a
> weak woman would not refuse to follow her unkind
> husband. (25)

Naturally enough such widespread and heartfelt
repentance as the exiles demanded was never
forthcoming from the English nation as a whole. At
the successful accession of Elizabeth this might well
have brought a blush of embarrassment to the cheeks
of those who had prophesied doom and destruction if
England remained obdurate. But, ever-resourceful,
the exiles turned yet again to the scriptures, and
replaced their picture of a revengeful Jehovah by
that of the ever merciful, loving Father, who would
not heap up his anger against even his most
undeserving children. This change of emphasis on the
principal characteristics of the deity did not come
about in quite the cynical way that I have indicated.
The exiles had indeed been depicting just such a
loving God throughout their sojourn overseas with
reference to the idea of plague as chastisement
rather than merely as punishment, and so only a small
adjustment was required to apply the Lord's loving
kindness to the whole nation rather than to the

elect. The fact that the exiles had been chary of
making too many distinctions between the elect and
the rest of the nation proved a positive bonus in the
making of this post-Marian adjustment. The exiles
did, however, keep some of their fire in reserve, and
warned England that if this signal proof of God's
mercy was not properly appreciated, then the plagues
would return with renewed vigour. It is interesting
that the implied covenant between God and the English
did not vanish when the contractual penalties were
waived; rather the reverse, since England's
miraculous deliverance then and in later years from
the threat of Spanish and papal domination served to
underline the special relationship between God and
the English nation. (26)

One further point needs to be made concerning
the Marian exiles' view of plague and divine
punishment, and that is the nature of the plagues.
With the exception of the chief persecutors the
plagues experienced in the present, and those to
follow in the future as a result of sins of the
people, are all temporal, that is, earthly rather
than heavenly. There is a conspicuous lack of the
kind of hell-fire and damnation rhetoric that one
might reasonably expect from such a group as the
Marian exiles, out of power, and out of England.
Various explanations for this concentration on
worldly rather than external punishments can be
suggested. Perhaps as the exiles sought to make the
maximum impact on the political, social, and
religious events in England, the threat of eventual
punishment in the afterlife was considered to be too
remote to perform this function. Or perhaps, more
simply, they felt that this threat of hell was so
immediately obvious as to require no special
emphasis; or is the answer that in the circumstances
of sixteenth century protestantism such rhetoric was
never in general use, and indeed belongs to a later
period, possibly the eighteenth century? Again, the
exiles' emphasis on Old Testament imagery, where hell
is not a concept much in evidence, and temporal
punishments are the general rule, could account for
this phenomenon. It is also relevant to consider
whether a belief in predestination tends to inhibit a
preacher or writer from speaking at length on the
question of a man's ultimate heavenly reward or
punishment, because to do so would imply that man can
influence his final destination by his behaviour on
earth, an argument that protestants since Luther had
been at considerable pains to deny. Punishment and
plagues as evidence of divine anger against sin

perhaps had to be described and experienced in temporal terms, for to suggest otherwise might be interpreted as presuming on the prerogative of God. However, the martyrs and others who suffered persecution under Mary do tend to stress the delights of heaven for those who have endured much for the faith, despite the exiles' failure to dwell on the eventual consequences of sin in the afterlife. Evidently no such inhibition as that attached to the discussion of hell applied in the same way to heaven.

The Marian exiles by the end of their sojourn abroad had found the solution to the problem facing them in 1553. By seizing on the complementary doctrines of the cause and effect mechanism operating between sin and divine punishment, and the importance of godly chastisement for the faithful, and refining and fitting them aptly to the circumstances which they faced, they had managed to account for the eclipse of English protestantism under Mary, and explain why the godly appeared to bear the brunt of the disaster. In so doing they had also made a significant contribution to the development of the link between English nationalism and the protestant faith, and had reinforced the assertion of Hugh Latimer, Bishop of Worcester, in 1537, that the English should render 'due thanks to our Lord God ... for verily he hath shewed himself God of England, or rather an English God.' (27)

Notes

1.   M. Coverdale, How and whether a Christian man ought to fly the horrible plague of pestilence by Andrew Osiander (1538), sig. A3v-4r.

2.   T. Wilson, The art of rhetoric (1553), fol. 36v-47r.

3.   W. Morrison, An invective against the great and detestable vice treason (1539), sig. D8.

4.   T. Becon, A comfortable epistle to God's faithful people in England (1554), sig. A5.

5.   Humble Supplication unto God (1554), sig. A7.

6.   For this see the article by G. Bowler below.

7.   H. Latimer, Sermons, ed. G.E. Corrie (Parker Society, Cambridge, 1844), p.91.

8.   II Thess. 2, v.10-12.

9.   Becon, Comfortable Epistle, sig. A7 v.

10.   J. Knox, The first blast of the trumpet against the monstrous regiment of women (1558), sig. D7 v.

11.   R. Edgeworth, <u>Sermons very fruitful and godly</u> (1557), p.275.
12.   II Timothy 2 v. 12.
13.   J. Knox, <u>The copy of an epistle</u> (1559), p.17.
14.   Hebrews 12 v 6.
15.   J. Pownoll, <u>A most pithy and excellent epistle to animate all true Christians unto the cross of Christ</u> (1556), sig. E4v-E5.
16.   J. Bradford, <u>Letters, treatises, remains</u>, ed. A. Townsend (Parker Society, Cambridge, 1553) p.36.
17.   T. Lever, <u>A treatise of the right way from danger of sin</u>, written in 1556 but printed in 1575, sig. G8.
18.   <u>An admonition to the bishops</u> (1553), sig. A5.
19.   <u>Supplication to the Queen's majesty</u> (1555?), sig. C8v.
20.   For these writers see the article by G. Bowler below.
21.   <u>A true mirror</u> (1556), sig. B3.
22.   <u>The copy of a letter sent by John Bradford to the right honourable lords the earls of Arundel, Derby, Shrewsbury and Pembroke</u> (1556), appended verses.
23.   I Kings 18 v. 21 and Lever, <u>Treatise</u>, sig. H7v.
24.   Musculus, <u>The temporiser</u> (1555), sig. G7v.
25.   Pownoll, <u>Epistle</u>, sig. G3r.-v.
26.   See the article by Lake below.
27.   H. Latimer, <u>Sermons and remains</u>, ed. G. Elwes (Parker Society, Cambridge, 1845), p.385.

Chapter Five

MARIAN PROTESTANTS AND THE IDEA OF VIOLENT RESISTANCE TO TYRANNY

Gerry Bowler

Though the Edwardian clergy had ceaselessly taught Englishmen that disobedience to civil authority was a sin equal to witchcraft, it did not take some protestants very long to urge violence when they found themselves under the rule of a Catholic queen. From the first to the last days of her reign Mary Tudor was faced with protestant subjects who felt themselves justified, on both religious and political grounds, in taking up arms against her regime. Her reign had hardly begun before a London pamphleteer was urging a protestant show of force:

> Noblemen and gentlemen favouring the word of God, take counsel together and join yourself with all your following! Withdraw yourselves from our virtuous lady Queen Mary ... Draw near to the Gospels and your guerdon shall be the crown of glory. (1)

This pamphlet war was to grow steadily more intense and the protestant attacks on her were to become utterly unrestrained. By 1558 Mary was being depicted as a blood-crazed monster and writers were calling for both her murder and a general massacre of her Catholic clergy. How protestants were able to justify this shift from preaching non-violent obedience to an advocacy of violence is a fascinating chapter in the history of ideas.

While still living under their 'godly Josias' Edwardian protestant publicists, in response to the unrest and rebellion which religious reform had prompted, produced a considerable body of what might be termed the literature of obedience. (2) Arguing from scripture, they showed how disobedience had never prospered. Princes, good and bad alike, were the anointed agents of divine rule and to oppose them

124

was to oppose God himself. The royal person was
sacred, shielded by God from assassination or
conspiracy - the very birds of the air would disclose
treason and rebels would always suffer for their
actions. These government apologists also claimed
that rebellion was a futile blow against the cosmic
order for had not God ordained everything and
everyone in a particular place with a particular
purpose? Thomas Cranmer told the rebels of Devonshire
in 1549:

> Standeth it with any reason to turn upside down
> the good order of the whole world, that is
> everywhere, and ever hath been, that is to say
> the commoners to be governed by the nobles and
> the servants by their master? Will you now have
> the subjects to govern their King, the villeins
> to rule the gentlemen, and the servants their
> masters? If men would suffer this, God will not.
> (3)

Disobedience to civil authority was clearly caused by
ignorance, greed or madness and would result in
political and economic disaster for all concerned.

Many protestants clung to this teaching even
when faced with the Marian persecution. One of them,
the jailed Edwin Sandys, refused to be liberated from
his prison by Wyatt's army or to sanction the 1554
rebellion, saying rather, 'If this rising be of God,
it will take place; if not, it will fall.' (4) Others
such as John Bradford, Latimer, Ridley, and Cranmer
submitted to a fiery martyrdom. Hundreds more fled to
the safety of protestant Europe where some wrote
works espousing the virtues of peaceful resistance.
Many of these exiles, however, went beyond this and
chose to preach a gospel of violence.

European protestantism had a tradition of
advocating armed resistance that was almost as old as
the reformation itself. Most of the reformed
movements' leaders, including Zwingli, Luther,
Bullinger, and Calvin, had written in defence of
forcibly withstanding tyranny. (5) It is not
surprising then that the first comprehensive call to
resistance issued by Marian protestants should be
based on a work first issued almost a quarter-century
earlier by Martin Luther. This was A faithfull
admonition of a certain true pastor by John Bale,
(6), playwright, polemicist and Edwardian Bishop of
Ossory, translated from the tract Warning to his Dear
German People. Prefacing Luther's text were calls for
resistance by Melanchthon and one by Bale writing as

'Eusebius Pamphilus'. Luther had claimed in his tract that defence of one's self and the true religion was legitimate and could not be termed rebellion or compared to the wild excesses of the Anabaptists. As the Emperor and Catholic forces in Germany were denying protestants the practice of their faith Luther counselled disobedience and, if need be, armed violence against those attempting to enforce ungodly worship.

Bale's translation was not entirely faithful to its original. Significantly, Bale seems to have made a decision to widen the grounds of justifiable resistance by including not only Luther's religious concerns but also the more secular threat of Catholic attacks on the lawful and ancient privileges of England. Should the papists triumph, claimed A faithful admonition, all classes of Englishmen, nobles, yeomen and commons alike, would be disinherited and destroyed. Aliens would set up new laws to their advantage, steal English land and ravish English women. (7)

In the section by Philip Melanchthon the themes of alien threat and the rights of self-defence are also found. Melanchthon proferred examples from scripture and antiquity to show that earthly powers need not always be obeyed and, indeed, may be resisted with violence. The resistance shown by Armenians to the Emperor Maximian in defence of their religion and the killing of a viceroy in self-defence showed, said the tract, that the actions 'in christian men are right and lawful and do please god well'. Yea they are special testimonies of the judgement of god against unlawful violence and intolerable pride and presumption of tyrants.' (8) The definitions of tyranny in this section also are not exclusively religious and include the importing of foreigners to subvert the commonwealth.

It is in Bale's own words that the equation of foreign Catholic domination with tyranny is most clearly seen. This threat that protestant Germany once faced was now menacing England and, unless action were taken, would result in slavery to aliens and the triumph of false religion. That England had come to such a sorry pass was a result of the sin and ingratitude of the people, first under Edward and now continued under Mary. Chiefly to be blamed was the nobility whose indolence and supine dissoluteness had brought the present plague on England. The religious hypocrisy of the nobles had cost some of them dearly and they were now called upon to repent. This repentance that Bale urged on the nation was a

vigorous change of heart and action based on true
obedience to the word of God. Note how in the
following passage where Bale asserts the legality of
his appeal he achieves the transition from a call for
disobedience into one for active resistance:

> And specially let no man misconstrue it, but
> read it with judgement as an instruction not to
> stir any man to unlawful rebellion (as I doubt
> not but the papists God's sworn adversaries will
> be ready to say, whereas they and none other are
> the authors of all mischief as may most
> manifestly appear to any that hath but half his
> right wit) but only as an advertisement that no
> man minister any aid or obedience to such
> tyrants as bend themselves against God and his
> word and to the subversion of their natural
> country in which case it is not only unlawful to
> obey them or in any wise to consent unto them,
> but also most lawful to stand in the defence of
> God's religion and of the laudable and ancient
> state of their country against such
> uncircumcised tyrants (they shall never be
> called magistrates of me till they show
> themselves worthy of that name) as go about such
> devilish enterprises. The God of heaven with his
> mighty hand confound them. (9)

Resistance then was not disobedience. To Bale
and all the exile authors who followed him in writing
on the topic it was, in fact, a truer form of
obedience in which one chose to heed the dictates of
a higher law than the civil power's.

Luther's original call for resistance had been
made to protestant German princes who, he believed,
were constitutionally empowered to oppose themselves
to an errant emperor. Bale did not feel that this
argument in favour of the rights of the inferior
magistracy was one that would be successful in the
England of 1554. There the nobility had proved
themselves to be mere lip-gospellers under Edward and
many were now supporting the return of the Roman
primacy. The apostasy of Northumberland and the
neutrality of most of the landed class during Wyatt's
rising further made it clear that an appeal to the
English inferior magistracy was out of the question.
Moreover the failure of the English people
wholeheartedly to support the Edwardian reformation
convinced Bale that religious arguments alone were
insufficient to induce the populace to rise against
the Marian regime – thus the constant description of

the threat to England, its constitution and people.
Bale's hope was to educate the nation in the legality
of resistance so that, should an opportunity and a
righteous leader (he looked for another Judas
Maccabee) arise, the country would be ready to follow
Bale's advice.

The year 1554 ended with a Catholic star in the
ascendant: Mary had wed her Prince Philip; the Queen
was rumoured to be pregnant with an heir to the
throne who would be three-quarters Spanish; England
had been officially restored to the Church of Rome.
Protestant exiles responded with another salvo in the
pamphlet war. This was the tract Certain Questions
Demanded and asked by the Noble Realm of England, of
her true natural children and Subjects of the same,
published in Wesel in the spring of 1555. (10) Like
Bale's work, Certain Questions mixed religious and
political concerns; unlike Bale, the anonymous
author ignored previous European writings and
concentrated on the issues of the moment; the Queen's
marriage and pregnancy, parliamentary bills, trials
and imprisonments and the future of an independent
England.

The pamphlet was framed as a series of forty-
eight questions, all designed to undermine the
authority of Queen Mary and her regime. Since most
Englishmen would have agreed that a usurper need not
be obeyed, (11) Certain Questions moved to attack the
legitimacy of Mary's claim to the throne. It pointed
out that Mary's succession rested on the terms of her
father's will, a document which specified that
failure to keep its conditions would result in
forfeiture of the crown:

> Item, whether the Princess be worthy to be her
> father's heir (who only by his last will called
> her unto) will not observe her father's will,
> and whether of right her father's will ought to
> prevail against all her practices, contrary to
> the same will or not? and what judgement shall
> follow that Princess which doth the contrary?
> (12)

But Mary was a usurper in more ways than one.
Certain Questions became the first of the exile works
to claim that no woman could legitimately rule when
it asked:

> whether the express word of God in the xxii.
> Chap(ter) of Deut(eronomy) forbid a woman to
> wear a sword, or wear spurs, as kings do in

their creation, or to wear any other weapon, or apparel of a man, saying: A woman shall not wear the weapons of a man, neither shall a man put on woman's rainment, for who so doeth it, is abomination unto the Lord God. (13)

Two further questions sought to emphasise accusations of usurpation by reminding the reader that the Queen was an illegitimate child, declared a bastard by the great universities of Europe and her own chancellor, Stephen Gardiner. (14)

Having made the case against Mary's usurpation, the tract then attacked the Queen as a tyrant, one who placed her will above the law. She was accused of imprisoning her sister Elizabeth illegally, perverting the law in the Nicholas Throgmorton case and unjustly putting to death Archbishop Cranmer and Lady Jane Grey. (15) Mary's seizure of the property of those of her opponents who had fled England was labelled 'oppression and extortion'. Her tyranny was also manifest in her persecution of protestantism which she had promised at her accession to protect and in her promotion of catholicism contrary to law and solemn oath.

The most damaging article, however, in <u>Certain Questions</u>' list of accusations must have been the portrayal of the Queen as a traitor to the realm because of her attempts to 'deliver up unto another foreign prince, the right title, tuition, and defence of (her) realm, without the consent of (her) lawful heir or heirs apparent and faithful subjects'. (16) Appealing to the strong English feelings of xenophobia the tract made much of the Spanish threat to England and Mary's part in abetting it. The Spaniards, it was said, would raise taxes, force Englishmen to pay Prince Philip's debts, make off with the nation's riches and destroy the native nobility. It pointed out that Philip coveted the English crown and that he would resort even to open warfare to obtain it. Fearing that the Queen was intent on crowning her Spanish consort, willing him the throne and making foreign interests predominant, the tract countered with the notion that Englishmen had a stake in their own nation and that the Queen could not sell it, give it away nor even marry without the consent of the Commons.

What could be done to remedy this tyranny? Appealing to nobility or to Parliament was not a possibility. The nobility ('notable fools' the tract called them) had assented to the Queen's actions and Parliament had been packed with royal supporters.

129

First, the English military, 'the chief Captain and
soldiers of any town, castle, or hold', were called
upon to disobey any command the Queen might give that
would turn their charge over to the enemy or leave
the realm defenceless. (17) More importantly, the
author of Certain Questions was prepared to boldly go
where Bale had feared openly to tread and to appeal
directly to the people for resistance to tyranny. He
urged Englishmen 'to look to their own safety, and to
the safety of the realm and to join themselves wholly
together, to put down such a Prince as seeketh all
means possible to deliver them, their lands, their
goods, their wives, their children and the whole
realm into the hands of the Spaniard'. This
deposition, it was said, was lawful both by the laws
of God and nature. (18)

Certain Questions was the most radical
resistance tract which main-stream protestantism had
yet produced. In using Mosaic law to deny the
legitimacy of female rule, in allowing both secular
and religious reasons for justified violence and in
its willingness to entrust the commons with the duty
of rebellion this work went beyond any of its
predecessors and set examples for many that were to
follow. The doctrines of Certain Questions, however,
seem to have had no influence on the next resistance
tract published by English protestant exiles. This
was A Treatise of the Cohabitation of the faithful
with the unfaithful, a work based on lectures given
at Strasbourg by the Italian reformer Peter Martyr
Vermigli. (19) Vermigli spoke to the exile colony
that had gathered around him about the problem which
in 1555 and with the start of executions for heresy
in England had taken on special significance - the
responsibility of a true Christian in the midst of
infidels and idolaters. In the context of this
discussion Vermigli defined the occasions when
violent resistance might justly be employed in the
defence of religion.

All believers, said The Cohabitation, were
obliged to disobey any order which would compel them
to commit idolatry. The alternatives to such ungodly
obedience were, for most people, either flight or
martyrdom. There were, however, certain officers of
the state, the inferior magistrates, who had a duty
to go beyond and to actively resist religious
tyranny. Because they derived their power from the
chief ruler, these magistrates shared in his
responsibilities which always included the
maintenance of true religion. If the ruler neglected
this responsibility and promoted idolatry, he had to

be disobeyed. Should reasoned persuasion fail the magistrates might take up arms against him and feel confident that in this resistance they were emulating the scriptural examples of the Maccabees and those who deposed Queen Athaliah. (20)

The Cohabitation was not nearly so bold as Certain Questions had been. It restricted the right of resistance to a certain class of official, denying it to the common people and even to the nobility who were not office-holders. The tract was also careful to limit the justifiable excuses for resistance to those instances where the laws of God were threatened. In civil matters inferior magistrates were told to give way to 'the unjust commandments and decrees of their higher Lords'. Though this work might have appeared more timid than those earlier exile works, the sanctioning of resistance by such a respected leader of the reformation must have been an encouragement for those protestants hoping to overthrow their tyrant Queen.

Of the next two resistance tracts published neither could properly be termed 'protestant'. A Warning for England, which alarmed the Marian authorities in the autumn of 1555, eschewed all mention of religion and concentrated on the fear of Spanish domination with its attendant high taxes, displacement of English office-holders and loss of national independence. (21) There are echoes of Certain Questions in its talk of Philip's adultery and the dreadful examples of Spanish rule in Naples but there are none of that work's religious dimensions, unless one includes the threat to holders of abbey lands posed by the reconciliation with Rome. A Warning was clearly aimed at the October parliament and was meant to cut across confessional lines to influence those who had much to lose by seeing Philip given the crown matrimonial.

In the spring of 1556 the English ambassador in Paris wrote Queen Mary to tell her that

> one Bradford is come here of late, who hath served a great lord of Spain about the King of England ... the said Bradford pretendeth to have learned great secret matters in his service, as well by word spoken by him as by his letters and writings which he saith he hath seen. Whereupon he hath made a book, the most seditious and as like to do hurt if it came abroad as any can be devised. (22)

The book was The Copy of a letter sent by John

Bradford to the ... Earls of Arundel, Derby, Shrewsbury and Pembroke, written as if from a Catholic Englishman, one loyal to the Queen's religion but opposed to her Hispanophile policies. Though the tract attacked the 'devilish devices of certain heretics' it is not certain that its professions of religious orthodoxy can be taken seriously. (23) There is no doubt however that the work sought to arouse violent xenophobic feelings by the revelation of plots which the author had overheard or read of while serving in the household of a Spanish noble of Prince Philip's entourage. Queen Mary, he claimed, was to be supplanted by a Spanish viceroy, the English nobility was to be crushed and English law would disappear. The way to counter this threat was for patriots of all classes and beliefs to unite and to disobey the Queen if she sought to aid the Spanish. Englishmen were called upon to man their coastal defences to prevent any sneak attack the Spaniards might launch and 'when necessity compelleth them, to take all wholly one perfect way, in defending their country and withstanding their enemies'. (24)

The edition of The Copy was not the end of Bradford's involvement with resistance. Within a year a second edition of the work appeared and Bradford had joined in a plot to invade England and depose the Queen. (25) The conspiracy was that of Thomas Stafford, grandson of that duke of Buckingham executed by Mary's father and nephew to Cardinal Pole. Stafford's pretensions to the throne were humoured by the French who, wishing to cause the English and their Spanish allies any trouble they could, aided him in his invasion. In April 1557, with a band of patriots and mercenaries which included John Bradford, Stafford seized Scarborough Castle and issued a proclamation stating his case and inviting Englishmen to join him. The proclamation drew heavily on The Copy and was almost certainly Bradford's work. It called for Mary's deposition on the grounds of her breaking her father's will and her treachery to England seen in her favours to the Spanish. She was accused of conspiring to deliver up castles to the foreigners, impoverishing the country and attempting to bring it under the rule of Spaniards. (26) England, however, ignored the call to arms and within a very short time Stafford, Bradford and the others were on their way to the gallows.

While Bradford's work and A Warning steered clear of any identification with the protestant cause another work of 1556 was not ashamed to fly its religious colours boldly. This was A Copy of a very fine and witty letter sent from the Right Reverend Lewes Lippomanus, a somewhat curious tract which appeared in two different editions. The pamphlet purported to be a translation by an English Catholic of a letter sent from the papal nuncio in Poland to a Venetian gentleman. In the supposed letter and the translator's preface the Catholic clergy is revealed as a bloodthirsty crew bent on the destruction 'by chopping of heads and other like violences' of the nobility and all who opposed the Roman prelacy. Given such dangerous clerical designs the tract called for resistance based on the natural law concept of the legitimacy of self-defence. Both the English nobility and people were told to 'put their hands and wits to pull their necks from under the tyranny of the Bishop of Rome (God and man's enemy) and such wicked practices and not willingly put their own necks in halters: but rather defend themselves, according to God's law and the law of nature, than to suffer themselves to be willfully murdered'. (27)

The policy of 'chopping of heads' was sadly very much in practice by mid-1556. Those leaders of the Edwardian church who chose to remain in England had been exterminated, leading exile laymen had been kidnapped and returned for trial and the dangerous Dudley conspiracy, which aimed at Mary's deposition, had been betrayed. In this grim time appeared the most articulate and sophisticated of the protestant resistance tracts, A Short Treatise of politic power and of the true Obedience which Subjects owe to Kings and other civil Governors with an Exhortation to all true natural Englishmen. (28) This was the product of John Ponet, Edwardian Bishop of Winchester who had fled England after the failure of Wyatt's rebellion in which he had taken part. Of all the protestant exile books A Short Treatise comes closest to being a considered work of political theory in its arguments against absolutism and its defence of the right to resist tyranny.

Ponet began by establishing the origins and purpose of civil government — it was divinely established to maintain justice and benefit the whole nation. (29) The particular form that government took was left to the discretion of the people and the authority to make and execute laws could rest in a variety of institutions. Ponet saw clear limits to a ruler's power to command and a subject's duty to obey. Princes could not demand obedience to commands which ran counter to the laws of God or nature since they could scarcely claim to be wiser than or

superior to Him who made those laws. Nor could they
even break positive law which had been ordained for
the good of the nation because this would be to
contravene the purpose for which rulers were
instituted - 'to do good, not to do evil ... to
procure the wealth and benefit of their subjects and
not to work their hurt or undoing'. (30)

Just as princes had limits to their power, so
had subjects in their obedience. Anabaptists, said
Ponet, carried their liberty to the point of the
licence while English Catholics went to the other
extreme and demanded obedience to any command.
However, any order against the will of God must be
disobeyed as must any that would violate civil
justice or would harm the commonwealth. The subject's
loyalty must be first to his country and not the
prince who was, after all, only a part of the whole
and not an indispensable one at that, as the numerous
examples of tyrannicide and deposition showed. Ponet
admitted that there was no positive law anywhere in
Christendom that would sanction the removal or murder
of a tyrant but pointed out that these practices had
a long and honourable tradition. The Old Testament
was full of examples of tyrannicide and even English
history could offer the fates of Edward II and
Richard II. Ponet also pointed out that Catholics
themselves believed in the justifiability of
deposition - popes had removed the kings throughout
European history and conciliarist theory held that
even popes could be removed from office if they
proved unfit. All the evidence seemed to Ponet to
back his conclusion that sovereignty in any community
rested in the whole body and that it was delegated to
the ruler as a proxy. Should the prince abuse his
power this power could be revoked and the ruler
removed or killed. (31)

Having staked out his position Ponet then
considered the specifics of the situation in England
where a manifest tyrant now reigned - one who forbade
the true religion and who oppressed her subjects with
high taxation and murder. The correction of tyrants
belonged, in the first instance, to institutions
entrusted with the responsibility: in England this
included Parliament, the office of high constable,
the judiciary and the nobility. Ponet however saw no
help coming from any of these. The constable's office
had fallen into disuse while the other three had
proven themselves servants of the tyrant. Parliament
had enacted oppressive laws, the nobility was greedy
above all and judges did the government's bidding. So
disgusted was Ponet by what he saw that he devoted a

whole chapter to the proposition that no trust was to
be given to princes or potentates.

From where then was resistance to come? Ponet
turned to the individual tyrannicide. This was a
remedy that pre-Christian man had seen in the natural
law of self-defence and one that was evident in the
Old Testament and in secular history. Even Christ
seemed to allude to it in the lesson of the
unfruitful tree that would be cast into the fire.
Ponet's own view was one that took into account the
need for certain order:

> I think it cannot be maintained by God's word
> that any private man may kill, except (when
> execution of just punishment upon tyrants,
> idolators and traitorous governors is by the
> whole state utterly neglected, or the prince
> with the nobility and council conspire the
> subversion or alteration of their country and
> people) any private man have some special
> commandment or surely proved motion of God: as
> Moses had to kill the Egyptian, Phineas the
> Lecherous, and Ahud, King Eglon, with such like:
> or be otherwise commanded or permitted by common
> authority upon just occasion and common
> necessity to kill. (32)

The situation that he described was one that mirrored
the England of 1556 and there is no doubt that Ponet
would have applauded the assassination of Queen Mary
as a lawful and godly act.

Ponet died before his book was published and for
some time thereafter English protestantism lacked an
exponent of resistance who combined his boldness and
his clarity of thought. The exile authors who
immediately followed him owed much to his arguments
but they were clearly not as sophisticated. The 1557
tract The Lamentation of England, for example, shared
Ponet's distrust of the nobility as well as his
belief that tyranny could be resisted for secular as
well as religious reasons. It was as xenophobic as
Ponet could have wished and also accused the Queen of
seeking to betray her country into the hand of the
Spaniards. However, The Lamentation avoided Ponet's
historical and constitutional insights and called
much more abruptly for a divinely-inspired assassin
and, in a rather vaguely-worded appeal, for patriotic
unity:

> it be the duty of every Christian and true-
> hearted Englishman and that man perceiveth that

his native country like to come in to ruin and
destruction and doth not endeavour himself by
all the means he can devise, for the
deliverance, thereof, the same is not worthy to
be counted a true hearted Englishman but a
traitor to his country. (33)

(The Lamentation appeared again in 1558 with an
appendix in the form of a warning to England not to
duplicate the fate of Calais which had fallen to the
French. Englishmen were told to improve their
defences and to pray fervently that God would remove
the country's wicked rulers.)
By that time Calais itself had already been
warned of impending doom by the tract An Admonition
to the Town of Calais written by the preacher Robert
Pownoll. He lamented that a city once known for the
strength of its 'gospel like profession' had now
backslid into papistry and idolatry. The fates of
England and Calais were linked claimed Pownoll, as
both were suffering religious persecution, declining
in strength and coveted by foreign kings. Pownoll
claimed that England still had nobles who would
defend it but that Calais was not so lucky. The only
way to maintain Calais's freedom and protestantism
was in a repentance that would lead to, and ensure
the success of, violent resistance. The city had cast
off its allegiance to the tyrant Mary and to defend
itself, actions lawful to God, the laws of the land
and nature. Nothing should stand in the way of this
resistance, he told Calais:

For thou art not so far sworn to obey as by
obedience to show thyself a traitoress to thine
own country: Neither are thou so subject to this
Queen as for her sake, to withdraw for ever thy
subjection from the crown of England and from
the rightful inheritors of the same. (34)

Despite Pownoll's admonition Calais fell to the
French, a victim of the Franco-Spanish war in which
England had unwisely joined. The war and other
circumstances in 1557 seem to have wrought a change
in exile literature. There was certainly less of it
produced; the death of authors such as Ponet and the
increased difficulties of smuggling literary
contraband into a country at war were responsible for
this. There was also an undeniable change in thinking
about resistance and a swing from a mixture of
secular and religious concerns to one that was purely
religious. Before 1557 English resistance theory had

manifested a wide definition of tyranny, a definition
that included many secular acts of oppression. High
taxation, murder of political opponents, varieties
of usurpation, treason, diminution of the realm,
violations of the fundamental constitution,
collusion with a foreign power were all named as
actions that could prompt justifiable violent
resistance. Discouragement that the Marian plague
had lasted so long and a kind of patriotism prompted
by England's entry into a war with France seem to
have played their parts in causing those who had
advanced such secular arguments to keep silent on
this issue for a time and to leave the field to those
whose arguments were uncompromisingly religious.

This frustration is evident in Bartholomew
Traheron's 1558 tract A Warning to England to Repent,
and to Turn to God from idolatry and popery by the
terrible example of Calais where the author's
discouragement and rage at the Marian tyranny were
such that he attacked the Queen with more
intemperance and comprehensiveness than any previous
work. Mary, he said, 'bathed herself and swimmeth in
the holy blood of the most innocent virtuous and
excellent personages ... She is despiteful, cruel,
bloody, wilful, furious, guileful, stuffed with
painted processes, with simulation and dissimulation, void of all seemly virtues'. (35) Traheron did
not look for help from the nobility for they were too
cowardly and effeminate, nor could he call on the
people for they were too enfeebled by poverty and
oppression. Only repentance could now save England.
However, Traheron did show that he could approve of
resistance when he praised the Wyatt rebellion as a
rising 'in defence of their country, which then began
to be betrayed'. (36)

In late 1557 the colony of English exiles in
Geneva considered the question of obedience when one
of their leaders, Christopher Goodman, preached from
the Book of Acts on 'whether it is better to obey God
or man'. The community asked Goodman to put his
sermon into book form and this was done early in 1558
when his How Superior Powers Ought to be Obeyed of
Their Subjects: and wherein they may lawfully by
God's Word be disobeyed and resisted appeared with a
preface by William Whittingham.

Goodman's book and those of his fellow-exile
John Knox show that the Genevan colony considered
that they were setting out a new sort of idea.
Goodman claimed that human reason had so far been
inadequate and that even godly and learned men had
taught 'that it was not lawful in any case to resist

137

and disobey the superior powers: but rather to lay down their heads and submit themselves to all kinds of punishments and tyranny.' (37) Why Goodman should ignore the English protestant resistance writings of the previous four years is an interesting question. The answer is that the Genevan colony tended to be somewhat alienated from other exile groupings on a number of issues and that Goodman probably found his predecessors' theories to be too secular and insufficiently grounded in scripture. Unlike many of the earlier works <u>Superior Powers</u> relied exclusively on biblical precepts, turning its back on arguments from secular history, the writers of antiquity, Church Fathers or constitutional law. Since scripture was the revealed word of God, it made no sense to Goodman to look farther.

The essential scriptural passage on obedience was to be found in Acts where the apostles Peter and John, forbidden by civil authority to preach, replied that it was better to obey God than men. England's lamentable state could be blamed on the country's failure to follow divine precepts and to follow human custom instead. This could be seen in the matter of Mary's succession to the crown where Goodman claimed scriptural instructions should have been heeded above English law. Had this been done, Mary would have been barred from the throne for being a woman, a bastard, an idolater and a traitor. (38) It was not enough simply to disobey the commands of such a usurper and tyrant; one must actively resist them, even violently. Goodman's catalogue of ungodly commands shows that he considered tyranny to be defined in merely religious terms: enforced attendance at mass or pilgrimage, persecution of protestants, or compulsion to submit to papal authority. In fact, Goodman specifically warned against rebellion for secular reasons or masking hope for private gain under a cloak of religious zeal.

Like some of his predecessors Goodman looked to the inferior magistracy to lead the resistance and like them he was pessimistic about the chances of their actually doing so. Though the English nobility and office-holders had been placed by God in their positions to defend against tyranny and idolatry they had, in fact, actively participated in the Queen's persecutions. In such a case Goodman turned to the people:

> And though it appeared at the first sight a
> great disorder that the people should take unto
> them the punishment of transgression, yet, when

the Magistrates and other officers cease to do
their duty, they are as it were without
officers, yea, worse then if they had none at
all, and then God giveth the sword in to the
people's hand and he himself is become
immediately their head. (39)

Goodman, in advancing this idea, held that England
was bound by the same covenant as the Old Testament
Israelites who were obliged to slay all idolaters.
Englishmen then should have butchered Mary and her
priests early in her reign and spared the country
much misery and oppression. Even now, he said, if
they showed repentance God would send them a leader
to cleanse the nation.

Ideas very similar to Goodman's were also
published in Geneva in 1558. They were those of John
Knox, Scottish rebel, Edwardian court preacher and
prolific exile writer. In his The First Blast of the
Trumpet Against the Monstrous regiment of women Knox
echoed Goodman's statement that the idea of
justifiable resistance originated with the Genevan
exiles and continued the attack on female rule. Knox
drew on a wider variety of sources than did Goodman
in his assault on gynocracy, bringing forward
arguments, not only from scripture, but also from
nature, history, civil law, the Church Fathers and
Aristotle. (40) Having shown how such rule was
repugnant to divine and natural law and subversive of
the state Knox concluded that the only sure guide in
political matters was scripture, particularly the
lessons on kingship found in Deuteronomy, where Knox
claimed to discern an everlasting command to exclude
women, idolaters and foreigners from civil rule.
Scripture also commanded the remedy for the mistake
of having permitted such a one, as was Queen Mary, to
reign: violent resistance, like that met by the
biblical usurper Queen Athaliah who was murdered
along with her idol-worshipping priests. The
inferior magistrates were to lead and the people were
to ensure that they acted with rigorous zeal. (41)
The application of this theory to England was plain:

And therefore fear not to affirm, that it had
been the duty of the nobility, judges, rulers
and people of England, not only to have resisted
and again standed Mary, that Jesabel, whom they
call their queen, but also to have punished her
to the death with all the sort of her idolatrous
priests, together with all such as should have
assisted her, what time that she and they openly

began to suppress Christ's Evangel. (42)

Knox's insistence that scriptural precepts be the foundation of political action was reiterated in The Appellation of John Knox published as a self-defence against his conviction in absentia by Scottish Catholics of heresy. Here he defined the chief duty of secular rulers to be the maintenance of true religion and asserted that should it be persecuted the inferior magistracy and the people had the right to use violence in its defence. Knox called on the Scottish nobility to do better than their English counterparts and to defend him and the true religion he preached.

In an appendix to The Appellation Knox set forth a summary of his proposed Second Blast which much resembled the content of Goodman's Superior Powers. In it Knox maintained that any claim to the throne must rest, not on royal lineage, but on the consonance of the choice with biblical precepts. No idolater or religious transgressor could ever rule in a Christian country and should such be chosen he might be deposed lawfully. (43) This was truly radical stuff and, had it ever been adopted, would have swept away English constitutional law and custom, the rule of women, dynastic monarchy and the possibility of anyone but an enthusiastic Calvinist male sitting on the throne. These ideas, however, found little favour either in England or on the continent and, in any event, Queen Mary was dead before the year was out and her protestant sister Elizabeth on the throne. The exiles soon disbanded their colonies and returned home to England, some to positions of power and influence, some, like Goodman, to suspicion and disfavour.

English protestants under Mary had developed some of the most far-reaching theories about resistance yet published. Writers such as Ponet, Bale and the author of Certain Questions had expanded the definition of tyranny to include secular offences. Many had gone far beyond their continental forbears in allowing the common people a role in overthrowing the tyrant and others had now made the ruler's sex a factor in determining the legitimacy of civil government. On their return home they did not, however, entirely abandon their beliefs about the justifiability of violence in response to tyranny. Though certain doctrines such as popular rebellion and antigynocracy were pushed to the background, English protestants remembered under Elizabeth the lessons they had learned under Mary. Veterans of the

exile such as John Knox and Laurence Humphrey
continued to advocate the lawfulness of resistance,
and annotations in English Bibles praised it.
Numerous works in favour of it were published
throughout the reign and, for a time, it even became
part of parliamentary debate when the country faced
the threat of yet another Catholic queen. (44)

Notes

1. Calendar of State Papers, Spanish, vol.
xi. ed. Royal Tyler (London, 1961), pp.173-4.
2. The best of these works are John Cheke's
The hurt of sedition (London, 1549), John Hooper's
Romaynes (Worcester, 1551) and Cranmer's homily 'An
Exhortation Concerning Good Order and Obedience'.
3. Thomas Cranmer, 'Answers to the Fifteen
Articles of the Rebels, Devon, Anno 1549' in
Miscellaneous Writings and Letters of Thomas
Cranmer, ed. John Edmund Cox (Parker Society,
Cambridge, 1848), p. 185.
4. The Sermons of Edwin Sandys, ed. John Ayre
(Parker Society, Cambridge, 1842), p.ix.
5. A good introduction to reformation
resistance theory is Quentin Skinner, Foundations of
Modern Political Thought, vol. 2 (CUP Cambridge,
1978).
6. The work was published twice in 1554: by
John Day? of London and Rihel of Strasbourg. For the
attribution of this tract to Bale see my 1981 London
Ph.D. dissertation 'English Protestants and
Resistance Writings, 1553-1603'.
7. Bale, A faithfull admonition, sigs. 12-K.
8. Ibid., sig. C.
9. Ibid., sigs. A5-A5v.
10. Certain Questions was published in Wesel
by Josse Lamprecht and seems to be the 'Seditious
book of questions in print' which alarmed the Privy
Council in the summer of 1555. Acts of the Privy
Council, 1554-56, ed. John Roche Dasent (London,
1892), pp. 153-4.
11. There was a long-standing consensus in
European thought against usurpation stretching from
John of Salisbury through Thomas Aquinas to popular
literature. See, for example John Lydate, The book of
Johan Bochas (London, 1527), p. 52.
12. Certain Questions, Sig. A2v.
13. Ibid., sig. A2v.
14. Ibid., sigs. A2v and A6.
15. Ibid., sigs. A3-3v.
16. Ibid., sig. A2.

17. Ibid., sig. A2.
18. Ibid., sigs. A3v and A5.
19. The editing of this tract, published by Rihel of Strasbourg in 1555, is sometimes attributed to Thomas Becon but any number of the exiles gathered about Peter Martyr Vermigli could have been responsible.
20. The Cohabitation, fo. 48v.
21. Anon., A Warning for England (Emden, 1555), sigs. A5v and A7v.
22. In Sheila R. Richards, Secret Writings in the Public Records. Henry VIII - George, vol. 3 (London, 1974), p.9. Wotton's letter identified an Englishman named Dunnill as the printer, with Antwerp as the place of publication.
23. Bradford's statements on doctrine are extremely ambiguous and some marginal notes and an appended poem are anti-Catholic. However, the Elizabethan puritan Sir Francis Hastings in a Watch-Word (London: 1598) and David Loades, 'The Authorship and Publication of The Copye' in Transactions of the Cambridge Bibliographical Society, vol. 3 (1960), pp. 155-60, take Bradford at his word.
24. The Copy, sig. G4v.
25. See Loades, 'The Authorship and Publication of The Copye' for more about this second version.
26. In John Strype, Ecclesiastical Memorials, vol. 3, no. 2 (Oxford, 1822), pp. 515-18.
27. Anon., A Copy of a very fine and witty letter (Emden and London?, 1550) Sigs. Av-A2.
28. John Ponet, A Short Treatise (Strasbourg, 1556).
29. Ibid., sigs. A4v-A5.
30. Ibid., sig. B5V.
31. Ibid., sig. D7.
32. Ibid., sigs. G8-G8v.
33. Anon. The Lamentation (n.p. 1557), p.11.
34. R(obert) P(ownall) An Admonition to the Town of Calais (n.p., 1557), p.15.
35. Bartholomew Traheron, A Warning to England to Repent (Wesel, 1558), Sig. A5.
36. Ibid., Sig. A3.
37. Christopher Goodman, Superior Powers (Geneva, 1558), p.30.
38. Ibid., pp. 49-57.
39. Ibid., p.185.
40. John Knox, The First Blast (Geneva, 1558), fo. 7-29v.
41. Ibid., fo. 35
42. Ibid., fo. 36.

43. John Knox, <u>The Appellation</u> (Geneva, 1558), fo. 77v-78.

44. Some notable Elizabethan works on resistance include John Knox, <u>History of the Reformation in Scotland</u> (London, 1587); Dudley Fenner, <u>Sacra Theologica</u> (London, 1586); Lawrence Humphrey, <u>The Nobles</u> (London, 1563), and certain annotations in the Geneva Bible (Geneva, 1560) and the Bishop's Bible (London, 1568). The parliamentary debates of 1572 on the fate of Mary, Queen of Scots are full of resistance theory. See T.E. Hartley (ed.), <u>Proceedings in the Parliaments of Elizabeth I</u> (Leicester University Press, Leicester, 1981). For this see G. Bowler, '"An axe or an acte": the parliament of 1572 and resistance theory in early Elizabethan England', <u>Canadian Journal of History</u>, vol. 19 (1984).

Chapter Six

'A RARE EXAMPLE OF GODLYNESS AMONGST GENTLEMEN': THE
ROLE OF THE KINGSMILL AND GIFFORD FAMILIES IN
PROMOTING THE REFORMATION IN HAMPSHIRE*

Ronald Harold Fritze

How did the reformation succeed in Tudor England?
This is a question with almost as many answers as
there are scholarly studies of English counties,
towns and various groups of people. This study
examines a crucial, perhaps the most crucial,
contribution to the transformation of the county of
Hampshire into a reasonably protestant county. That
element was the creation of a group of protestant
gentry capable of helping to implement and to
maintain the Elizabethan religious settlement in
their county. There were other manifestations of
protestantism in Hampshire in addition to its
appearance among the gentry. Protestant scholars in
Winchester College waged guerrilla warfare against
what they considered were the corrupt superstitions
of the old religion. Protestant preachers roamed the
county spreading their version of the gospel and
suffering persecution for their labours. (1) But, in
spite of these efforts, the crucial development for
the ultimate success of protestantism was still the
conversion of an inter-related group of families of
the gentry who also served as justices of the peace.
It was the efforts of this ruling segment of the
county's population that ensured the success of the
reformation.
        How this protestant conversion of a significant
segment of the gentry in Hampshire came about cannot
be fully determined. The thoughts, questions and
decisions these people made in the course of their
various spiritual journeys have been lost. However,
evidence of the protestant J.P.s' impact on Hampshire
is unmistakable. So, while it is not possible to
identify exactly how their conversion to
protestantism took place, it is possible to chart the
growth of protestantism among the gentry of Hampshire
and its ultimate domination of the county's rulers.

144

In this process the efforts of the families of Kingsmill and Gifford were paramount.

By the late fifteenth century both the Kingsmill and the Gifford families had long resided in Hampshire. Neither family had a pre-eminent place among the magisterial gentry of the county. Of the two the Kingsmills were the more obscure but John Kingsmill I, the son and heir of Richard Kingsmill, showed the type of talent and potential as a lawyer that made him a reasonable match for Jane, the daughter of John Gifford, an esquire of Ichell, Hampshire. The two families arranged a marriage indenture on 1 August 1490 which provided the young couple with the generous sum of 48 li 13s and 4d a year to live on. (2) This amount was in addition to John's earnings as a lawyer.

Following his marriage John Kingsmill I continued to be a great success as a lawyer. By 1499 his skills were so well known throughout England that William Eleson could advise Sir Robert Plumpton of Yorkshire to secure Kingsmill's service for 'it were well done that he (Kingsmill) were with you, for his authority and worship'. Eleson also added this caution 'his (Kingsmill's) coming will be costly to you' which further verifies the reality of his successful legal practice. (3) Royal recognition of his talents also continued with appointments to a number of offices. By 2 October 1502, John Kingsmill I had become the fourth Justice of Common Pleas and entered the third position in 1507. (4)

Just how much further John Kingsmill I would have risen in the legal profession and royal service cannot be answered for on 11 May 1509 he died. He left, besides his wife Jane, at least four surviving children: John, Alice, Morpheta and Mary. (5) The task of carrying on the Kingsmill family's name and fortune lay with the son and heir John Kingsmill II, who was about twelve years old at the time of his father's death. Following in the footsteps of his father, he took the educational path leading to a legal career. Lincoln's Inn admitted him in October 1516 and on 9 May 1521 he was called to the bar at the approximate age of twenty-four. (6) During the same period, John II also began a family of his own. He signed a marriage indenture with John Goring of Burton, Sussex for his daughter Constance on 7 November 1519. He completed that agreement on 5 March 1521 by placing all his lands in Basingstoke, Hampshire in use to his wife. (7)

Unlike his father, John II did not rise steadily through the legal profession. Instead he began to

participate in the typical local activities of a
fledgling member of the Tudor gentry. By 1533 he had
achieved only modest success for a thirty-six year
old gentleman, especially one with John Kingsmill
II's family background. His fortunes, however, were
soon to improve.

The 1530s were a time of opportunity for a
person with protestant leanings, few scruples, or
both. If a person could enter Thomas Cromwell's
service or become one of his local agents,
advancement and enrichment would most likely follow.
Fortunately for John Kingsmill II, he possessed both
a contact with Cromwell and budding protestant
credentials. His wife's family, the Gorings, were the
source of both of these timely assets.

The Gorings of Burton, Sussex were an old yet
undistinguished family of that county's gentry. John
Goring had married well and so was able to enter the
ranks of the magisterial gentry. Judging from their
wills, they were an extremely religious family
whether they were following the old or the reformed
faiths. (8) William Goring, the son and heir of John,
converted to protestantism quite clearly in the
1530s. About the same time he developed an
association with Thomas Cromwell which was
maintained through to the principal secretary's
execution in 1540. One of Goring's most important
services to the central government involved his
participation during 1538 in the revelation of the
Marquis of Exeter's conspiracy. Cromwell rewarded
Goring's efforts by supporting his election as one of
Sussex's two knights of the shire. (9) This
connection with Cromwell proved rewarding not just
for Goring but also for the members of his extended
family.

John Kingsmill II also started to exhibit signs
of a conversion to protestantism and entered into
association with Thomas Cromwell in the latter 1530s.
His relationship with the Goring family was probably
instrumental in helping to bring about these changes.
He was certainly not the only husband of a Goring
woman to later become a protestant. Still, it must
have been a confusing time for him since his sister
Morpheta was first a prioress and then abbess of
Wherwell Abbey since at least 1529. Apparently the
entire Kingsmill family came over to protestantism
including Morpheta, who after the dissolution
returned to her family and lived with them in a
friendly manner until her death early in Elizabeth's
reign. (10) Meanwhile John Kingsmill II started to
cooperate closely with Sir Thomas Wriothesley, a

trusted and influential associate of Cromwell's, who was building up a great landed estate in Hampshire through the acquisition of monastic lands. By June 1538 Kingsmill had been conducting business for Wriothesley in Hampshire for some time and asked Wriothesley to secure favours for him from Cromwell through his office as lord privy seal. (11) Not surprisingly, his affiliation with Wriothesley and Cromwell brought Kingsmill the honour and privilege of holding important local government offices. He appeared as a J.P. for the first time in 1537 and was appointed sheriff of Hampshire on 15 November 1538. (12) Very quickly John Kingsmill II rose to become Wriothesley's and Cromwell's most important adherent in Hampshire.

Kingsmill's rise to local leadership of Cromwell's following and the nascent protestant gentry in Hampshire is not surprising. The year 1538 was a time of great flux among the group of gentry in Hampshire that supported protestantism and Cromwell's policies. Previous leaders had died, some had returned to the conservative fold, the family of Sir William Paulet was starting to set its own independent course in local politics, and Bishop Stephen Gardiner had returned to Winchester to reassert his episcopal power and the conservative way. All of these things had caused a deterioration in strength of Cromwell's local following. Their situation was further weakened by Thomas Wriothesley's absence on a diplomatic mission to Flanders during the winter of 1538/39. Not surprisingly the local leadership of Cromwell's followers and local protestants devolved on to John Kingsmill II. (13) The choice of Kingsmill was quite reasonable: he was well-connected with the rest of the local gentry, a convinced protestant and a loyal follower of Cromwell and Thomas Wriothesley.

Events during the spring of 1539 tested Kingsmill's capacity for local leadership. On 21 March, Henry VIII called a new parliament to provide for national defence and to formulate a religious settlement that would end the growing religious divisions in the nation. Cromwell wanted a parliament consisting of men that supported his policies. To obtain such men, he assigned William Fitzwilliam, the Earl of Southampton and William Paulet, newly created Lord St John, to supervise the elections in Surrey, Sussex and Hampshire. As sheriff of Hampshire, John Kingsmill II occupied a pivotal position from which to manage the elections of Hampshire's two knights of the shire. He used his office to good effect and with

147

the help of Fitzwilliam and Paulet managed to return the Cromwellian candidates, Thomas Wriothesley and Richard Worsley, as the county's knights. Their efforts, however, were not unopposed because Stephen Gardiner, the conservative Bishop of Winchester and his followers disapproved of Cromwell's policies and Wriothesley's spoliation of St Swithun's Priory. Fortunately, for Kingsmill, the preponderance of power still rested with his side in the spring of 1539. (14) In the aftermath of the election however, he warned Wriothesley that the enemies of protestantism continued to hope that 'the bishop (Gardiner) may get favour that then they shall be restored again to their old dominions.' Gardiner's people might make amends with Wriothesley but they treated Kingsmill coldly. As he described his situation, 'I do not see much peace when I know above all other (I) am most in his (Gardiner's) displeasure with him and all his.' (15)

The immediate future did not bring a fulfilment of Kingsmill's pessimistic prediction. Thomas Wriothesley arrived a few days after the election and his commanding presence brought about an apparent reconciliation of the local rulers during the quarter sessions held at Winchester. (16) Protestantism's growing strength seemed unstoppable in Hampshire. Its final triumph, however, was not yet at hand for in 1540 protestantism's dominance in Hampshire still depended on the protection of Thomas Cromwell. Cromwell's removal from power and his swift execution left the adherents of the reformation with too few people holding significant positions in local society. Henry VIII's last years were a time when both John Kingsmill II's fortunes and protestantism's influence suffered a severe setback. He was right not to see much peace for himself in the immediate future. (17)

Time, however, was on the side of Kingsmill and the reformation in Hampshire in spite of the grim events of the early 1540s. A new generation of inter-related magisterial gentry with protestant leanings was growing up in Hampshire. This network of people was centred on John Kingsmill and his family and its existence made the ultimate triumph of the Elizabethan religious settlement considerably easier than it might have been in such a religiously conservative county as Hampshire. Therefore, the best way to describe the development of a solid protestant foundation in Hampshire's society from 1547 to 1570 is to trace the growth of the Kingsmill family's local and protestant connections.

148

John Kingsmill II belonged to a family well-connected with the gentry of Hampshire. Two of these connections, in particular, formed the nucleus of the growing protestant group in the county. Richard Gifford of Kings Somborne was a first cousin of John Kingsmill II since Richard's father William and John's mother Jane were both the children of John Gifford of Ichell. Another possibly more significant connection between the two men was that they both married daughters of John Goring of Burton, Sussex: John to Constance and Richard to Anne. (18) This connection also made both men brothers-in-law of Sir William Goring, already mentioned as a committed protestant by the early 1530s. Given what is known about the role of women in the spread of protestantism among both the well-to-do and poorer segments of society, it is highly possible that Constance and Anne provided the initial impetus toward reformed beliefs in their new families. (19) This seems especially likely in light of the distinctive level of religious commitment practised by the Goring family and the similar degree of faith exhibited by Constance Kingsmill and some of her children. (20)

From this solid core of protestantism, it is possible to trace a growing circle of other gentry who came to share their beliefs with the passing years. This expansion principally took place by means of the children of the Kingsmill and the Giffords. Male children provided potential J.P.s while both male and female children made useful marriage alliances possible.

John and Constance Kingsmill were a prolific couple and produced at least fourteen children: nine boys and five girls. Obviously Constance was incredibly strong of body as well as of faith. William Kingsmill, their eldest son and heir gained a place as a J.P. in the first years of Elizabeth's reign which he retained throughout his life except during his terms as sheriff of Hampshire. In this position, he provided leadership in local government and supported the preservation and extension of the protestant reformation in Hampshire. His marriage to Bridget Raleigh of Warwickshire did not create any local marriage alliance but such a purpose normally did not form the only priority in such decisions. (21) Andrew Kingsmill, apparently the second son, contributed his talents to the protestant ministry. Attending Oxford University, he received a fellowship from All Souls College. At the beginning of Elizabeth's reign he decided to move to Geneva and

then to Lausanne in order to observe and to learn
directly the practices of the best reformed ministry.
Presumably he intended to return to England and share
the benefits of his experience with his countrymen
but illness prematurely ended his life and career.
His legacy was simply some small devotional books
posthumously published by a friend. (22)

Richard Kingsmill, a younger son, sought his
fortune in the law and attended Lincoln's Inn. He
established a reputation as a good lawyer like his
grandfather John I before him, which along with his
protestant convictions helped to get him preferments
in the Court of Wards and Liveries from its master
William Cecil. Besides serving as a J.P. in Hampshire
during most of Elizabeth's reign, he was also an
active parliament man and served as a burgess for
Calne, Wiltshire in 1559, a burgess for Heytesbury,
Wiltshire in 1563 and a knight of the shire for
Hampshire in 1584 and 1586. He married the daughter
and heir of Richard Fawkner of Hurstborne, Hampshire
which became his home. As early as 1559 he served as
a commissioner to bring true religion to the north of
England. (23)

Henry Kingsmill never became a J.P. but
continued the family policy of supporting
protestantism. During the reign of Queen Mary, he
went into exile with the Earl of Bedford. Upon his
return to England, he entered into Queen Elizabeth's
service and in 1563 sat as a burgess for Downton,
Wiltshire. (24) John Kingsmill III, like his older
brother Andrew, attended Oxford and became a fellow
of the protestant infested Magdalen College in 1556.
By 1570 he had become Bishop Robert Horne's
chancellor for the diocese of Winchester replacing
the academically talented but morally dissolute
George Acworth and so helped to make Horne's
difficult episcopate somewhat easier. In addition,
he received election as a burgess for Ludgershall,
Wiltshire in 1584 and 1586. (25) George Kingsmill,
who was very much younger than the rest of his
brothers, chose a career in the law like his older
brother Richard. Following his father's and
brother's examples, he entered Lincoln's Inn and
played a prominent part in the life of the society.
Eventually he rose to be a serjeant at law in 1594, a
Queen's serjeant in 1595 and a justice of Common
Pleas in 1599. During the parliaments of 1584 and
1586 he sat as a burgess for Stockbridge, Hampshire.
In addition by the 1590s he was serving as a justice
of the peace for Hampshire with his older brother.
(26) Thomas Kingsmill followed the academic path of

his brothers Andrew and John and also demonstrated once again the family's talent for learning. Staying at Oxford, he became the first Regius Professor of Hebrew there and so made his contribution to furthering the reformation from that position in the university. (27) Nothing is known about John Kingsmill II's two remaining sons Arthur and Roger, which indicates that they were either nonentities or died before reaching adulthood.

John Kingsmill II's daughters also did their part to expand the reformation and make it secure. Catherine Kingsmill's marriage to Richard Norton, the son and heir of John Norton of East Tisted, Hampshire, provided the protestant cause with a great coup. John Norton, a contemporary of John Kingsmill II's, had been a leading supporter of Bishop Stephen Gardiner but by the beginning of Elizabeth's reign his son was in the protestant camp. From at least 1561 Richard Norton served as a J.P. for Hampshire and sat as a knight of the shire for the county in 1571 and 1572. Whether his wife Catherine Kingsmill helped to convert him to protestantism is not known but she certainly gave him a closer connection to the protestant Kingsmill-Gifford group. (28) Margaret Kingsmill married John Thornborough of Shotesdon, Hampshire. This marriage further increased the number of magisterial gentry bound together by ties of family and protestantism. Thornborough served as a J.P. for Hampshire from 1564 to 1591. (29) A further prestigious connection for the Kingsmill-Gifford group was the marriage between Alice Kingsmill and James Pilkington, a Marian exile and the first protestant bishop of Durham from 1561 to 1576. Pilkington maintained close and cordial relations with his Kingsmill in-laws and helped advance Richard's career in the Court of Wards. In addition, such a family relationship could only help the efforts of the Elizabethan episcopate and its local supporters to continue the progress of the protestant cause. It also provided the Kingsmill-Gifford group with one of its several friends in high places in the Elizabethan central government. (30) Jane Kingsmill's marriage to John Cupper was not nearly as important in producing significant religious and political alliances. Cupper died prior to 2 May 1566 and it was probably this family tragedy that inspired Andrew Kingsmill to write his devotional tract A Most Excellent and Comfortable Treatise .... (31) Elizabeth, the fifth daughter, does not appear to have married. Thus John Kingsmill II's children provided a potent addition to the increasing strength and cohesion of Elizabethan protestantism both nationally and locally in Hampshire.

The marriage of Richard Gifford and Anne Goring did not match the fecundity of that of John and Constance Kingsmill. Still, their three sons and one daughter also made a significant contribution to the protestant cause in Hampshire. Compared with most of the Kingsmill men, Henry Gifford, the eldest son and heir of Richard, played a rather modest role in the group of Hampshire protestants. In spite of his having the support of Bishop Robert Horne in 1564, Henry did not obtain any important local government offices until much later. He served as sheriff of Hampshire in 1578/79 and as a J.P. from 1583. His election to Parliament as a burgess for Stockbridge in 1572 can be attributed to his family's control of considerable land and thus patronage in the immediate area. (32) John Gifford of Bentley made soldiering his career and served in Ireland as a captain of the horse under Sir Henry Sidney. His personal relations with Sidney were excellent. As a result it seems likely that Sidney persuaded the Earl of Bedford or Sir William Cecil to secure his election as a burgess for Camelford in Cornwall in 1572. John Gifford's direct involvement in Hampshire was thus slight but in his will he did remember his brother-in-law Sir Henry Wallop with the gift of a horse and the office of overseer of the will. (33) Richard Gifford's third son William appears to have been a nonentity in his local society.

Richard Gifford's daughter Anne secured possibly the most important local marriage alliance for the Kingsmill-Gifford group. Sometime after 29 August 1545, she married Henry Wallop, the son of Sir Oliver Wallop and the heir of his uncle the courtier Sir John Wallop. This marriage brought a powerful and previously religiously conservative family into the protestant faction. That talent and power were now devoted to the cause of the reformed religion. Throughout his career during the reign of Elizabeth, Sir Henry Wallop provided formidable leadership and support for the Kingsmill-Gifford group and protestantism in Hampshire. He was joined in this effort by his father Sir Oliver Wallop and his younger brother William Wallop. (34) Thus the protestant cause was substantially strengthened by Anne Gifford's marriage to Henry Wallop, while the Catholic cause was immeasurably weakened.

Other less direct connections of family and friendship also served to strengthen the position of protestantism in Hampshire during the early years of

Elizabeth's reign. Richard Gifford's sister Jane had married Thomas Haydok, a member of Hampshire's gentry and a J.P. Although Thomas Haydok remained faithful to his old religion, his son James had joined his uncle Richard Gifford and the other adherents of protestantism in the 1560s. (35) Nicholas Dering, a J.P. for Hampshire, had been a close friend of John Kingsmill II, and it is not surprising to find his son Thomas supporting the Kingsmill-Gifford group in his position as an Elizabethan J.P. for Hampshire. (36) William Uvedale of Wickham was connected to Hampshire's protestant faction by sentiment, friendship and family. It seems likely that he was Bishop Robert Horne's steward for the diocese of Winchester and the Bishop certainly considered him a favourer of the reformed religion. Uvedale felt ties of friendship and trust strong enough to appoint his fellow J.P.s Henry Wallop and Richard Norton and the future J.P. Richard Ingpen as the overseers of his will on 3 February 1567. In addition, he called Ingpen his 'cousin'. (37) Richard Ingpen was the son of Francis Ingpen of Galaker, Hampshire and Alice, the daughter of Richard Norton, the grandfather of the protestant Richard Norton. This connection made Richard Ingpen the first cousin of the protestant Richard Norton as well as of William Uvedale. His grandfather Thomas Ingpen also served briefly as a J.P. in the early 1560s but showed no leanings toward protestantism. Richard, however, did. In addition to his family connections to the Nortons and Uvedale, he belonged to a group of protestant Middle Temple lawyers associated with the Earl of Bedford, a patron of the Kingsmills. Of course such lesser family connections did not necessarily obligate a person to give his foremost allegiance to his relatives. (38) Overall, however, the Kingsmill-Gifford grouping was based on a firm foundation of family ties reinforced by protestant convictions.

John Kingsmill II's children were a generally quite succesful group and contributed mightily to the furtherance of the reformation both locally and nationally in England. During Elizabeth's reign there was a Kingsmill judge of Common Pleas, a Kingsmill attorney and surveyor of the Court of Wards, a Regius Professor of Hebrew at Oxford, two protestant ministers of religion, a bishop's wife and two wives of local J.P.s. In addition, three of his sons served as J.P.s in Hampshire and one as its sheriff. Apart from the children of John Kingsmill II, the other members of the Kingsmill-Gifford group contributed another twelve long-serving members of the magisterial bench by 1578. They also provided six sheriffs during the first twenty years of Elizabeth's reign, not counting the shrievalty of William Kingsmill in 1563/64. (39) This meant that during the years 1558-78 there was always a significant number of men from the Kingsmill-Gifford group on the bench of Hampshire. United by a common faith and family ties, they presented a formidable front to those who opposed them and were a convenient source of allies for whoever served as the protestant bishop of Winchester.

John Kingsmill II died on 11 August 1556 in the midst of the reign of the Catholic Mary Tudor. (40) Considering his protestant convictions, he must have departed this world with little hope for the future of the reformation in England. On 25 May 1554, Mary was wedded with Philip II, soon to be King of Spain, making the possibility of another protestant succession seem impossibly remote. Religious persecution was also starting against the English protestants. However, the Kingsmill-Gifford group clearly continued to be the focus of a vigorous and committed protestant community among the Hampshire gentry. Even before Elizabeth's reign, they attempted to resist and subvert the burning of a relative, Thomas Bembridge, as a heretic. This episode took place on 29 July 1558 and was the only Marian burning to take place in Hampshire and it could not have been called a success for the Queen and her followers. Bembridge was a bachelor and so without any direct heirs to his property. Prior to his execution, therefore, he executed an indenture on 26 April 1558 which left his land to Richard and Anne Gifford, Anne being called his 'kinswoman'. In default of their heirs, his property was to go to Constance Kingsmill of Sidmontan, Bembridge's 'cousin' and the widow of John Kingsmill the protestant J.P. (41) Thus the only heretic burned in Hampshire came from the respectable gentry and was not just a radical artisan sectary.

The events leading up to Bembridge's arrest by John White, the Bishop of Winchester, are not known. During his imprisonment and trial he made no attempt to conceal or deny his heretical opinions. In his examination before Bishop White, he denied the papal supremacy, admitted only the three major sacraments and denied the existence of both purgatory and transubstantiation. Bembridge also managed to bring out that he thought 'Martin Luther died a good Christian man, whose doctrine and life he did approve and allow', even though his examiners had not even

154

asked him about it. Inevitably he was condemned as a
heretic and handed over for execution to Sir Richard
Pexsall, then sheriff of Hampshire and son-in-law of
William Paulet, first Marquis of Winchester. Once the
fire was lit and started to burn him, Bembridge's
courage failed and he called out his recantation. In
response to his cry, some of his friends came forward
and removed him from the fire, which was illegal. As
a result Pexsall was forced to place them in prison.
Pexsall himself was not a very determined persecutor
and instead of continuing the interrupted execution,
simply sent Bembridge back to prison. This irresolute
action subsequently resulted in Pexsall's confine-
ment in the Fleet prison for a period of time by the
Privy Council. After one week in prison Bembridge had
reconsidered and took back his recantation.
Meanwhile orders had arrived from the Privy Council
commanding Pexsall to burn Bembridge according to
proper procedure, which did not recognise
recantations made after the lighting of the fire.
(42) So after considerable trouble Bembridge was
finally burned and received his reward in a mention
from John Foxe. His execution left a legacy of
bitterness in the county as acerbic mention was made
of it during the disputed parliamentary by-election
of 1566. (43)

By the early years of Elizabeth's reign, the
Kingsmill-Gifford group had come to constitute one of
the two leading political factions in Hampshire.
Because protestantism played such a dominant role in
the formation of this political grouping, it is not
surprising that Robert Horne, the new protestant
Bishop of Winchester became its close ally. The
Paulet family and their adherents formed the only
other important political faction in the county.
William Paulet, the first Marquis of Winchester and
many people in this faction were religious
conservatives. This made them either active or
passive resistors to the Elizabethan religious
settlement and any extension of it by convinced
protestants like Horne and the Kingsmill-Gifford
group. Since Bishop Horne's major task was the
implementation of protestant religion in Hampshire,
it was fortunate for him that the Kingsmill-Gifford
group was there to lend him their support. Without
them, his task would have been well-nigh impossible
in the face of the powerful Paulet's opposition in a
basically religiously conservative county. Therefore, it is not surprising that members of the
Kingsmill-Gifford group dominated the new Bishop's
listing in 1564 of those J.P.s who supported the

Elizabethan religious settlement. (44)

The episode that most clearly shows the protestant group's cooperation with Bishop Horne was the disputed parliamentary election of 1566. It pitted the Paulets' candidate Sir John Berkeley against Henry Wallop, a leading member of the protestant faction. Both the electoral rolls and subsequent legal actions in the Star Chamber clearly show members of the Kingsmill-Gifford group as the leaders of a drive to elect another staunch protestant as the new Knight of the Shire of Hampshire. These efforts received significant support from Horne. Although their combined efforts failed to elect Wallop due to the unfair electoral practices of the sheriff, Sir Richard Pexsall, a grandson of the Marquis of Winchester, the Kingsmill-Gifford group had formed a lasting political alliance. (45) They supported the bishop again in 1569 in a dispute with conservatives over local office-holding. (46) By 1570 they had gained sufficient strength to get their candidates elected knights of the shire for Hampshire while the local power of the Paulets went into a period of decline. (47) Thanks to the Kingsmill-Gifford group, Bishop Horne arrived in Hampshire to find a conservative county that contained a significant protestant presence. Without this group as allies, his task of establishing and securing the Elizabethan settlement would have been nowhere near as successful. The presence of a mere two or three families becoming protestants at a formative stage of the reformation made all the difference to its success in Hampshire.

* The quote in the title of this chapter is taken from Andrew Kingsmill's <u>A View of Mans Estate</u> (London, 1574), 'To the Reader' by Francis Mills, who was the editor of Kingsmill's writings and wrote a description of the author's character. I would like to thank Dr Frederic Youngs, Dr Roger Manning, Dr William Robinson, Dr Peter Lake for reading and commenting on this paper.

Notes

1. John Gough Nichols, (ed.) <u>Narratives of the Days of the Reformation</u> (Camden Society, Old Series, 72, 1860), pp.29-30 and 71-2.

2. <u>Kingsmill Manuscripts, National Repository of Archives Report, Calendar and Transcripts</u> (Winchester, 1963) (typescript), no. 1088. Hereafter referred to as <u>Kingsmill MS</u>.

3.   Thomas Stapleton (ed.), <u>Plumpton Corres-</u>
<u>pondence: A Series of Letters, Chiefly Domestick</u>
<u>written in the Reigns of Edward IV, Richard III,</u>
<u>Henry VII, and Henry VIII</u> (Camden Society, Old
Series, 4, 1839), pp.132-5.
4.   A.B. Emden, <u>A Biographical Register of the</u>
<u>University of Oxford to A.D. 1500</u>, 3 vols (Oxford,
1957-9), II, p.1074; J.H. Baker (ed.), <u>The Reports of</u>
<u>Sir John Spelman</u>, 2 vols (Selden Society, London
1977-8), II, pp. 371 and 387; and <u>Calendar of Patent</u>
<u>Rolls Preserved in the Public Record Office: Henry</u>
<u>VII</u>, 2 vols (London, 1914-16), vol. 2, pp.314-54.
5.   Baker, <u>Spelman</u>, II, p.371; <u>Herald's Visit.</u>
<u>Hants.</u>, pp.2-3; and <u>Kingsmill MS.</u>, no. 1301.
6.   <u>Lincoln's Inn Admissions</u>, vol. 1, p.38 and
<u>Lincoln's Inn Black Book</u>, vol. 1, p.201.
7.   <u>Kingsmill MS.</u>, no. 1099.
8.   PROB 11/20/5, will of John Goring; PROB
11/37/38, will of William Goring; and PROB 11/42A/21,
will of Elizabeth Goring. These wills contain strong
evidence of individual religious conviction in their
bequests and funeral arrangements.
9.   P.W. Hasler (ed.), <u>The History of</u>
<u>Parliament: The House of Commons 1558-1603</u>, 3 vols
(London, 1981), v. 'Goring, Sir William'. Hereafter
referred to as Hasler, <u>Hist. Parl.</u>
10.   <u>Letters and Papers Henry VIII</u>, IV, pt.3,
no.5838, and <u>Kingsmill MS.</u>, no. 1301.
11.   SP 1/133/42-43. All documents are from the
Public Record Office of Great Britain unless
otherwise specified in the citation.
12.   E 372/382/Villa Sutht. Res Sutht. and <u>List</u>
<u>of Sheriffs for England and Wales</u> (Public Record
Office list and Indexes Series IX, rpt. New York,
1963), p.56.
13.   Ronald Harold Fritze, 'Faith and Faction:
Religious Changes, National Politics and the
Development of Local Factionalism in Hampshire,
1485-1570' (Ph.D. thesis, University of Cambridge,
1982), pp.151-66.
14.   Ibid., pp. 176-90; Stanford E. Lehmberg,
<u>The Later Parliaments of Henry VIII, 1536-1547</u> (CUP,
Cambridge, 1977), pp.41-3 and G.R. Elton, 'Thomas
Cromwell's Decline and Fall', in <u>Studies in Tudor and</u>
<u>Stuart Politics and Government: Papers and Reviews</u>
<u>1946-1972</u>, 2 vols (CUP, Cambridge, 1974), vol. 1,
pp.202-4.
15.   SP 1/146/fo. 237-40.
16.   SP 1/150/138-9.
17.   Fritze, 'Faith and Faction', pp.190-201.
18.   <u>Herald's Visit. Hants.</u>, pp.2-3 and 16-17

and The Victoria History of the Counties of England: A History of Hampshire and the Isle of Wight, 5 vols (London, 1900-12), vol. 4, pp.516-18. The herald's visitation is incorrect in regard to Richard Gifford's parentage.

19. Patrick Collinson, 'The Role of Women in the English Reformation illustrated by the Life and Friendships of Anne Locke', in Studies in Church History, vol. 2, edited by G.J. Cuming (Blackwell, Oxford, 1965), pp.258-72; Claire Cross, '"Great reasoners in scripture": the Activities of Women Lollards, 1380-1530' in Derek Baker (ed.), Medieval Women: Studies in Church History (Blackwell, Oxford, 1978), pp.359-80; Natalie Zemon Davis, 'City Women and Religious Change', in Society and Culture in Early Modern France (Stanford, 1975), pp.65-95; and Richard L. Greaves, 'The Role of Women in Early English Noncomformity', Church History, vol. 52 (Sept. 1983), pp.299-311.

20. See above note 8; Andrew Kingsmill, A Most Excellent and Comfortable Treatise, for all such as are any manner of way either troubled in mind or afflicted in body (London, 1577), passim, and PROB 11/63/24, will of Constance Kingsmill, dated 1579. Throughout his text Andrew Kingsmill refers to the importance and actual practice of Christian devotion by his family. His mother Constance was a great giver of Geneva Bibles in her will. Also see Andrew Kingsmill's A Godly Advice touching Marriage at the end of his treatise A View of Man's Estate (London, 1574), sigs. Jii-(Miv) in which he advises a sister on how to choose a godly husband.

21. Herald's Visit. Hants., pp.2-3; List of Sheriffs, p.56; and E 372/405-46/Villa Sutht. Res Sutht.

22. Dictionary of National Biography, 22 vols, ed. Leslie Stephens and Sidney Lee (London, rpt. 1980-9), v 'Kingsmill, Andrew', Anthony A. Wood, Athenae Oxonienses 4 vols. (Oxford, 1813-20), vol. 1, pp.373-4 and 550; and C.M. Dent, Protestant Reformers in Elizabethan Oxford (OUP, Oxford, 1983), pp.22, 38-9 and 94.

23. Herald's Visit. Hants., pp.2-3; Hasler, Hist. Parl., v 'Kingsmill, Richard'; Hastings Robinson (ed.), Zurich Letters, 2 vols (Parker Society, Cambridge, 1842-5), vol. 1, pp.72- and note; British Library Lansdowne MS. 8/fo. 212, James Pilkington to William Cecil; and SP 12/1/43.

24. Hasler, Hist. Parl, v 'Kingsmill, Henry'. Also see Henry Kingsmill as a historian in Bodleian Library Rawlinson MS. D. 168 especially fo. 1-2. I

would like to thank Prof. M.A.R. Graves of the
University of Auckland for this reference.
    25. Halser, <u>Hist. Parl.</u>, v 'Kingsmill, John'.
However see Hampshire Record Office, Consistory
Court Book 34, for 10 March 1570/1 for a more
accurate dating of John Kingsmill III's earliest
appearance as Chancellor of the Diocese of
Winchester.
    26. Hasler, <u>Hist. Parl.</u>, v 'Kingsmill,
George'.
    27. Wood, <u>Athenae Oxon.</u>, vol. 1, p.758 and
Dent, <u>Protestant Reformers</u>, p.39 for an example of
Thomas Kingsmill's commitment to protestantism.
    28. Hasler, <u>Hist. Parl.</u>, v 'Norton, Richard';
Fritze, 'Faith and Faction', pp.428-30 and C
219/28/108.
    29. <u>Herald's Visit. Hants.</u>, pp.49-51; <u>CPR Eliz.</u>, vol. 3, no. 140; and Hatfield House MS.
278/fo. 40-41.
    30. <u>Wills and Inventories from the Registry at Durham</u>, edited by William Greenwell (Surtees
Society, 38, 1860) pp.8-11, the will of Bishop James
Pilkington and British Library Lansdowne MS. 8/fo.
212.
    31. <u>CPR Eliz.</u>, vol. 4, p.20 and Kingsmill, <u>A Most Excellent and Comfortable Treatise</u>, sigs.
Aiiir-Aiii4.
    32. Hasler, <u>Hist. Parl.</u> v 'Gifford, Henry' and
Mary Bateson (ed.), 'A Collection of Original Letters
from the Bishops to the Privy Council, 1564, with
returns of the Justices of the Peace and others
within their respective dioceses, classified
according to their Religious Convictions' in <u>Camden Miscellany</u>, IX (Camden Society, New Series, 53,
1895), p.54. Printed edition reads Henry Clifford
rather than Henry Gifford which is correct.
    33. Hasler, <u>Hist. Parl.</u>, v Gifford, John.
    34. Hampshire Record Office 5M53/935; Bateson,
'Bishops' Letters', pp.53-6; and Hasler, <u>Hist. Parl.</u>, v 'Wallop, Sir Henry' and 'Wallop, William'.
    35. <u>Herald's Visit. Hants.</u>, pp.11 and STAC
5/245/38. The election return (C219/28/108) for 14
April 1572 may also show James Haydok supporting the
Kingsmill-Gifford group's candidate in that election
but the surname in the entry is too obscured for
certainty.
    36. SP 1/146/fo. 236-40 and Bateson, 'Bishops'
Letters', pp.55.
    37. Ibid., pp.53-6; PROB 11/51/17; and Ronald
H. Fritze, 'The Role of Family and Religion in the
Local Politics of Early Elizabethan England: The Case

of Hampshire in the 1560s', <u>The Historical Journal</u>, vol. 25 (June 1982), p.275.

38. <u>Herald's Visit. Hants.</u>, p.30; PROB 11/51/17; and Hatfield House MS. 202/fo. 73-4 in which Bishop Robert Horne writes to William Cecil on 21 Jan. 1569 and suggests that Richard Ingpen be made a J.P. among other things.

39. The J.P.s were Richard Norton, John Thornborough, Richard Gifford, Henry Gifford, Henry Wallop, William Wallop, Thomas Dering, James Haydok, William Uvedale, Richard Ingpen, Oliver Wallop and William Jephson.

The sheriffs were Oliver Wallop, 1558-9; William Uvedale, 1560; Richard Norton, 1564-5; William Jephson, 1572-3; John Thornborough, 1577-8; and Henry Gifford, 1578-79.

40. C 142/110/142.

41. John Foxe, <u>Acts and Monuments</u>, 8 vols, edited by S.R. Cattley and George Townshend (London, 1837-41), vol. 8, pp.490-2 and C 142/115/47.

42. Foxe, <u>Acts and Monuments</u>, vol. 8, pp.490-2 and John Roche Dasent, <u>Acts of the Privy Council of England</u>, 32 vols (London, 1890-1907), vol. 6, pp.361 and 371-2.

43. STAC5/W36/33, interrogatories for the part of Henry Wallop, question no. 42 and STAC 5/P30/32, depositions of William Kingsmill, Richard Norton and John Fisher, answer no 16.

44. Bateson, 'Bishops' Letters', pp.53-6 and Fritze, 'Role of Family and Religion', pp.276-9.

45. Ibid., pp.279-85.

46. Hatfield House MS. 202/fo. 73-4.

47. C 219/28/108. For the collapse of Paulet power at the centre, particularly in the Exchequer, see C. Coleman, 'Artifice or accident? The reorganisation of the exchequer of receipt, c. 1554-72', in C. Coleman and D. Sarkey (eds), <u>Revolution Reassessed</u> (OUP, Oxford, 1986), especially pp.190-8. This shows again the interdependence of local and central politics. The establishment of protestantism amongst prominent minorities like the group centred on the Kingsmill and Gifford families ensured that when the Elizabethan regime looked to base itself on ideologically reliable provincial elites it found at least the kernel of such cadres already there. Thus when the attractions of local power and of agreeing with the government were added to the more spiritual appeal of the gospel things could change really quite fast. The shift within Hampshire seems to have been part of a general trend, dating from the early 1570s when, in the aftermath of the revolt of the northern

earls and the Ridolphi plot, the regime sought for
determinedly protestant provincial support. For this
see C. Cross, <u>The Puritan Earl</u> (Macmillan, London,
1966) and D. McCulloch, 'Catholic and puritan in
Elizabethan Suffolk; a county community polarises',
<u>Archiv für reformationsgeschichte,</u> vol. 72 (1981).

Chapter Seven

JOHN FOXE AND THE DEFENCE OF THE ENGLISH CHURCH

Jane Facey

Many of the themes which have been raised by the essays in this book come together in the person of John Foxe. Indeed, Foxe might be taken to have provided the first definitive account of the problematic relations between the true church of gathered believers and the English nation, with which this book has largely concerned itself. Setting himself to answer the basic question, posed by the papists, 'where was your church before Luther?', Foxe took up Bale's division between the true and false churches and used it to produce a systematic history of the struggle between Christ and Antichrist. With Jewel and other protestant apologists, Foxe was concerned to argue that it was the Church of Rome that had departed from 'primitive perfection' and that the English reformation, far from introducing novelty and schism into the church, represented a 'renewing of the old, ancient church of Christ'. (1) Foxe, however, did not limit his case to demonstrating the English Church's succession to the doctrinal purity of the apostles and early Fathers. He was concerned to argue that the cause of the church had always been kept alive by gathered groups of true believers, who, even at the height of Antichrist's power, had never succumbed completely to popery.

In his history therefore Foxe needed to show the gradual progress of change and corruption within the church and to identify the growing presence of Antichrist within the papacy. He also needed to identify a true church tradition of groups which had remained free from popish corruption and able to recognise the Antichristian claims of the papacy. Under popery, Foxe claimed, the true church existed like leaven in an otherwise corrupt mass of dough. When the parish churches had been given over to

popery, 'Christ's approved churches' were to be
sought among those whom Foxe called the 'secret
multitude of true professors'. (2) Foxe identified
the true church with these secret groups, who
maintained the true church in opposition to the false
church of Rome.

The grounds of his identification of the true
church were essentially doctrinal. The true church
was 'not bound to any certain place or person, but
only to faith, so that wheresoever the true faith
was, there was the church of Christ'. (3) The church
was founded on a 'form of doctrine':

> planted by the apostles, and taught by true
> bishops; afterward decayed and now reformed
> again. Although it was not received nor admitted
> of the pope's clergy before Luther's time,
> neither yet is; yet it was received of others,
> in whose hearts it pleased the Lord secretly to
> work; and that of a great number, who both
> professed and suffered for the same, as in the
> former times of this history may appear. (4)

Foxe's aim in the <u>Acts and Monuments</u> was, as he wrote
in 1563, to describe the fate of this church under
'the great persecution and horrible troubles that
have been wrought and practised by the Romish
prelates'. (5)

In discharging this task Foxe was not merely
engaging in an exercise of formal anti-papal polemic;
he was also reformulating a question which the
previous history of the English reformation had posed
for Elizabethan protestants in rather an urgent form
- how could a religion whose progress hitherto had
been based on cells of true believers, who had often
seen themselves as operating within and in opposition
to a corrupt, indifferent and sometimes hostile mass,
transmute itself into the official ideology of an
inclusive national church? In so doing he committed
himself to a number of propositions or assumptions
about the nature of the true Church and its
opposition to popery which raised problems for his
later defence of the Church of England as a national
church. It is with the nature of these assumptions
and the difficulties and constraints which they
produced that this essay is concerned.

The structure of Foxe's narrative was provided
by a periodisation taken from the prophetic books of
scripture and applied to the facts of church history
as Foxe discerned them. In his Latin play <u>Christus
Triumphans</u> Foxe personified the major forces which he

saw in conflict in the history of the church in a
number of characters. Satan was bound at Christ's
incarnation for a thousand years. (6) Once that
period had expired, Satan conquered the church by
cunning devices. Foxe introduced the characters
Pseudamnus (or Antichrist) and Dioctes, the
persecutor, at this point. Satan ordered Pseudamnus
to 'go to Babylon', where you will besiege the abode
of the pontiff' and gave him the advice that:

> when you have gotten through to the highest, be
> careful to conduct yourself discreetly as
> pontiff. You will appear as the unique vicar of
> Christ, and as such, you will be applauded. (7)

Antichrist then persecuted the true church of Christ,
Ecclesias, who was forced to go into hiding.
Eventually, however, the true preaching of the gospel
was revived and concurrently Antichrist was
revealed, Ecclesia came out of hiding to await the
coming of the bridegroom.

By the 1570 edition of the Acts and Monuments
the basic apocalyptic framework within which Foxe set
out the fruits of his historical researches was set.
The period between 'the primitive time' and the
'latter days' was divided into five sub-periods.
First, 'the suffering time of the church' for the
first three hundred years after Christ; secondly, the
'flourishing and growing time of the church' for the
next three hundred years; thirdly, 'the declining
time of the church and of true religion' for another
three hundred years. Fourth came the 'time of
Antichrist reigning and raging in the church since
the loosing of Satan'; and last was 'the reforming
time of Christ's church, in these latter three
hundred years'. (8)

The divisions established between these periods
were not hard and fast, however. Despite the binding
of Satan:

> the church and see of Rome was not altogether
> void and clear from all corruption during the
> whole time of the first thousand years after
> Christ our saviour, but eftsoon before the full
> thousand years was expired, certain enormities
> and absurdities began to creep into the heads of
> the clergy. (9)

Thus the rise of popery was a gradual process, and
Foxe did not feel able to pin-point an exact date at
which the Church of Rome had become corrupt and the

true church had gone definitely into hiding. However,
by the fourth period the separation had become
complete. This was 'the time of Antichrist, and
loosing of Satan, or desolation of the church' (10)
and roughly equated by Foxe with the period from
'Gregory VII, called Hildebrand, Innocent III ...
till the time of John Wyclif and John Huss', (11)
whom together Foxe held to have ushered in the last
reforming age of the church. However, just as the
rise of Antichrist had been a gradual process and
thus not susceptible to precise dating, so too was
the re-emergence of the true church. For when the
Church of Rome had ceased to be a true church, God
still had to have his church on earth. Thus, Foxe
concluded, during this period the true church:

> although it durst not openly appear in the face
> of the world, oppressed by tyranny; yet neither
> was it so invisible or unknown but by the
> providence of the Lord, some remnant always
> remained, from time to time, which not only
> showed secret good affection to sincere
> doctrine, but also stood in open defiance of
> truth against the disordered Church of Rome.
> (12)

Thus for Foxe there were 'divers and sundry groups'
who well before Wyclif's times had 'wrestled and
laboured in the same cause and quarrel'. (13)
     We need to examine and analyse Foxe's treatment
of some of these groups and individuals in order to
gain some sense of the characteristics which Foxe saw
as qualifying people for inclusion within the true
church. The point here is not to examine or evaluate
Foxe's skills as an historian; the veracity or
otherwise of his account of these groups is
immaterial for the present purpose. Rather we are
concerned, through an analysis of the way in which
Foxe presented his material in the Acts and
Monuments, to establish how his basic polemical aim -
to establish a long-standing lineage for the
protestant Church of England - conditioned his
attitude to the nature of true religion and the
'church'.
     The Waldenses can be taken as an example. The
date of their foundation, 1260, corresponded, Foxe
claimed, with the 1260 days mentioned in Revelation
12 as the length of time the woman (a figure for the
true church) was in hiding in the desert. He also
associated it with the prophecy of Joachim of Fiore,
that Antichrist would be born in 1260. One thousand,

two hundred and sixty days was also mentioned in
Revelation 11, referring to the witnesses of the
truth who would counteract Antichrist's presence:
'and I will give power to my two witnesses, and they
will prophesy for 1,260 days clothed in sackcloth'.
(14) Founded by Peter Waldus of Lyons, who began by
giving out 'certain rudiments of the scriptures'
which he had translated into French, the Waldenses
turned away from popish superstition to the true
repentance 'and the sincere worship of God and true
piety'. (15) The bishops of Rome, Foxe observed,
'could neither abide that the scriptures should be
translated and declared by any other'; and the more
diligent Waldus was 'in setting forth the true
doctrine of Christ against the errors of Antichrist,
the more maliciously their fierceness' raged against
him. (15) The Waldenses were persecuted and forced to
flee from Lyons, scattering all over France and
especially to Provence and Piedmont, where Waldenses
continued to be found until the sixteenth century.
(16)

Foxe was able to claim a number of close
parallels between the beliefs of the Waldenses and
those of later protestants. They held, for instance,
that 'only the holy scriptures is to be believed in
matters pertaining to salvation' and that nothing was
to be admitted in religion 'but only what is
commanded in the word of God'. (17) They insisted on
two sacraments only; they repudiated the invocation
of saints, purgatory, masses for the dead;

> fasts, superfluous holy days, ... orders of
> priests, monks and nuns, vows, benedictions,
> pilgrimages and all the rabblement of rites and
> ceremonies brought in by man.

They rejected the Pope's pardons and indulgences,
they held the marriage of priests to be godly, and
above all saw the Church of Rome as the 'very Babylon
spoken of in the Apocalypse'. (18) These articles of
belief imputed to the Waldenses by Foxe matched very
closely with a list of twenty 'principles and
infallible truths' of scripture which Foxe listed
elsewhere in the <u>Acts and Monuments</u> as the
'touchstone' by which all 'other doctrines and
opinions of men' may be tried and examined so that
they may 'the more easily be judged whether they be
true or the contrary, and whether they make against
the scripture or not'. (19)

Starting at the point when the reign of
Antichrist began in earnest, and stretching to the

very reformation itself, for Foxe the Waldenses
represented the 'first beginning of the restoring and
maintaining of the true doctrine of Christ's gospel,
against the proud proceedings of popish errors'. (20)
As such they provided a paradigm for Foxe's view of
the true church. For Foxe, popery had come to enjoy
'but the name only of Christ, and the outward form of
his religion'. Popish religion was a religion of
externals, full of 'fond traditions and vain
ceremonies'. (21) The true church was kept alive by
small groups who used the Bible to produce a critique
both of the tyrannical claims of the Pope and the
false outward forms of popish religion, in favour of
a properly inward profession of Christianity. Popery
tended to be seen in this context as a clericalist
conspiracy, whose natural response to any attempt to
make the word of scripture available to the people
was persecution.

Thus, Wyclif, who was presented by Foxe as
ushering in the last reforming age of the church's
history, when the struggle between Christ and
Antichrist would be particularly sharp, (22) had,
Foxe claimed, initially argued the case for
scriptural equality and religious poverty against
the entrenched wealth and privilege of the
ecclesiastical hierarchy, the monastic orders and
the papacy. From there he had progressed to urging
the authority of the scripture and the vocation of
preaching against the authority claimed by the
priesthood in the administration of the sacraments,
and ended by challenging the doctrine of
transubstantiation itself. Like his predecessors in
the true church, Wyclif believed that Peter had
enjoyed no power over the rest of the apostles and
that 'the Church of Rome is not the head of all
churches'; that scripture was 'a rule sufficient of
itself to rule the life of every Christian man' and
that all other external rules of man's invention 'do
add no more perfection to the gospel'. (23) There was
therefore a basic opposition being established here
between the human authority of the church and the
authority of scripture, between clerical wealth and
power and an active, scripturally based lay piety.

Wherever Foxe found criticism of either the
claims of the Pope or of popish religious practice on
the one hand, and persecution by the Church of Rome
on the other, there he claimed to discern the true
church. Of course his touchstone of true belief was
essentially doctrinal, and he did his best to square
the positions adopted by the underground groups he
enlisted as members of the true church with later

protestantism; but such a position left ample room to explain away or ignore apparent doctrinal inconsistency or backsliding. Thus Foxe was forced to concede that Huss and the Bohemians had not rejected the central error of transubstantiation. Huss neither 'spoke against the seven sacraments and almost in all their papist opinions was a papist with them'. But his denunciation 'of the doings of the Pope to be Antichrist like', his putting of the scriptures before the traditions of men, his Christ-centred life and Christ-like death at the hands of the popish persecutors were all enough to claim him as a member of the true church (24).

Indeed, many of the different individuals and groups whom Foxe claimed in the <u>Acts and Monuments</u> as members of the true church had little or nothing in common except opposition to some aspect of popery. For instance, Richard Armachanus, the Primate of Ireland, was one of many who opposed the friars. Since, Foxe claimed, in the 'idle and beggarly sect of friars' the reader 'may well perceive Antichrist plainly reigning and fighting against the church', (25) anyone who attacked them must be taken to have been on the side of the true church. In a remarkable interview with the Pope, Armachanus, according to Foxe, maintained 'the true doctrine and cause of the church, against the pestiferous canker creeping in by these friars'. (26) Alongside these learned protagonists of the church's cause Foxe listed many ordinary people who had opposed popery. Joan John, for instance, although she 'attributed too much honour to the true saints of God's departed ... for lack of better instruction or knowledge' still 'did abhor the idolatrous worshipping of dead images' and knew that God disliked holy days and fast days. (27) Then there were the people of Merindol who went to the church but:

> prayed with their backs turned to the images, offering no candles to them and doing no reverence to crucifixes. They never caused priests to say any masses or dirges; nor took any holy water; they thought pilgrimages, vows to saints and the buying of pardons as unlawful. (28)

Thus Foxe felt able to conclude that:

> amongst and besides the great number of the faithful martyrs ... I find recorded ... the names of divers other persons, both men and

women, who in the fullness of that dark and
misty time of ignorance, had also some portion
of God's good spirit, which induced them to the
knowledge of his truth and gospel, and were
diversely troubled, persecuted and imprisoned
for the same. (29)

In fact Foxe tended to include any anti-papal
group or individual who was persecuted by Rome, as he
almost admitted in the following quotation:

and if they think this doctrine be so new that
it was not heard of before Luther's time, how
then came such a persecution before Luther's
time, here in England? If these were of the same
profession which they were of, then was their
cruelty so unreasonable, to persecute their own
catholic fraternity? And if they were
otherwise, how then is this doctrine of the
gospel so new, or how are the professors therein
so late started up, as they pretend them to be?
(30)

This approach to the history of the true church
reached its logical conclusion in Foxe's treatment of
the Albigensians. All the records concerning this
group, Foxe admitted, presented them as 'worse than
the Turks and infidels'. (31) But by using a simple
formula which equated those whom Rome persecuted with
the membership of the true church, Foxe was able to
conclude that the opinions of the Albigensians must
have been 'sound enough'. They can be presumed to
have been professing:

nothing else, but against the wanton wealth,
pride and tyranny of the prelates, denying the
Pope's authority to have ground of the
scriptures: neither could they away with their
ceremonies and traditions, as images, pardons,
purgatory, of the Romish Church, calling them,
as some say, blasphemous occupyings. (32)

Since Foxe put these words into the Albigensians'
mouths, they can safely be accepted as a sure
indication of what Foxe was looking for in members of
the true church before Luther.

Foxe was able to take such liberties and ignore
such lacunae in his evidence because of the basic
conceptual foundations upon which his case rested.
For Foxe's essentially eschatological view of
history allowed him to see virtually all groups and

169

individuals who had been persecuted by Rome as
members of a true church, whose existence could be
assumed on scriptural rather than historical ground.
It was axiomatic for Foxe that such a church must
exist and that its members 'could never be utterly
destroyed, nor yet compelled to yield to the
superstitions and false religion of the church of
Rome'. (33)

The privileged insight which Foxe's knowledge
of scripture gave him into the historical process
thus allowed him to see all such groups progressing
to the final consummation of the true church in a
full protestant reformation of the visible church.
This in turn enabled him to iron out or explain away
the discrepancies and inconsistencies which clearly
existed within his version of the true Christian
tradition. For the inevitability of the triumph of
the true over the false church produced a progressive
view of the revelation of doctrinal truth as the
forces of Christ gradually triumphed over those of
Antichrist. This allowed Foxe to explain the lapses
of many of his 'true believers' in terms of the
popish corruptions and superstitions with which they
were still surrounded. Thus many of the members of
the true church were pictured by Foxe as possessing
only a portion of the truth. What with the 'proud,
cruel and bloody rage of the catholic seat' and 'the
weakness and frailty of their own nature (not then
fully strengthened by God)', (34) it was not
surprising that they recanted and erred on many
occasions. The testimony of even those opponents of
Rome who recanted or had been themselves subject to
errors was still valuable to Foxe since it
demonstrated:

> the continuance and consent of the true Church
> ... touching the chief points of our faith
> (though not in like perfection of knowledge and
> constancy in all). (35)

And yet for Foxe the doctrine of justification
by faith, which represented 'the divine knowledge of
salvation' and the church's 'chief consolation', had
only been restored to the church by Luther. (36)
Before Luther, he admitted:

> of our justification by faith, of grace, and of
> the promises of God in Christ, of the strength
> of the law, of the horror of sin, of the
> difference between law and the gospel, of the
> true liberty of conscience, no mention was made

170

> or very little was heard. Wherefore, in this so
> blind a time of darkness it was much needful and
> requisite, that the Lord of his mercy should
> look upon his church, and send down his gracious
> reformation ... through the glorious exhort-
> ation of God, came Martin Luther. (37)

How could earlier groups be enlisted to a true church
defined largely in terms of succession to right
doctrine if the central doctrine necessary to
overthrow popery had hardly been known? Here Foxe's
basic dichotomy between a view of popery as concerned
almost entirely with external observance and
ceremonies of human devising and a scripturally based
and therefore spiritual and properly inward true
religion came to his rescue. For such an opposition
between inward and outward, spiritual and carnal
religious forms, anticipated that opposition between
the law and the gospel, which was grounded on the
crucial insight of justification by faith and was
central to Foxe's whole vision of the protestant
message. Thus justification by faith might represent
Luther's crucial contribution to the true church, but
the opposition maintained by earlier groups between
their own inward and scripturally based spirituality
and the empty formalism of popery ensured that there
was a Luther-shaped hole at the heart of the true
church tradition even before the great German prophet
began his evangelical mission. It was that which
explained the alacrity with which, Foxe claimed,
groups like the Waldenses and the Lollards embraced
the 'new' protestant preaching. Here Foxe quoted
Sleidan's claim that although the Waldenses had ever
'used a manner of doctrine more pure than the rest',
yet they had 'increased in more knowledge and
perfection of judgement' with the coming of Luther.
(38) In short, Foxe felt able to hail the reformation
as the culmination and vindication of all the efforts
and sufferings of those earlier groups and
individuals who had struggled with popery to keep the
religion alive:

> If John Huss, or good Jerome of Prague, or John
> Wyclif before them both, or William Brute,
> Thorpe, Sunderby or the Lord Cobham; if Zisca
> with all the company of the Bohemians; if the
> earl Reimund with all the Toulousians; if the
> Waldois, or the Albigensians, with infinite
> others, had either been in this our time now, or
> else had seen then this ruin of the pope, and
> revealing of antichrist, which the Lord now hath

171

dispensed unto us, what joy, and triumph would they have made! (39)

Foxe saw the reformation as the spiritual victory of the true church over the 'false-coloured religion of the Romish see, wherein many a true man hath been drowned'. (40) Antichrist had now been revealed and the scriptures were now freely available. In his preface to the 1570 edition of the Acts and Monuments Foxe expressed his confidence that Queen Elizabeth would:

> furnish all quarters and countries of this your realm with the voice of Christ's gospel and faithful preaching of his word. (41)

The true church had come out of hiding, and, as knowledge of the gospel increased, so would the church's membership. In England at least, the church was no longer a gathered group of true believers, cowering under the cross of persecution; it was a national institution. Much though that transition was to be welcomed, it nevertheless raised difficulties for Foxe. For amongst the members of the church thus defined were numbered the godly as well as the not-so-godly, those still 'in shadow', who needed further instruction and spiritual counsel if their formal membership of the church was to become a full participation in the spiritual body of Christ. (42) The contrast with the underground groups of true believers who had hitherto comprised Foxe's vision of the true church was marked. The people of Merindol and Cabriers in Provence were typical of the underground communities to which Foxe habitually referred. According to Foxe, they lived 'so godly, so uprightly and so justly' that the:

> little light of true knowledge which God had given them, they laboured by all means to kindle and increase daily, more and more. (43)

In taking such groups as his paradigm for the true church, Foxe was admitting that the Elizabethan Church was bound to seek to induce a similar zeal and spiritual warmth in its own members. But, as Foxe conceded, 'the fervent zeal of those Christian days seemed much superior to these our days and times'. (44) For:

> To see their travail, their earnest seekings, their burning zeal, their readings, their

watchings, their sweet assemblies, their love
and concord, their godly living, their faithful
demeaning with the faithful may make us now, in
these days of free profession, to blush for
shame. (45)

Foxe here returned to a problem which had
afflicted both the Edwardian and the Marian
protestants. Once the English church had ceased to be
a small fused group of true believers and had become
a synonym for the population at prayer, how could
English protestants handle the fact that the majority
of the members of that church were not even formally
or properly protestant let alone personally godly?
Under Edward even the irenic Foxe had become moved to
advocate the use of excommunication to dragoon the
English at least into an outward godliness. (46) As
Catharine Davies has argued, even under Edward VI the
sins of the nation had seemed to cry out for divine
retribution, and, as Joy Shakespeare has pointed out,
the Marian exiles had rapidly adopted that view in
order to explain their own predicament. Things
however, looked very different after 1559. Viewing
the sufferings of the godly under Mary from the
perspective of the providential return of the gospel
at the hands of Queen Elizabeth, Foxe was able to
present the sufferings of the martyrs as having
vindicated the English church as a true church in the
eyes of God and man. Persecuted by Antichrist yet
constant in faith, the English martyrs were obviously
members of the true church. In the Old Testament
sense of blood confirming the covenant of the Lord
with his people, (47) their blood provided the final
seal on the English church's claims to be a true
church. As Foxe wrote in the dedication of the 1563
edition of the <u>Acts and Monuments</u>, 'the argument of
both churches are here set out, fortified by the
strongest and most forcible testimony of blood'. (48)
The true church might be defended by learned and
godly writings, but its standing was confirmed by the
blood of the martyrs. In Revelation 19 the heavenly
rider on the white horse who is called 'faithful' and
'true' and 'the word of God' is clothed in 'a robe
dipped in blood', the blood of the saints 'who bore
testimony to Jesus'. (49) The Church of England, Foxe
concluded, does:

receive so great and manifold benefits by these
martyrs, with whose blood it is watered, by
whose ashes it is enlarged, by whose constancy
it is confirmed, by whose testimony it is

> witnessed and finally through whose agonies and
> victories the truth of the gospel doth
> gloriously triumph. (50)

For Foxe the example of the martyrs should help the
English church to grow in strength and numbers.
There could be no better way to vindicate the English
reformation and inspire the godly than the 'godly end
of the gospellers, full of hope, and constant in
faith'. (51) The martyrs, he had no doubt, were
'registered in the book of life' and although their
salvation 'need not the commemoration of our stories,
yet for the more confirmation of the church, I
thought it not unprofitable'. (52)

At one level this might appear to have been, and
indeed was, a triumphant resolution of the tension
between the godly minority and the profane mass that
bedevilled English protestant thought up until that
point. And yet many of the difficulties had not been
resolved so much as suppressed, or transferred on to
another level of analysis. Foxe's analysis of the
conflict between the true and false churches had
involved a direct opposition between the inward and
outward forms of religion, between the inner truths
of scriptural doctrine and the empty forms of human
tradition and authority. That worked well enough when
the true church was identified with small groups of
true believers and the false church with the
institutional structures and jurisdictional claims
of the Church of Rome. Now, however, the English
church was a national institution with claims and
structures of its own, so how were these to be
squared with the internal dynamic of true religion
which had dominated Foxe's account of the true church
thus far?

Obviously enough, none of the groups cited by
Foxe had enjoyed the services of public ministers,
let alone the government of bishops and the Christian
prince, yet unsurprisingly these figures stood at the
centre of Foxe's defence of the English church. Thus
Foxe was later to write of the minister, that 'I know
that there is nothing in human affairs more excellent
than the sacred function' of those 'who are truly
trained to rule their portion and province of the
flock of the Lord'. (53) The duties to be performed
by the minister Foxe summarised as follows:

> to preach the word, to minister the sacrament,
> to pray, to bind and loose, where cause urgently
> requireth, to judge in spiritual causes, to
> publish and denounce free reconciliation and

remission in the name of Christ, to erect and
comfort troubled consciences with the rich
grace of the gospel, to teach the people the
true difference betwixt the law and the gospel
... to admonish also the magistrates erring or
transgressing in their office. (54)

These of course were functions central to the well-
being of the church, and yet nearly all the groups
which comprised Foxe's true church tradition had been
forced to exist without them. Moreover, such powers
conferred great status and authority on the clergy,
but Foxe's true churches had been comprised almost
exclusively of the laity, and clerical power had
almost become synonymous with popery in Foxe's
history.

In <u>Christus Triumphans</u> Foxe had Pornopolis (the
whore of Babylon) and Pseudamnus (Antichrist)
lamenting that the laity were both reading the
scriptures and seeing through the corruptions of
popery:

We are already a common story on everybody's
lips. They are all diligently reading
scriptures - stonecutters, smiths, potters,
everybody. And what I think is bad, the dregs of
the people are starting to be wise now. What is
more, they even weigh our traditions on the
scales of the scriptures. (55)

In Foxe's history it was usually the laity rather
than the clergy who perceived the truths revealed in
scripture and repudiated popery. If popery was, in
part at least, a clericalist conspiracy against the
laity, it was natural for the leaders of the clergy,
the bishops, to seek to uphold and extend traditions
and claims which maintained and enhanced their own
power and authority. Here Foxe cited the struggles
between 'King William and Lanfranc, King Henry I and
Anselm, King Stephen and Theobald, King Henry II and
Becket, King John and Stephen Langton, Henry III and
Boniface'. (56) Foxe asked his readers to consider
the mischief done by such churchmen who 'commonly
being set up by the Pope, especially since the time
of the conquest, have put the kings of this land to
much sorrow and trouble'. Foxe lamented the:

vain superstition or vile slavery of the
churchmen of those days, who, (being not content
with their own natural prince and king, given
them of God) must seek further to the Pope. (57)

Such crude self-interest led, he claimed, to 'a lamentable decay of true Christianity amongst the Christian bishops' who were so 'enflamed with glorious ambition' and so anxious to contend 'for honour' that they put their own position as bishops before their faith and remained deaf to the arguments of scripture. (58) Obviously there had to be some good bishops. Grosseteste for one was thought by Foxe to be 'a godly and learned bishop' (59) and a member of the true church. In Lanfranc's time also Foxe mentioned 'divers good bishops' who took the side of the married clergy against the popish monks, but 'this godly enterprise was stopped by stout Lanfranc ... that lusty prelate'. (60) On the whole, therefore, the history of the corruption of the Church of Rome included the English parishes with their clergy. The Antichristian nature of the papacy was reflected in the bishops and archbishops who made up the popish hierarchy throughout the church. Under popery the clergy were usually the agents of Antichrist.

Over against the clergy, Foxe singled out ordinary professors drawn from the ranks of the laity and often from the lower orders as 'the standard bearers of Christ's army'. For, as Foxe observed, 'God chooseth the weak things of the world to confound mighty things ... God is no respecter in degree of persons'. God has called 'all sorts of men to confirm his truth and to bear witness unto his assured and infallible word'. (61) The godly martyrs of the Acts and Monuments had been able to maintain the truth without the help of any clergy and without the supervision of any bishops. Indeed, only by virtue of being a populist underground movement had such groups managed to defy the popish authorities in church and state and to maintain themselves as the true church. In the process of thus resisting the popish repression of the papist clergy many of these groups had delivered themselves of several anti-clerical dicta which Foxe quoted with approval. Thus the 'learned answers' of William Thorpe, which were cited by Foxe in full, contained the assertion that:

> if a good priest fails, as they do now often, in
> such a case, St. Augustine saith that a man may
> lawfully commune and take counsel of a virtuous
> and secular man. (62)

The Lollards held, according to Foxe, that 'every goodman, although he be unlearned, is a priest'. (63) And yet even without priests and the approval

176

and encouragement of public authority, Foxe claimed that:

> the secret multitude of true professors was not much unequal; certes and fervent zeal of those days and times seemed much superior to these our days and times; as manifestly may appear by their sitting up all night reading and hearing. (64)

For 'in secret knowledge and understanding they seemed then little or nothing inferior to these our times of public reformation'. (65) If so much could be achieved by the laity, unaided by the clergy, and if all forms of clerical power, particularly the powers of the prelates, had been integrally linked to the rise and maintenance of popery, what sort of consequences or implications for the organisation of the Elizabethan Church might Foxe's argument hold?

In part, Foxe was able to defuse the potential radicalism of his position by stressing the different circumstances in which the church had to operate. Foxe distinguished hard between the church under the cross of persecution and in times of relative prosperity. Thus he denounced Stephen's second epistle (66) as spurious since it purported to deal with questions of ecclesiastical order and hierarchy during a time of persecution when such questions were entirely inappropriate to the church's situation. Under the cross of persecution the church could not concern itself with such matters. In that situation, if the word of truth did multiply the numbers of the godly notwithstanding 'the rarity of books and the want of teachers' this was due to the 'marvellous workings of God's almighty power'. (67) Thus, since the spiritual achievements of the true church under popery were a direct result of the autonomous action of the Holy Spirit during a time of persecution, they could provide no very direct precedent for the conduct of Elizabethan protestants living under a godly prince. Moreover, even the underground groups at the centre of Foxe's account had tried to establish or retain a public ministry of the word amongst them. According to Foxe, the Waldenses had ministers who taught them using Bibles translated into their own language. (68) Similarly, during 'the days of darkness' the people of Angrogne had had 'certain to preach the word and minister the sacraments to them privately'. (69) When in Luther's time it pleased God 'to set forth the light of his gospel more clearly' the Waldenses, Foxe claimed, 'never spared anything to establish the true and pure ministry of the word of God and his sacraments'. (70) However, even in a settled church in full possession of the gospel, Foxe held the minister's authority was a direct function of his ministry being 'exercised in righteousness' and with 'the gift of teaching'. (71) Given the role of clerical self-aggrandisement in the rise of popery, Foxe could hardly give the clergy unlimited spiritual power over the laity. Such power was not bound 'to any ordinary place or to any succession of chair, nor to worthiness of blood' but conferred by God's free mercy and grace. (72) For:

> the administration of the spiritual kingdom comes by heavenly virtue and grace of divine election; the succession is made not by the office but by the life, the doctrine and the corresponding conduct. (73)

For Foxe, therefore, the clergy were the ordinary and optimum holders of spiritual power in the church, but only if their doctrine was sound and their lives righteous. Should they lapse, God would raise up laymen in their stead, as he had in the true church under popery. Foxe did not specify how the laity could or should judge the righteousness or orthodoxy of the clergy and certainly suggested no institutional means whereby the perceptions and judgements of the ordinary laity could be brought to bear on or allowed to limit the powers of the clergy. Given the absence of such mechanisms in the Elizabethan church, such silence is understandable, but, added to Foxe's warning about the dangers of too great an accretion of power in the hands of the clergy, it ensured both that this position was ambiguous and that it retained the potential for the generation of a powerful critique of the Elizabethan ecclesiastical status quo.

The same ambiguity surrounds Foxe's treatment of the ecclesiastical hierarchy. At times he was prepared to ground such a hierarchy on scripture. 'By the scripture he appointed or by the primitive Church allowed, a hierarchy of archbishops, bishops, minister and deacons,' he claimed:

> ... in which four degrees as we grant diversity of office, so we admit in the same also diversity of dignity, neither denying that which is due to each degree, neither yet maintaining the ambition of any singular person. For, as we give to the minister place

above the deacon, to the bishop above the
minister, to the archbishop above the bishop, so
we see no cause of inequality why one minister
should be above another minister, one bishop in
his degree above another bishop to deal in his
diocese, or one archbishop above another
archbishop; and this is to keep an order duly
and truly in the church. (74)

As we have seen, Foxe held that such a concern for
external order was only appropriate 'when the church
began to be settled in more prosperity and order';
only then was it necessary for 'every man to know his
degree and the limits of his authority'. (75) Such
considerations were not necessary for the being of
the true church, but only for its well-being in times
of prosperity. External order and hierarchy might be
conducive to the process of edification which built
the temple made of lively stones which was the true
church, (76) but it could and should not be confused
with it. Nor, however, should it be confused with the
opposite; illegitimate clerical power led to popery,
but that did not mean that all clerical power or
external hierarchy in the church was illegitimate.

Apart from the purity of their doctrine, the
other crucial determinant of the clergy's legitimacy
was the maintenance of right relations with the power
of the prince. Along with nearly all other English
protestants Foxe gave the Christian prince or
magistrate a very exalted role in the life of the
church. He was to:

see the law of God maintained, to promote
Christ's glory and gospel, in setting up and
sending out good preachers, in maintaining the
same, in providing bishops to be elected that be
faithful, in removing or else correcting the
same being faulty or negligent, in congregating
the clergy when need is of any counsel or
election, or hear their learning in causes
propounded, and according to the truth learned,
to direct his judgement, in disposing such rites
and ordinances for the church as make to
edification, not to the destruction thereof; in
conserving the discipline of the church and
setting all things in congruous order. (77)

Of course, the attempted usurpation of these just and
necessary powers by the clergy was a central strand
in Foxe's vision of popery and his narrative of its
rise to power in the church. Yet his own historical

179

researches showed that princes had proved relatively
easy prey for the ambitions of the papacy; too easy
certainly to provide a crucial or essential element
in the being of a true church. In the <u>Acts and
Monuments</u> Foxe did his best to portray relations
between the kings of England and the papacy as a
struggle. He delineated an early period characterised by a just supremacy enjoyed by the prince over the
church. This represented things as they ought to be
and provided an English precedent for the situation
under Elizabeth. There followed a period of
progressive deterioration in the monarchs' power
over the church, as the papacy ate more and more into
the jurisdiction of the crown. Only with the Tudors
was the full authority of the crown restored to its
pristine state.

One notable example of early English Christian
kingship cited by Foxe was the reign of King Alfred,
who was 'worthy of high renown and commendation'. He
divided his goods, 'into two equal parts; the one
appertaining to uses secular, the other to uses
spiritual and ecclesiastical'. (78) A patron of
learning and religion, Alfred brought to England the
'godly divine and learned philosopher' John Scot,
despite his being out of favour at Rome. Alfred was
successful in war against the Danes and zealous for
the 'common peace and tranquillity of the weal
public'. A lover of good letters, he translated many
books into English himself, including the psalter
from Latin for the use of his own people. Alfred
then, provided Foxe with an English model of
Christian kingship, whose example he dwelt on:

> to move other rulers and princes in these our
> days to his imitation, or else to show them what
> hath been in times past in their ancestors,
> which ought to be, and yet is not found in them.
> (79)

However, by the reign of Edward the balance was
beginning to turn in favour of popery. It was
monasticism which first gained a foothold for
Antichrist on English soil. Foxe lamented the
misguided zeal of this king for the:

> blind ignorance and superstition ... in
> esteeming Christ's religion chiefly to consist
> in giving to churches and in maintaining of
> monkery, falsely being persuaded that remission
> of sins and remedy of their souls therein did be
> in building monasteries, erecting churches and

cloisters, and in placing monks in the same ...
wherein appeareth how ignorant that time was of
the true doctrine of Christ's faith, and of the
free grace of the gospel. (80)

With the coming of the Normans, the balance finally
tilted in the papacy's favour. Henry II struggled
against Antichrist in the person of Becket, 'a plain
rebel against his prince', and much of Richard's
reign was taken up with dissensions caused by
Archbishop Baldwin and his monks. (81) All this
showed, Foxe argued, 'how little kings could then do
in their own realms, for the Pope'. (82) Of course
the peak of papal interference in England was reached
during John's reign, when the pope unnaturally
released his subjects from their oath of obedience.
(83) Foxe's narrative of the succeeding reigns
consisted of repeated declarations of 'the Pope's
unreasonable gatherings, exactions and oppressions'.
(84) Gradually, therefore, the English kings had come
to be completely under the religious, political and
economic sway of the papacy. At one level while Foxe
was concentrating on the Antichristian nature of
popery and the complete incompatibility of the claims
of the Pope with true Christian kingship, he was able
to score a number of solid polemical points. Once
however attention was focussed on the Christian
prince as a major bulwark against popery, the rather
inadequate record of English monarchs in resisting
the claims of the papacy became a source of potential
embarrassment.

Foxe's portrayal of the restoration of princely
rights by the Tudors redressed the balance a little.
It was after all Henry VIII who freed the English
crown from 'the usurped dominion' of the papacy,
something which no previous monarch had dared even to
attempt. (85) While on the one hand this restoration
of the powers of the Christian prince in England was
seen by Foxe as a turning point in the history of the
English Church Foxe was forced to admit that the
struggle between the true and false churches
continued, through the rivalry between Gardiner and
Cromwell and various 'variable changes and mutations
of religion'. (86) After the fall of Cromwell, Foxe
argued, 'the state of religion more and more decayed
during the residue of King Henry's reign'. (87) For
all his efforts to present relations between the
English crown and the papacy as a struggle, Foxe was
ultimately unable to equate that struggle with the
conflict between the true and false churches. What
had kept the true church alive under popery had been

the spiritual self-help of quite humble men and women. For a great deal of the <u>Acts and Monuments'</u> arguments grounded on a populist vision of true religion and the community of the godly were being used to justify the claim of English monarchs to rule the church.

Unsurprisingly, the tension inherent in any view of Christian kingship developed in such a context shows in Foxe's account of Mary's reign. In condemning her 'unlucky and rueful reign', Foxe was at pains to point out that he was not dismissing Mary's God-given powers as a prince or ruler. He intended, he claimed, no 'detraction to her place and state royal, whereunto she was called unto the Lord'. However, in giving up her sovereignty to the Pope Mary had, in Foxe's estimation, gone over to the side of Antichrist and 'the Lord did work against her therefore'. (88) Such political quietism was easy enough in retrospect, but confronted by the sufferings and struggles of the French protestants, Foxe found insouciance difficult to sustain. He dealt with events in France in a Paul's Cross sermon, which he later had to justify to the privy council following complaints by the French ambassador. Foxe contended that the protestants in arms in France were in fact fighting against the pope's tyrannical hold over the king and were hence playing the part of loyal subjects:

> They be not rebels against his person, crown and dignity but rather like good subjects ... (they wanted) to take his part and to defend his honour and royal estate, to have a full and perfect King over them, whom the Pope would not make a subject. (89)

Foxe was here using his own very exalted view of Christian kingship to extend the usual protestant injunction to obey God rather than man so as to include not merely passive disobedience in religious matters, but, through an extension of the notion of the king's two bodies, also to justify political opposition to the policies of a papist king, in the name of the inherently anti-papal institution of Christian kingship.

For Foxe true order was a matter of non-popery. Any authority, clerical or lay, which lapsed into popery became in some sense illegitimate. Under popery the laity were allowed the spiritual self defence of scriptural study and the maintenance in secret of true belief, whatever the popish clergy might tell them or do to them. In his apology for the French protestants Foxe came perilously close to asserting a parallel right to political self defence. All this ensured that Foxe's defence of the Elizabethan church could not but be ambiguous. On the one hand he held the powers of the magistrate and the minister, the prince and the bishop, to be essential to the well being of the church; yet on the other, it had been those very external authorities which had, in the past, shown themselves to be likely, in the case of the clergy, to introduce and establish, and, in the case of the prince, to succumb to and maintain, popery. The real internal history of the true church had taken place without the services of either prince or bishop - it had been a result of an interaction between the word, the autonomous action of the Holy Spirit and the spiritual self-help of the godly.

It was one of the ironies of Foxe's position that the resultant gathered groups of the true believers could be identified with the true church with certainty only when the church itself was in hiding under the cross of persecution. For then the sufferings and martyrdom of the godly provided irrefutable evidence of the purity of their profession. This situation was reversed when the church basked in the favour of the Christian Prince. For then the membership of the church expanded to include ungodly, hypocritical and crypto-popish professors. Thus when the church was at the zenith of its visibility and outward power, the presence of the saving remnant of genuinely true believers within it became all but invisible. Foxe's close proximity to the events of the mid-Tudor period and in particular to the Marian burnings allowed him to evade the consequences of this paradox in a striking and novel way. The irrefutable evidence of the burnings could be used to counterbalance the patent imperfections of belief and conversation which afflicted the newly expanded membership of the Elizabethan church. The burnings enabled Foxe both to link the Elizabethan Church to his version of the underground tradition of the true church, and thus refute popish accusations of novelty, and also to assume that, within the perfectly sensible institutional structures provided by the Elizabethan church for the maintenance of religious order, there could be found the living body of Christ, personified in the lives in ordinary men and women, of the sort who had gone to the stake under Mary and would do so again if they had to.

It has been argued here, however, that there

remained inherent in Foxe's position certain tensions between a definition of the church in terms of the internal spiritual dynamic involved in the creation and maintenance of such groups and one which concentrated on the external ordinances of prince, bishop and minister. Foxe himself chose not to dwell on those tensions. And yet his own career, his refusal to take office within the Elizabethan establishment and the distanced irony and gentle humour with which he addressed those of his friends who did, (90) surely show that he retained a certain ambiguity of attitude towards the external forms of ecclesiastical power and the practical institutional arrangements established within the Elizabethan Church. Of course, the whole thrust of his argument allowed him to avoid having to defend the practicalities of the Elizabethan settlement. To take one central example; as we have seen, under Edward the ungodliness even of professed gospellers had led him to advocate excommunication, to be imposed by each and every minister, as a means of enforcing certain minimum standards of conduct on the laity. (91) To have continued to advocate such a course of action under Elizabeth would have been overtly to criticise the Elizabethan church, and Foxe lapsed into silence on the issue. He was able to do so because by the 1560's both the sufferings of the godly under Mary and the providential return of the gospel under Elizabeth had provided validation enough for the English church.

For Foxe the establishment of the Elizabethan church resolved the tension between the saving remnant and the national community once and for all. His stress on the native origins of the reformation and the true church, in Wyclif and the Lollards, together with his attempts to present relations between the English crown and the papacy as a struggle, now really bore fruit. Foxe had always tried to portray popery as in some sense foreign and un-English. In rejecting popery the true protestant England had asserted itself and in so doing there was a sense in which the saving minority of the godly had become the national community. The leader of that community had embraced the gospel and thus reduced, if not removed, the tension between the inward and outward government of the church. Under popery the outward hierarchies of church and state had always been the agents of corruption; now, under the tutelage of the Christian prince, they had become agents of the gospel. Through the reforming activities of the Queen and the proselytising efforts of a godly learned clergy the gospel now had free access to the nation. From being a saving minority within a corrupt mass, the godly themselves had become agents of edification, providing the solid core for an ever-expanding mystical body or spiritual temple of true believers, constructed not only within but in and through the external ordinances provided by the godly prince and the clergy. (92) Through Elizabeth the 'brightness of God's word was set up again', thereby confounding Antichrist, and the true temple of Christ was 're-edified'. Foxe prayed that, with God's help, Elizabeth and her subjects together might 'proceed in all faithfulness to build and keep up the house and temple of the Lord'. (93)

Of course, some protestants of a later generation, whose relationship with the events of the mid-century was more remote, were to take up elements within Foxe's version of the protestant tradition with which to back up an assault on central features of the Elizabethan church. In the Admonition controversy Cartwright no less than Whitgift had recourse to Foxeian arguments. (94) Foxe's great book did indeed represent a magnificent attempt to contain the considerable tension between the little flock of Christ and the national community within a stable and yet evangelically dynamic synthesis. However, both the institutional peculiarities and failings of the English church and indeed the inherently perennial nature of that tension rendered it unsusceptible to final or definitive resolution. It is a tribute to Foxe's stature as an ideologist for English protestantism that his book should have stood not only at the end of one phase of protestant thought and debate but at the very beginning of the next.

Notes

1. 'The Acts and Monuments of John Foxe', J. Pratt (ed.) in The Church Historians of England (London, 1853-70) (hereafter cited as A.M.), vol. 1, p.9. See also A.M., vol. 1, pp.519-20.
Cf. J. Jewel, 'An Apology of the Church of England' in Rev. J. Ayre (ed.), The Works of John Jewel, Bishop of Salisbury (The Parker Society, Cambridge, 1845) (hereafter cited as Works), vol. 3, pp.92, 100 & 106; and his Challenge Sermon, Works, vol. 1, pp.3-25 and pp.20-1.
Cf. A.W. Pollard and G.R. Redgrave (eds.), A short-title catalogue of Books Printed in England, Scotland and Ireland, and of English Books Printed

Abroad, 1475-1640, London 1928 (hereafter referred
to as STC), 2961, M. Parker (ed.), The Gospels of the
Four Evangelists translated in the old Saxons' time
out of the Latin into the vulgar tongue of the Saxons
(London, 1571), Preface by Foxe, sigs. Aijr-v and
9ijr-v; Foxe stated that Parker was trying to prove
'how the religion presently ... professed ... is no
new reformation of things lately begun ... but rather
a reduction of the Church to the Pristine State of
old conformity'. See also STC, 159. A testimony of
Antiquity, showing the ancient faith in the Church of
England touching the sacrament of the body and blood
of the Lord, here publicly preached and also received
in the Saxons' time, above 600 years ago, J. Josselyn
(ed.) (London, 1566), Preface by Parker, sig. Qjv,
who was convinced that the Elizabethan church had
revived many of the beliefs once held by the Anglo-
Saxon church.
    V.N. Olsen, John Foxe and the Elizabethan Church
(University of California Press, Berkeley, 1973),
pp.51ff. and 114.
    J.F. Mozley, John Foxe and his Book (SPCK,
London, 1940), Chapter 5.
    2. A.M., vol. 4, p.218.
    3. A.M., vol. 1, p.8.
    4. A.M., vol. 4, p.217.
    5. STC, 11222, J. Foxe, Acts and Monuments of
these latter and perillous dayes, touching matters of
the church, wherein are comprehended and described
the great persecutions and horrible troubles that
have been wrought and practised by the Romish
prelates, specially in this realm of England and
Scotland, from the time of our Lord 1000, until the
time now present. Gathered and collected according to
the true copies and writings certificatory, as well
of the parties themselves that suffered, as also out
of the bishops' Registers, which were the doers
thereof (London, 1563) (hereafter cited as A.M.
1563).
    6. J. Foxe, 'Christus Triumphans' in J.H.
Smith (ed.), Two Latin Comedies by John Foxe the
Martyrologist (Renaissance Text Series 4), (Cornell
University Press, Ithaca, 1973), Preface, sig. A5v.
Foxe considered that in this play he had transferred
'from the sacred writings to the theatre, what was
most pertinent to ecclesiastical affairs'.
    Revelation 20: 1-3.
    R.K. Emmerson, Antichrist in the Middle Ages
(Manchester, University Press, 1981), pp.232-5.
    R. Bauckham, Tudor Apocalypse (Courtenay
Library of Reformation Classics, Appleford, 1978),

pp.45-9.
   7. Foxe, Christus Triumphans, vol. 4, pp.61-119.
        Revelation 20:7-8; 'When the thousand years are over, Satan will be released from his prison and will go out to deceive the nations.'
   8. STC, 11223, The Ecclesiastical History, Containing the Acts and Monuments of Thinges passed in every King's time in this Realm especially in the Church of England principally to be noted ... from the primitive time till the reign of K. Henry VIII, 2nd ed., London 1570 (hereafter cited as A.M. (1570) vol. 1, p.49).
   9. A.M. (1563), vol. 1, p.1.
   10. A.M. vol. 1, p.5, 'in which time both doctrine and sincerity of life were utterly, almost, extinguished; namely in the chief heads and rulers of this west church, through the means of the Roman bishops'. Matthew 24:15; 'standing in the holy place "the abomination that causes desolation" spoken of in Daniel 9:27, 11:31, & 12:11. Foxe was not concerned to calculate the exact dating of Antichrist's reign: 'as touching the just number of the year and time, we will not be very curious or careful about it at present', A.M., vol. 2, p.792; Olsen, John Foxe, pp.70-4.
   11. Ibid.
   12. A.M. (1570), Preface; 'To the true and faithfull Congregation, of Christ's Universal Church', sig. iiin. See also A.M., vol. 3, p.724.
   13. A.M., vol. 2, p.790.
   14. A.M., vol. 2, p. 726 (the prophecy of Joachim of Floris; Liber Concordie Novi ac Veteris Testamenti (Ventijs, 1519); Olsen, John Foxe, pp.31-2, 34-5 & 114. Revelation 11: 3-4 & 12:6. K.R. Firth, The Apocalyptic Tradition in Reformation Britain 1530-1645 (OUP, Oxford 1979), p.103.
   15. A.M., vol. 2, pp.263-4. See also A.M., vol. 2, pp.268-9 (the godly manners and customs of the Waldenses). The historicity of the Acts and Monuments does not concern us here, but for a summary and bibliography of Maitland's attack on Foxe, see Olsen, John Foxe, pp. 88-92 (S.R. Maitland, A Review of Foxe the Martyrologist's History of the Waldenses (London, 1837)).
   16. A.M., vol. 2, pp.264-5.
   17. Ibid.
   18. A.M., vol. 2, p.265 (Revelation 17 & 18).
   19. A.M., vol. 1, pp.62-71 at p.71.
   20. A.M., vol. 2, p.265.
   21. A.M., vol. 1, p.69. Members of the true

church were those who 'by election inwardly are joined to Christ' as opposed to by 'outward profession only' (A.M., vol. 1, p.88).

22. A.M., vol. 2, p.791, 'at whose time this furious fire of persecution seemed to take his first original and beginning'. See also A.M., vol. 2, p.796; 'by God's providence', Wyclif rose up 'through whom the Lord would first waken and raise up against the world' which was in such 'horrible darkness'. But 'this boil or sore could not be touched without the great grief and pain of the whole world'. Olsen, John Foxe, p.38.

23. A.M., vol. 3, p.4.

24. A.M., vol. 3, p.510. Nevertheless, Huss was condemned by the papists because 'he spoke against the pomp, pride and avarice and other enormities of the Pope, cardinals and prelates of the church' (ibid), and, as knowledge of the gospel increased through his preaching, Pope Alexander V began to 'stir up the coals and directeth his bull' against his followers (A.M., vol. 3, pp.405ff). A.M., vol. 3, pp.491-2; Foxe described the Christ-like degradation and death of Huss at some length. The putting on of the garment of the priesthood, for instance, reminded Foxe of 'the white vesture which Herod put on Jesus Christ to mock him withal. So likewise, in all other things, he did comfort himself by the example of Christ.'

25. A.M., vol. 2, pp.755-6. Those mentioned by Foxe opposing the friars included Gulielmus de Sancto Amore (A.M., vol. 2, pp.510 ff); and Johannes Poliaco (A.M., vol. 2, p.710). These men were listed with others in a catalogue of 'learned and zealous defenders of Christ against Antichrist' whom the Lord was raising up in the 1360s (A.M., vol. 2, p.749).

26. A.M., vol. 2, pp.755-65, at p.756.

27. A.M., vol. 4, pp.176ff. Using the city registers, Foxe referred to forty men and women who were brought to examination before Richard Fitzjames, Bishop of London 1509-18. Joan Baker refused to set any store by the crucifix, pilgrimages or the pope's pardons (A.M., vol. 4, p.174); William Pottier accused priests of worshipping concubines instead of God (A.M., vol. 4, p.175); and Roger Hilliar spoke out against pilgrimages, the carnal presence in the sacrament, and praying to saints (ibid.). These examples are typical of the contents of many other city registers to which Foxe referred (Cf. A.M., vol. 4, pp.217ff. for an account of the Lincoln registers.)

28. A.M., vol. 4, p.490.

29. A.M., vol. 4, p.173.
30. A.M., vol. 4, p.217.
31. A.M., vol. 2, p.356.
32. Ibid. Foxe's representation of the
Waldenses and Albigensians as members of the true
church prior to the reformation caused considerable
debate amongst nineteenth century historians: see
Olsen, John Foxe, p.90.
33. A.M., vol. 4, p.508.
34. A.M., vol. 4, p.174.
35. Ibid.
36. R. Fritze, 'Root or Link? Luther's
position in the historical debate over the legitimacy
of the Church of England', Journal of Ecclesiastical
History, 1985. W.A. Clebsch, 'The Elizabethans on
Luther' in J. Pelikan (ed.), Interpreters of Luther
(Philadelphia, 1968), pp.97ff. Olsen, John Foxe,
pp.17-18.
38. A.M., vol. 4, p.172.
38. A.M., vol. 4, p.506. Luther 'gave the
stroke, and plucked down the foundation, and all by
opening one vein long hid before, wherein lieth the
touchstone of all truth and doctrine, as the only
principal origin of our salvation, which is, our free
justifying by faith only, in Christ the Son of God'
(A.M., vol. 4, p.259). W. Haller, Foxe's Book of
Martyrs and the Elect Nation (Cape, London, 1963),
pp.165 & 174; 'Foxe was as certain as Aylmer that
Wyclif begot Huss, Huss begot Luther and Luther begot
truth, but it did not occur to him that England
should wait for truth to come to her from Germany.
It had come to England straight from the apostles and
had remained there ever since through all
vicissitudes'. (But for critcism of Haller's 'elect
nation' conclusion see Olsen, John Foxe, pp.40-3;
Bauckham, Tudor Apocalypse, pp.11 and 87; and Firth,
Apocalyptic Tradition, pp.106-8).
39. A.M., vol. 4, p.553. See also A.M. (1570),
Preface 'To the True and Faithful Congregation', sig.
iiiir; and A.M. vol. 3, p.530 (the vision of Huss).
40. A.M., vol. 8, p.253.
41. A.M. (1570), Preface 'To the Right
Virtuous, Most Excellent, and Noble Princess, Queen
Elizabeth', sig. iiv.
42. A.M., vol. 1, p.69; 'brought in under the
shadow of Christianity; wherein remaineth almost
nothing else but the name only of Christ and the
outward form of his religion'.
43. A.M., vol. 4, p.475.
44. A.M. vol. 4, p.217.
45. A.M., vol. 4, p.218.

46. <u>STC</u>, 11233, J. Foxe, <u>De Censura sive</u>
<u>excommunicatione Ecclesiastica rectoque eius usu, ad</u>
<u>illustrissimum patrem Archiepiscopum cantuariensem,</u>
<u>reliquosque huius ordinis Episcopos pastores, ac</u>
<u>ministros Ecclesiae Anglicanae ubicunque constitutos</u>
<u>interpellatio</u>, London, 1551.
    47. Exodus, 24:8.
    48. <u>A.M.</u> (1563), Dedication to the Duke of
Norfolk, dated September 1559.
    49. Revelation, 17:6 & 19:11-13.
    50. <u>A.M.</u>, vol. 6, p.275.
    51. <u>A.M.</u>, vol. 8, p.668.
    52. <u>A.M.</u>, vol. 4, p.126. See also <u>A.M.</u>, vol. 8,
pp.378-9.
    53. <u>STC</u>, 11237, J. Foxe, <u>Eicasmi sev</u>
<u>Meditationes in Sacram Apocalypsin</u> (London, 1587),
p.18. 'A Letter of John Foxe to Archbishop Whitgift',
Lambeth Palace Library MS, No. 2010 fol. 120; cited
in Olsen, <u>John Foxe</u>, p.169. Cf. <u>STC</u>, 11234, J. Foxe,
<u>De Christo gratis justificante</u>; or <u>Of Free</u>
<u>Justification by Christ</u> (London, 1694), p.338; and
<u>A.M.</u>, vol. 8, p.12 (1 Tim. 3 & Titus 1).
    54. <u>A.M.</u>, vol. 1, p.26.
    55. Foxe, <u>Christus Triumphans</u>, pp.97-8.
    56. <u>A.M.</u>, vol. 2, p.296.
    57. <u>A.M.</u>, vol. 2, p.213.
    58. <u>A.M.</u>, vol. 2, p.113.
    59. <u>A.M.</u>, vol. 2, pp.523-4; Grosseteste
accused the pope of many enormities, as 'all kinds of
avarice, usury, simony, and extortion, all kinds of
filthiness, fleshly lust, gluttony and sumptuous
apparel', and refused to admit a young nephew of the
Pope to be canon of his church, for which he was
excommunicated (<u>A.M.</u>, vol. 2, p.531). Peacock was
another godly bishop praised by Foxe (<u>A.M.</u>, vol. 3,
pp.730-4), and both Hooper and Cranmer were
considered to fulfil the description of a godly
bishop found in 1 Tim. 3 (<u>A.M.</u>, vol. 8, p.12) and as
martyrs provided a useful link for Foxe between
outward church hierarchy and membership of the true
Church Universal (<u>A.M.</u>, vol. 6, pp.639, 644-5, 652-9
(Hooper), & vol. 8, pp.13-15, 19 and 22 (Cranmer)).
See also <u>A.M.</u>, vol. 1, p.350.
    60. <u>A.M.</u>, vol. 2, p.114. Foxe concluded that:
'it is not to be doubted that the Lord, even amongst
them (bishops), hath his remainder who have not bowed
their knees unto Baal ... although that these kind
of people are very rare and hard to be found' (<u>A.M.</u>,
vol. 3, p.724).
    61. <u>A.M.</u>, vol. 8, pp.140, 423.
    62. <u>A.M.</u>, vol. 3, pp.277. William Thorpe, 'the

constant servant of God', was examined by Archbishop
Arundel in 1407. Foxe printed his story in full so
that the readers could marvel at 'the marvellous
force and strength of the Lord's might, spirit and
grace, working and fighting in his soldiers, and also
speaking in their mouths' (A.M., vol. 3, pp.249-85 at
p.249). Cf. STC, 11235, J. Foxe, De non Plectendis
Morte Adulteris Consultatio (London, 1548), cited in
Mozley, John Foxe, p.32; 'the corruption of our times
is largely due to the wickedness of priests ... on
the whole laymen would rule the church better. None
but inspired men of God should be admitted into the
ministry'.

63. A.M., vol. 3, p.198 (article 12); and
'every layman in every place may teach and preach the
gospel'. C. Cross, Church and People 1450-1660
(Fontana, NP, 1976), pp.113-19. Cross has noticed
that in the beliefs of the laity described by Foxe
there was 'something of a theory of lay ministry'.
Edmund Allin, a miller, for instance, who maintained
that true Christians 'are all kings to rule our
affections, priests to preach out the virtues and
word of God ... and lively stones to give light to
each other ...' (A.M., vol. 8, pp.322-3. See also
A.M., vol. 8, pp.464, 125.)

64. A.M., vol. 4, p.218.

65. A.M., vol. 7, p.218.

66. A.M., vol. 1, p.194-5. (AD 250-3).

67. A.M., vol. 4, p.218.

68. A.M., vol. 4, p.508, 'their ministers
instructed them secretly, to avoid the fury of their
enemies, who could not abide the light'.

69. A.M., vol. 4, p.510.

70. A.M., vol. 4, p.508-9.

71. A Letter from John Foxe to Archbishop
Whitgift, fol. 120. Cf. De Censura, sig. C8vo, where
Foxe expressed his desire for a godly ministry that
was both dignified and virtuous.

72. A.M., vol. 7, p.269.

73. Foxe, Eicasmi, p.138.

74. J. Whitgift, The Works of John Whitgift, J.
Ayre ed. (Parker Society, Cambridge, 1851-3), 3 vols,
vol. 2, pp.333-4. A.M., vol. 1, p.50. Olsen, John
Foxe, chapter IV. See also Foxe, Of Free
Justification, p.338.

75. A.M., vol. 1, pp.194-5.

76. Under the control of Elizabeth, the
Christian prince and magistrate, the 'church of God
began to be edified again in England', A.M., vol. 8,
p.286. N.L. Jones, 'Elizabeth, Edification and the
Latin prayer book of 1560', Church History (June

1984), pp.174 ff.
77. A.M., vol. 1, p.26.
78. A.M., vol. 2, p.26.
79. A.M., vol. 2, p.21.
80. A.M., vol. 2, pp.102-3.
81. A.M., vol. 4, p.197 (Becket), & vol. 2, pp.287-95 (Baldwin & the monks).
82. A.M., vol. 2, p.296.
83. A.M., vol. 2, p.329.
84. A.M., vol. 2, pp.328, 420.
85. A.M., vol. 5, p.61; King Henry brought about 'a prosperous and happy change for us ... he was rid by divorcement, not only from the unlawful marriage ... but also from his miserable yoke of the Pope's usurped dominion'. A.M., vol. 5, p.46; Henry brought about what had 'durst be attempted before of any prince within this realm ... (the) overthrow of the Pope's supremacy'.
86. A.M., vol. 5, p.260.
87. Ibid.
88   A.M., vol. 8, p.628.
89. 'Letters to and from John Foxe', Harleian MSS, no. 417, fol. 131.
90. For instance, a letter written in 1561 to Laurence Humphrey who had been made president of Magdalen College, Oxford, quoted by Mozley, John Foxe, p.66; 'Come now, tell me, my friend, have you really deserted your flock and order? ... I change not my degree nor order, which is that of the mendicant brothers, or if you will, the preaching brothers ... But now you have left our company and gone up higher, riding as they say, in a white chariot'. Simeon Foxe, 'The Life of Mr. John Fox', included in the introduction to A.M., vol. 1, on p.45. See Mozley, op.cit. pp.64-6.
91. Foxe, De Censura sigs. A7-A7vo; 7 D8vo.
92. See J.S. Coolidge, The Pauline Renaissance in England Puritanism and the Bible (OUP, Oxford, 1970), chapter 2. See also A.M., vol. 3, p.282 (the godly answers of William Thorpe).
93. A.M., vol. 7, p.466.
94. Olsen, John Foxe, pp.152-5. Whitgift, Works, vol. 2, p.333-6.

Chapter Eight

PRESBYTERIANISM, THE IDEA OF A NATIONAL CHURCH AND THE ARGUMENT FROM DIVINE RIGHT

Peter Lake

English protestantism has emerged from the essays collected here as an ideology not well suited to produce a convincing rationale for a genuinely national church. The progress of the English reformation had relied heavily on small groups of true believers working at both the local and national levels to confer protestant meanings on what were at best ambiguous official policies. Of course the fate of the gospel was never wholly dependent on the efforts of these groups to control their own destiny but rather on the twists and turns of a high politics dominated, at least until 1559, by the peculiar marital history of Henry VIII's reign. As protestants struggled to impose a legitimating necessity on their otherwise meaninglessly contingent experience, they came to see in it the workings of the providence of God responding to the achievements and failures of the English reformation. Such a vision raised in a fairly acute form the problem of the relationship between the nation and the minority of true believers within it. This was a topic which caused protestants continuing ideological difficulty throughout the century. Even under Edward VI, as Catharine Davies has pointed out, the self image of the saving remnant, the leaven that leavened the whole lump, seemed more appropriate to protestant experience than a triumphalist imperialism, organised around the defence of the royal supremacy.

Of course the cause of national reformation had always been inextricably linked to the resumption by the Christian prince of his rights over the church. However, it is difficult to see an argument which came so naturally to Stephen Gardiner as distinctively protestant, and certainly the subsequent history of the Tudor monarchy, and in particular of the Marian persecution, left the

193

protestant relationship to that nexus of concerns at best ambiguous. As Gerry Bowler has pointed out the populist appeal to the people against a tyrannical Queen and lick-spittle aristocracy to which the Marian resistance writers were reduced was not, as Professor Skinner claims, a sign of confidence in support of the people, but rather an indication of the extent to which protestants felt themselves estranged from the national community and its natural leaders. (1) Protestantism was rescued from the most extreme consequences of this impasse by the events of 1558/9. The providentialist view of their history which protestants had adopted meant that if the Marian persecution acquired the status of a direct expression of divine wrath at the failings of the Edwardian reformation, then the restoration of the gospel by Elizabeth must, by the same token, represent a divine response to the sufferings of Mary's reign, which had purged the nation of its guilt and in some sense affirmed the standing of the English as an essentially protestant people. That at least was the reading produced by John Foxe in whose work the two major elements in the self image of English protestants - the national strand organised around the dominating figure of the Christian prince, and the view of the true church as a little flock of Christ, a saving remnant - came together in a compelling vision of a triumphantly protestant England. These two levels in Foxe's polemic were held together by the notion of the power of the gospel restored and now propagated with the active sponsorship of the prince to the entire nation.

As Jane Facey has argued, however, there remained difficulties and tensions within Foxe's thought. To begin with there was the whole question of the standing and authority of the clergy and its relationship to the rights and spiritual autonomy of the godly community. Moreover, while since Henry VIII's reign it had been possible to claim direct divine sanction for the powers of the Christian prince, the whole middle range of ecclesiastical government, which linked the general overseeing authority of the prince to the efforts of individual pastors and their flocks, was devoid of direct scriptural sanction, or even of a properly protestant rationale. All this might not have mattered had not the poverty of the church's resources of money and trained manpower ensured that it could not even make the gospel available to the majority of the population, let alone convert them to a version of true religion recognisable to a protestant engagé.

It was under these circumstances of shortage that the constituent elements in the protestant tradition, as it had been formulated by Foxe, split apart and the whole question of what a protestant national church should look like was thrown open in the debate about presbyterianism. Presbyterianism represented the first attempt systematically to think through how the demands made by protestant ideology on the English church might institutionally be met. Taking the individual congregation as its basic unit, presbyterianism allowed no one congregation or minister any intrinsic authority over another. Each church thus defined was governed by two ministers and a panel of lay elders. These were elected by the congregation and between them they governed the parish. In so far as presbyterianism retained any co-ordinating authority lodged in the national church that authority was exercised by a hierarchy of synods to which each congregation sent representatives. The theoretical advantages of such an arrangement for protestants were clear; the presbyterian platform offered a preaching ministry in every parish and a congregationally based scriptural discipline, which by using a range of spiritual sanctions, starting with private admonition and ending with excommunication, could enforce godly conversation on all church members. Moreover, the resulting system of church government could claim direct spiritual sanction; it reflected, so the argument ran, the style of church government used and enjoined in perpetuity by the apostles and described in scripture. (2)

This is not the place to rehash the history of Elizabethan presbyterianism. What I want to do here is set both the presbyterian platform and the positions on church government worked out in opposition to it, in the context provided by the essays in this book; to see it, in short, not merely or mainly as a foreign import grafted on to a native protestant tradition which was ill suited to receive it, but as the product and extension of long term trends and tendencies within English protestant thought and feeling. The Foxeian synthesis represented an attempt to arrest the dialectic between the demands of external order and the spiritual dynamic of edification or, if you prefer, between a view of the church centred on the Christian prince and one centred on the godly community. However, both the inner logic of the ideas themselves and the practical failings of the English church as a proselytising institution combined to make Foxe's attempt to effect an ideological closure premature. As J.S. Coolidge has pointed out recently, puritanism, defined as the rejection of certain allegedly popish ceremonies and vestments enjoyed by the Prayer Book, always opposed the demands of godly consciousness to those of external order as they were defined by the prince. The ceremonies in question were not deemed ritually impure because they were popish, rather their popish origins were held to involve an inevitable encouragement of essentially popish opinions amongst the people, and the consequent offence of those members of the church who had a proper understanding of true religion and Christian liberty. As William Fulke argued, in a country where the effects of the gospel had been so uneven 'there cannot be such an uniformity of orders in all places as shall be profitable for all'. To argue that there could be was fatally to confuse the demands of external uniformity and decency with those of edification. From the 1560s, puritanism represented the product of a clash between the internal spiritual dynamic of edification and the growth of godly consciousness on the one hand and the demands of external order and formal obedience to the prince on the other. (3)

Presbyterianism merely developed and deepened that split, by shifting the Christian prince from the centre to the periphery of protestant concern and effectively handing control of the church to the godly. On the subject of the prince and the royal supremacy there was considerable justice in the presbyterians' claim that in theory there was really no difference between their view and that of the conformists. No protestant held that the prince should reform the church as the mood took him; all were agreed that the prince's will was objectively limited by scripture. His duty was to reform the church according to God's will. Admittedly under popery that duty was a question of a largely private transaction between the prince's conscience and the word of God. But in more normal times, when godly learned ministers were not in such short supply, the dictates of scripture should be mediated through the exegetical skills and interpretative authority of the clergy. All that the presbyterians were claiming was that the extent of positive scriptural injunction was not limited to the realm of doctrine, but included the external government of the church too. They were merely trying to inform the prince of this important discovery, so that she could modify her policies accordingly. (4)

However, whatever the theoretical similarities between presbyterian and conformist views of the royal supremacy, in practice the discipline left the prince no ordinary, quotidian role in the government of the church. According to Thomas Cartwright all the godly princes cited by Whitgift were either, like Constantine, Justinian or Jehoshaphat, merely executing 'that which is commanded by scripture' or were, like David, Moses or Solomon, themselves divinely inspired prophets, responding to the promptings of the spirit. Admittedly, in contradistinction to the papists, Cartwright allowed the prince a right to reform the church unilaterally if and when it had fallen so deeply into corruption as to be unable to reform itself. He also retained a residual right to ignore, revoke and indeed punish the illegitimate use of excommunication by the ecclesiastical authorities. Similarly, the prince could claim a right to prior consultation before, and active participation in, church councils, but ordinarily it remained the case that the 'church and commonwealth are distinguished as well under a Christian prince as under an unchristian' and the secular magistrate was, therefore, excluded from an active role in the government of the church. (5)

Having just excluded the prince, presbyterianism then proceeded to hand the government of the church over, lock, stock and barrel, to the godly. For the discipline provided the institutional means through which the godly could be called together by the word preached, separated from the corrupt mass of the population through the systematic use of the spiritual sanctions of the church and then handed control of those sanctions through their sole right to elect the elders and ministers who in practice ran the church. This represented a brutally simple resolution of the tension between the godly minority and the national church; under presbyterianism the one would simply be given control of the other.

Things of course were not quite as simple as all that. Even the presbyterians were prepared to acknowledge the dangers of too great a popularity in the government of the church. There remained too the problem of the relationship between the authority of the clergy and the rights and spiritual autonomy of the laity. It was all very well for Cartwright to lambast the bishops' usurpation of the people's right to choose their own pastors, a right bought by the death of Christ on the cross, but how did that square with the need to revamp and revalue the standing of

the ordinary minister of the word which provided no
less central an element in presbyterian ideology? (6)
There was certainly a strident clericalism at
the centre of much presbyterian polemic. The ordinary
minister of the word was variously described as a
father, a mother, a leader, a guide and a builder,
whose job it was to 'make a temple for his people
which are living stones for God to dwell in forever'.
(7) Imposing though that image was, it needs to be
remembered that it tied the standing of the minister
very closely to edification; the minister's standing
was effectively dependent on the efficacy of his
efforts in the pulpit and the quality of his
relationship with his flock. It was this which
produced the presbyterian claim that no one should be
ordained before they had received a call to minister
to a specific flock. Of ordination without such a
call, William Fulke observed 'how filthily it
stinketh of the popish indelible character'. John
Udall claimed that the standing of true ministers was
a function of God's spirit working in and through
them. As for the people, they should be able to 'try
the spirits' and judge 'who walk after the word of
God and who do not.' (8)
Of course such sentiments were the common coin
of protestant denunciations of the clericalist
tyranny of the papists. What presbyterianism was
trying to do was to give institutional shape and form
to those impulses through the peculiar balance
maintained in the political structure of the
discipline. Thus, as both William Fulke and Dudley
Fenner claimed, while the authority conceded to the
minister under presbyterianism was considerable it
was scarcely unlimited. 'While we entreat of the
authority of the pastors we must take heed that we
open not a window to popish tyranny instead of
pastoral authority,' wrote Fulke. The discipline did
this, he claimed, by ensuring that 'the pastor,
bishop or elder hath none authority by himself
separated from other'. According to Fenner the
discipline did not 'by the stairs of Rome' 'descend
from two to one' but ascended 'by the stairs of
Christ from one to two, from two to many'. (9)
Fulke discerned two types of authority wielded
by the minister, one inside the congregation, the
other outside. Both could only be exercised in
association with others. Inside the congregation 'he
may do nothing without the consent of the church'
while outside his authority could only be used
together with the 'whole synod or assembly whereof he
is a member'. For Walter Travers the discipline was

Presbyterianism

the very opposite of the spiritual tyranny inscribed
within episcopacy, 'the institution being such as
that no one carryeth any cause but all things are
guided by the consent of a number most fearing God
and of best ability for that purpose'. (10)
    That was fair enough for synods, of course, but
as Fulke himself admitted, his claim that the
government of individual congregations should be
conducted 'with the consent of the church' was rather
vague. In fact the authority of the people was
exercised by proxy through the activities of the
elected lay elders whose duty it was 'to have the
hearing, examination and determining of all matters
pertaining to discipline and government'. This was
necessary since as Fulke acknowledged 'the judgement
of the multitude is confuse'. In this way, so he
claimed, the extremes of clerical tyranny on the one
hand, and populist confusion and disorder on the
other, were avoided. Tyranny was averted because
under presbyterianism no man could 'do anything in
the church without the advice and consent of others
that be godly and wise and authorised by the consent
of the church. Confusion is prevented by the grave
counsel and orderly assembly of elders unto whom the
church hath committed her authority'. Lastly, the
rights and liberties of the people were safeguarded
by their continuing right to have the results of the
elders' deliberations propounded 'to the whole
multitude that it may be confirmed by their consent'.
(11)
    As both their conformist adversaries and modern
historians have been quick to point out there were
enough ambiguities in the presbyterians' account of
both the relations between the people and their
governors in the individual congregation and between
individual congregations and the authority of the
synods to provide plenty of room for conflict, had
the discipline ever been put into practice. (12) The
fact remains, however, that in theory and in prospect
the presbyterian platform represented the first
developed institutional answer to the problem of the
national church produced by English protestants.
Within it both the tension between the authority and
standing of the ministry and the rights and spiritual
autonomy of the laity and between the idea of a
national church and existing protestant attitudes to
the godly community were confronted and at least
notionally overcome.
    It was this which accounted for the note of
essentially eschatological excitement and expect-
ation with which the presbyterians referred to the

discipline. For inscribed at the heart of the presbyterian project lay a moment of transcendence when the division between the internal and the external government of the church was dissolved and Christ's spiritual body became visible, embodied in the community of the godly which had been called together and sustained by the purely scriptural ordinances and offices of the discipline. It is true that such claims were not perhaps quite as central to presbyterians' polemic as their conformist opponents – anxious to denounce them as Anabaptist incendiaries – would have liked. The presbyterian platform could be and was canvassed through thousands of pages of polemic on the basis of a simple protestant legalism – it was in the Bible, God had enjoined it and men should obey his injunctions. However, the tendency was there and showed clearly in the way presbyterians talked about the discipline. For Walter Travers it was part of the kingdom of Christ; for Dudley Fenner it was part of Christ's body, the establishment of which would be a 'major increase in the kingdom and glory of Christ' and would serve mightily to the 'suppression of the tyranny of Satan'. William Fulke agreed; it was the only 'form of regiment' which God had 'authorised' and 'promised to bless'. For Travers the 'assurance of God's favourable blessing of his own ordinance' guaranteed the orthodoxy and equity of the judgements of presbyterian synods. (13)

In this context Travers explicitly denied the conformists' habitual distinction between the inward and outward government of the church. The discipline was laid down by Christ and as such simply necessary for the process of spiritual edification to take place. There was a complete congruence between the spiritual gifts necessary to maintain the existence of the church and the offices contained in the discipline. Indeed, those offices represented the constituent parts of a body whose spiritual head was Christ. As such it was a divinely designed machine for the furtherance of that process of spiritual building which alone created and sustained the spiritual body of Christ in his church. Thus the presbyterians felt entirely justified in applying the rhetoric of spiritual building and edification directly to the implementation of the discipline. According to Thomas Cartwright, under presbyterianism 'our saviour Christ sitteth wholly and fully not only in his chair to teach but also in his throne to rule, not alone in the hearts of everyone by his spirit but also generally and in the visible government of his church, by those laws of discipline which he hath prescribed'. (14)

At one point Cartwright advanced the striking argument that since 'good men, that is to say the church' were the 'foundation of the world' it was only fitting that the government of the state should accommodate itself to that of the church and not vice versa. That, of course, was an assertion about the government of the visible church, yet under pressure from Whitgift Cartwright later glossed it as a statement about the invisible church of the elect. All that he had meant to say was that the fact that 'the full number of the elect is not yet gathered' was 'the cause why this world endureth'. That was uncontroversial enough but it could scarcely be construed as having any direct application either to the government of the visible church or the state. In short, it rendered the original exchange meaningless. This incident shows more than Cartwright wriggling to escape the radical implications of his own rhetoric; it stands for a far more general tendency within presbyterian thought, a tendency to refer to the discipline as a part of Christ's kingdom or body, to collapse the godly community recruited and defined through the discipline into the elect and to equate the edification of Christ's spiritual body with the implementation of the discipline. (15)

Of course the test of visible godliness applied through the discipline did not allow Cartwright to enlist his church members as 'members of the book of life' with anything like absolute certainty. But as he told Whitgift, for practical purposes that hardly mattered. For if the test of visible godliness did not separate the elect from the reprobate, or, in Cartwright's phrase, the sheep from the goats, it was quite sufficient effectively to exclude the visibly ungodly (pigs as Cartwright called them, pursuing his farmyard analogy). Left inside the church were only hypocrites, who, since they aped the behaviour of the godly so carefully, scarcely mattered, and true believers. As for those members of the elect whose lapses from grace had temporarily excluded them from the church, their status as elect vessels of God ensured that sooner or later they would start to act the part, repent and take their place as full members of Christ's body, the church. On other occasions presbyterians could let their underlying assumptions show with even greater candour. For all Cartwright's qualifications Walter Travers was quite happy to refer to the full members of the church under presbyterianism as 'saints'. (16)

Presbyterianism

If Cartwright's passage about the church providing the foundation of the world neatly illustrates this tendency to equate the visibly godly with the elect, it also highlights another unacknowledged but nevertheless common enough presbyterian habit - the extension of an active citizenship to be exercised only by the godly from the church to the state. At one level, of course, the presbyterians held that the church and state existed in completely separate spheres. The maintenance of such a distinction enabled them to argue, against conformist allegations of subversion, that the introduction of the discipline in the church would have no necessary effects on the structure of authority in the state. (17) They were able to argue this point with such complaisance because they believed that, in England, the church and the state shared essentially the same political structure. They both enjoyed the best form of polity as the ancient philosophers had described it, the mixed polity. In the discipline the monarchical element was provided by Christ, in the English state by the Queen; in the discipline the pastors and elders played the part of the aristocracy, in the state that role was filled by the privy council; in the discipline the democratic element came from the people, in the state it came from Parliament. (18) Moreover, the presbyterians attributed a common populist theory of power to both the church and the state; in both, power originated in the whole people only to be granted away to certain rulers who then exercised it, within the limits imposed by the mixed polity, in the name of both the social whole and of God.

However, if the discipline would not have changed the structure of the state (at least as the presbyterians conceived it) it would undoubtedly have had a direct effect on the personnel running the machinery of government. Nearly all the presbyterians were agreed that far from being subversive, the discipline would operate as a sort of cross between a secret police force and a system of social control. As such it would inhibit and inform the magistrate about the activities of papists, familists and sinners of all sorts. When Cartwright's very wide definition of what constituted popery is added to his dictum that in choosing secular magistrates the prince should limit herself to 'those who fear the Lord' (19) it becomes clear just how exclusive the godly oligarchy to whom the presbyterians wanted to entrust the government of church and state would have been. In the mixed polity of England the Queen might still rule, but only with the consent and co-operation of the godly.

Before we join Whitgift and the other conformists in writing this vision off as impossibly radical and un-English in its attitude to the power of the prince, it is worth pausing to consider just how closely such an interpretation fitted the situation and early history of the Elizabethan regime, as recent research has revealed it. The progress of the English reformation had after all been based on cells of protestants co-operating together to further the cause of the gospel both locally and nationally. It would, of course, be an exaggeration to claim that the accession of Elizabeth served simply to transfer power to such groups. The regime relied heavily on the acquiescence of families like the Stanleys, the Talbots or the Paulets, none of which could be described as repositories of protestant zeal. And yet, as Simon Adams has recently argued, from the outset the inner circle of the regime was dominated by a knot of committed protestants who shared an essentially similar view of the regime's situation and enemies. The incessant and apparently growing threat of popery made it increasingly natural to equate protestant zeal with political loyalty and under the persistent pressure exerted by the threat of popish subversion the regime came to rely more and more on determindely protestant local elites. This was a process by no means uniform in either its timing or its impact across the country. Yet, as Dermott McCulloch has shown, in Suffolk at least the interaction between local disputes and the intervention of the central government served effectively to transfer government of the county to a protestant, indeed puritan, group. In Hampshire Ron Fritze has argued that a protestant interest which stretched back to Thomas Cromwell's patronage network of the 1530s formed the nucleus for a protestant grouping which by the 1570s had overcome the conservative Paulet faction and come to dominate the county. (20)

Nationally, after 1571 Catholics were formally excluded from Parliament. Now however 'revisionist' a view one takes of the political power wielded by that institution, the effective hijack of the representative body of the whole realm for protestantism cannot have been without a certain symbolic significance. And of course, it had a political significance too. The effective domination of the lower house by protestants had provided the

203

occasion for a series of attempts dating from the 1560s to push the Queen's religious, foreign and marital policies in more firmly protestant directions. These manoeuvres were almost certainly connived at, if not stage managed, by the Queen's own councillors, in league with vocally protestant elements in the House of Commons. After the failure of one such attempt to get the Queen to settle the succession, Cecil drew up a contingency plan for the event of the Queen's sudden death. Government should pass to the privy council, until Parliament could be called to settle the succession. The aristocratic and democratic elements in Cartwright's view of the mixed polity of England were evidently to co-operate in order to reconstitute the monarchical element in a suitably protestant form. (21)

Dr Graves' recent reinterpretation of the parliamentary events of 1572 sees a campaign against Mary Stuart emanating from the very centre of the regime and sustained in the lower house by 'council men of business'. Gerry Bowler's article on the content of the debates finds arguments taken straight from the Marian resistance literature being used by bishops and parliament men to justify killing the Queen of Scots. Clearly radical protestant ideas had penetrated very close to the centre of the Elizabethan regime. On this view, therefore, the vision of Parliament as the locus for an open ended dialogue between the Queen and her subjects over issues of national significance which was inscribed within Sir John Neale's political narratives, can be retained. But if the 'rise' of Parliament as a political institution can still be discerned during Elizabeth's reign, its causes need no longer be sought in either a conspiratorial view of puritanism or the rise of the gentry, but in the problematic relations pertaining between the Queen and many of her councillors and in the reliance of those councillors, in the face of the Queen's mortality and the threat of popery, on the support of an emergent protestant ruling class. When the reliance of those same local elites on the backing of the centre is added to the equation the ambiguity of the political relationships involved becomes clear and the role of men like Thomas Norton as 'council men of business' appears a little less like a 'one way street'. (22)

This evidence had been adduced here not to argue that the Elizabethan regime was in fact organised around such populist, protestant principles, but merely to show that elements central to the presbyterian vision of England as a godly commonwealth could be found very close to the heart of the Elizabethan establishment. Thus not only could presbyterians see in the discipline the final triumph of the true over the false church, as the corrupt forces of clericalist pride and tyranny, personified now in the cause of episcopacy, succumbed before the gospel, they could also see in it the logical extension of existing political trends and attitudes. As such the discipline represented both an essential defence of the progress already made by protestantism and the means to inaugurate a new golden age of protestant purity and zeal.

For the discipline operated at a number of levels. Not only was it a shopping list of institutional adjustments and reforms designed to improve the proselytising performance of the English church, it was also an organism of divine origin whose adoption would be a symbolic act of national submission to the divine will, which would set the seal on the process of reformation and call down the blessings of God upon the nation in unprecedented profusion. Rejecting conformist claims that there were not enough trained ministers to meet the needs of the discipline, Thomas Cartwright claimed that men lawfully elected to office in the reformed church would automatically receive from God the spiritual gifts necessary for the fulfilment of their new duties. Where the will of God was concerned the politics of the possible no longer applied. God would overcome all obstacles. In short, the discipline was the 'policy of policies', 'even the most excellent policy in the world to glorify God' and thus conducive both to the 'destruction of our enemies' and the 'maintenance of our peace'. (23)

But if the presbyterian vision of the discipline as but a continuation and culmination of existing ideological and political trends has more than a grain of truth in it, there remained a crucial difference between attitudes which only achieved their clearest expression at moments of crisis, unacknowledged, unsystematic and geographically uneven trends and tendencies and full scale systems of government. The price for the presbyterians' failure to notice that difference was complete political failure.

If the survival of a protestant England was taken to depend on the nation fulfilling its covenant with God and instituting a presbyterian reformation, those who advocated such a reformation, even in the face of repeated failure and official repression, took on the mantle of a saving remnant, whose

205

continued efforts to institute the discipline stood
almost alone between England and the judgement of
God. To one set of petitioners, at least, a process
of further reformation undertaken by Parliament was
the only way left for the nation to regain God's
favour. Walter Travers pictured the efforts of 'the
faithful servants of God that kneel before him day
and night to be merciful to us' (together with the
presence of so many foreign refugees sheltering from
the popish wolf) as all that stood between England
and the wrath of God. (24)

The presbyterians' rhetoric turned on a series
of harsh either/or choices between reform and
corruption, renewed divine favour or judgement and
the threat of destruction. Once it became clear that
reality was not about to shape itself according to
the dictates of scripture the presbyterians were
forced to marginalise themselves within a Foxeian
rhetoric of the saving remnant, languishing under the
persecution of the false church. It was no accident,
therefore, that the 1580s ended with Martin
Marprelate vapouring on about the blood of martyrs
which the discipline had yet to inspire or episcopal
tyranny to claim. (25)

The complete failure of presbyterianism to make
any political headway ensured that its major long
term contribution to the development of a genuinely
protestant legitimation for the national church lay
in the reaction it provoked from other Elizabethan
divines. Initially that reaction was organised
around the twin Foxeian poles of the power of the
prince in governing and the role of right doctrine in
validating the Church of England as a true church.
These certainly provided John Whitgift with his most
effective arguments against Thomas Cartwright.
However, the polemical constraints inherent in the
confrontation with presbyterianism ensured that
Whitgift could hardly give Foxeian emphasis to the
evangelical mission of the English church. His drive
to label as anabaptist Cartwright's identification
of the discipline and the godly community it existed
to create and define with Christ's body or kingdom,
together with the practical deficiencies of the
English church as a proselytising institution
rendered the nexus of protestant concerns centred on
the concept of edification a source of embarrassment
for Whitgift. As a proponent of conformity as it was
then being enforced, Whitgift had to prefer the
demands of external order and uniformity to those of
edification. The result, as Coolidge has argued, was
an impoverished understanding of the concept which

collapsed it into a synonym for the transfer of improving information, rather than retaining it as a figure for the construction, within the structures provided by the visible church, of a spiritual temple built only of lively stones or true believers. This was a polemical double bind which was to afflict even the most evangelically minded conformists, until the 1590s when Hooker was able to escape the attentions of the Calvinist thought police for long enough to invest ceremony and ritual practice with a positively edifying role in the life of the church and thus break with the austerely word-centred style of piety which had hitherto dominated the Elizabethan church. (26)

There were, however, other ways of evolving a positive protestant response to the problem of the national church, a response which exploited rather than evaded the austere scripturalism which united nearly all Elizabethan protestant divines. These involved the virtual appropriation of presbyterian modes of argument for the defence of central elements within the ecclesiastical status quo. The breakthrough came with the development of *iure divino* arguments for episcopacy. It has recently been argued that this represented no real change from Whitgift's position and that there was a consensus amongst Elizabethan conformist divines that while episcopacy was of apostolic origins and therefore the best, it was not the only legitimate form of church government. This statement contrives to be both formally true and essentially misleading at the same time. For while such a formulation represented a sediment of common opinion, it did so rather as a basic datum or lowest common denominator than as an actively shared belief or principle. (27)

Whitgift had stressed the variety and variability of apostolic practice in order to allow the secular magistrate a large measure of autonomy in framing the government of the church to that of the state. With Foxe Whitgift had argued that the government of the church should vary with circumstances. Primarily it must accommodate itself to the structure of the secular state in which it had to exist. On this view presbyterianism limited the royal supremacy not merely by excluding the magistrate from the government of the church, but also by removing his right to change the government of the church to suit the structure of the state. This was a claim which the presbyterians turned back on conformist arguments for episcopacy, asking, if episcopacy was indeed of apostolic foundation, what freedom did that leave the magistrate to order the church as he saw fit? It was in part to meet such objections that early conformists like Whitgift and Matthew Hutton grounded the superiority of episcopacy as a form of church government not so much on its apostolic origins as its congruence with the monarchical structure of the English state. (28)

The position adopted by the conformist writers of the late 1580s and early 1590s was rather different. Unlike Whitgift they accepted the presbyterian premise that there was one form of church government contained in and commended by scripture. John Bridges was the first conformist to advance that claim in print and a range of contemporary opinion, stretching from Martin Marprelate through Walter Travers and Sir Francis Knollys to Richard Hooker, acknowledged that he was breaking new ground. (29) From that base the conformists proceeded to argue that the form of church government enjoined in scripture was episcopal not presbyterian. The structure of the arguments that they used to maintain this position replicated almost exactly those employed by the presbyterians. Thus the presbyterians argued that since the church was Christ's household he could not, without blasphemy, be held to have left its internal government unprovided for. Moses had left detailed instructions for the government of the church under the law and it was absurd to assume that Christ would have been any the less careful for the welfare of his flock under the gospel. Thomas Bilson virtually reproduced these arguments before proceeding, just as the presbyterians had, to apply the precedents and injunctions of scripture directly to contemporary circumstances. (30)

The testimony of Jerome that episcopacy was a tradition of the church, introduced by men in order to control the heresy and schism which the principle of ministerial parity was allowing to run rife, had been used by earlier protestants (the young Bridges amongst them) to prove that the origins of episcopacy were indeed human. Now that passage was glossed rather differently as applying to the time of the apostles. Thus episcopacy might have been founded by men but those men also happened to have been apostles and so its origins were rather more than merely human. Timothy and Titus were the first bishops, their authority came directly from Paul who had thus established the model for what Thomas Bilson termed 'the perpetual government of Christ's church'. (31)

It is true that the iure divino apologists for

episcopacy made rather greater play with arguments
drawn from the Fathers and church history than did
the presbyterians, but that was because both the
Fathers and the history of the church seemed to
support their claims that the church had not been
governed other than by bishops from the time of the
apostles until the reformation. Such a claim was
scarcely open to the presbyterians, for whom the
dominance of the early church by episcopacy provided
sure evidence of the presence and gradual rise to
power of Antichrist. In forming their different
versions of these events both sides displayed a
remarkable degree of agreement about the facts of
early church history. Walter Travers and Thomas
Bilson produced virtually identical accounts of the
rise of episcopacy in the early church, but where
Travers could see only decay and decline Bilson
discerned a process of institutional fine tuning
whereby the government of the bishop was integrated
with the authority of church councils and the
Christian prince. Ultimately these divergent
interpretations were grounded on fundamentally
different premises about the nature of church
government, premises which were presented as
different readings of scripture. (32)

It is important to emphasise this point, because
it was only the scriptural basis of their arguments
that allowed the conformists to advance what had
become by the 1590s some very exalted claims for the
episcopal government of the English church. As
Hadrian Saravia triumphantly concluded, 'the form of
government which was ordained of God and delivered of
the apostles and confirmed of the fathers ought to
remain and continue in like sort'. For Richard
Bancroft the government of the church of England was
'apostolical and far to be preferred before any other
that is received this day by any reformed church of
Christendom'. Matthew Sutcliffe agreed; 'the
government of the church of England is most
conformable to the government both under the law and
the gospel and hath testimony of scriptures,
confirmation of antiquity and was never gainsaid but
of late days when factious companions and clouters
and tinkers and merchants and men of occupation
aspired to church government'. Even the temperate
Bilson was ready to claim that the present government
of the English church came very close to the
'sincerity of the scriptures and society of the
ancient and uncorrupt church of Christ'. Bridges
himself held that England possessed 'the regiment of
the church which God hath blessed'. (33)

Whitgift, Hutton and the young Bridges had not
used language like this. (34) Nor had they argued as
Sutcliffe, Saravia and Bancroft all did that to
remove episcopacy from a church for any reasons other
than necessity was a sin comparable to that of Arius.
Such a position while it did not unchurch the
reformed churches left them subject to the enormous
condescension of an English church whose external
government no less than its doctrine could now claim
to reflect an apostolic purity. Such claims had not
been open to Whitgift precisely because he had not
based his case for episcopacy as directly and
exclusively on scripture as did the later
conformists. Once that move had been made the austere
scripturalism which united nearly all Elizabethan
protestants made a language almost as exalted as that
employed by the presbyterians about the discipline
available to the conformists. (35)

If there were differences of substance as well
as tone separating Whitgift from the later
conformists it remains true, as Margaret Sommerville
has usefully reminded us, that the considerable
polemical advantages that accrued to the conformist
case from a <u>iure divino</u> defence of episcopacy were
not achieved by any major conceptual breakthrough,
but by a small shift of emphasis from one aspect of
Whitgift's case to another. Indeed, that case had
always looked like a rather uncomfortable halfway
house as Dudley Fenner and other presbyterians were
only too ready to point out. (36) Why, therefore, did
it take nearly twenty years for conformists to
resolve those difficulties when all they had to do
was play up Whitgift's view of the apostolic origins
of episcopal power and play down the erastian
relativism with which he had surrounded it?

The answer to that question surely lies not in
the intellectual but the political history of the
period. As the old guard of Elizabethan councillors
died off in the late 1580s a new group, centred on
Whitgift and Hatton and linked to the Queen by a
common hatred of puritan indiscipline, seized the
initiative in ecclesiastical affairs. Riding high on
a tide of carefully orchestrated anti-presbyterian-
ism and helped by the extremity of tone which had
crept into much late presbyterian polemic, the
clerical ideologues of this faction inserted the <u>iure
divino</u> defence of episcopacy into the centre of the
conformist propaganda effort. Sir Francis Knollys'
attack on the <u>iure divino</u> case as an affront to and
infringement on the royal supremacy typified the
ideological forces which had for so long inhibited

the development and open expression of the argument
from divine right. By the late 1580s and early 1590s
however that strain of erastian, anti-prelatical if
not anti-clerical, opinion was no longer dominant at
court. Knollys' protests came to nothing and by the
early 1590s the <u>iure divino</u> case was established as
the new orthodoxy, as Hooker's belated and rather
half-hearted adoption of it shows. (37)

This development marked a significant staging
post on the long road back from the brutal
erastianism of the Edwardian and early Elizabethan
reformations. The Christian prince had long enjoyed
the sanction of scripture, through the direct
application of scriptural models of divine kingship
to the Tudor monarchy. Now the godly bishop had
joined the Christian prince on the pedestal of
divinely ordained power. The next stage came with the
extension of the <u>iure divino</u> argument to tithes. For
whilst the aura of prestige and enhanced status which
the <u>iure divino</u> case afforded the bishops could not
but reflect on the whole clerical estate (or so
Saravia and Hooker piously hoped) such claims did
nothing to improve the economic condition and hence
the status of the ordinary minister. (38) The massive
transfer of wealth from the clergy to the laity which
had fed the progress of the English reformation had
placed the issue of the wealth of the church, the
remuneration of the clergy and the encroachments of
the laity thereon at the centre of clerical concern.
This was a topic which united men of strikingly
different opinions on other issues in strident
denunciations of the rapacity and sacrilege of the
laity. Bancroft no less than Cartwright, Saravia no
less than Travers waxed lyrical on the subject of the
rights of the church and the greed of the laity. (39)
And yet, as far as I can find, no Elizabethan
conformist divine advanced a <u>iure divino</u> defence of
tithes. (40) They limited themselves to asserting the
general obligation to yield the clergy a sufficient
maintenance and characterised the dereliction of
that duty as sacrilege. As for the tenth it was part
of the Mosaic law and as such abrogated by Christ,
who had left the precise calculation of the clergy's
wages to the relevant human authorities.

Nevertheless, just as with episcopacy, the
argument from divine right was lying there waiting to
be used. As early as the late 1580s in his D.D.
thesis (which was to remain unpublished until the
1640s) Lancelot Andrewes had toyed with the argument
only to lay it aside lest its controversial novelty
detract from the general acceptance of his basic

claims about the sacrilegious nature of lay
encroachment on the rights of the clergy. (41) In
fact, no one dared deploy the full iure divino case
for tithes until 1606 when George Carleton claimed
that the obligation to pay tithes was directly based
on scripture; the tenth had not been abrogated by
Christ as part of the Mosaic law, but like episcopacy
its continuing validity should be construed as an
expression of Christ's concern for his household the
church. The structure of the arguments deployed by
Carleton and subsequent proponents of the same case
ran precisely parallel to that used by both the
presbyterians and the iure divino apologists for
episcopacy. The argument applied scriptural texts
culled from both the Old and New Testaments directly
to contemporary circumstances and only had recourse
to arguments from human law and church history as an
afterthought. Certainly, there was no attempt to
mediate the dictates of scripture through the
decisions of intervening human authorities. (42)

Carleton's book was dedicated to Bancroft whose
protection, Carleton claimed, was necessary for the
open expression of ideas made novel and potentially
offensive by long neglect. Bancroft's 'wisdom and
courage for the advancement of the church's oppressed
state' made Carleton the more ready to rely on the
Archbishop's patronage. R. Eburne made a similar
point in dedicating another early statement of the
iure divino case to James Montague, Bishop of Bath
and Wells. (43) These dedications to the two leading
lights of the early Jacobean ecclesiastical
establishment may betray a pseudo-official campaign
on the issue, prompted by Bancroft's longstanding
desire to 'do something' about impropriations.
Certainly by 1618 at the latest the iure divino case
had acquired the status of an official orthodoxy, for
in that year Selden was twice personally rebuked by
James himself and forced to explain himself before
the High Commission at Lambeth for daring to demur in
print from the argument from divine right. Just as
with episcopacy, the full development of the iure
divino case was retarded not by a conceptual
difficulty intrinsic to the subject, but by the
presence of lay interests and opinion likely to be
offended by any move in that direction. Only when
backing at the highest political level had been
obtained were such arguments risked in print. (44)

With the announcement of the iure divino case
for tithes virtually every aspect of the structure
and observances of the English church had acquired a
directly scriptural sanction. Here it is worth

recalling Ken Parker's findings on the general acceptance amongst English divines of the doctrine of sabbatarianism. Not for nothing did one author compare the donation of one tenth of the nation's wealth to the clergy to the dedication of one seventh of its time to divine worship. Both offerings, he claimed, perfectly reflected the arrangements laid down in scripture. (45) Add to this the divinely ordained government of the Christian prince and the godly bishop and the orthodox Calvinism, which for divines like Carleton still represented the official doctrinal position of the English church, and one can gain a sense of the extent to which, for Calvinist episcopalians at least, Jacobean England represented the epitome of a godly commonwealth.

This was no small achievement and much of the credit for it must go to James I himself. He personally backed the <u>iure divino</u> case for both bishops and tithes and, through his sponsorship of the oath of allegiance controversy, sought to place the 'imperial strand' in the anti-papal tradition at the very forefront of the regime's public image. Thus not only had presbyterianism been overthrown as a political force, the presbyterian image of the godly commonwealth had been replaced by an equally compelling vision, based on precisely the same scripturalist premises that had underpinned the discipline. (46) However, these polemical advantages were only obtained at a certain price. We started this paper with an analysis of the Foxeian version of the protestant tradition, balanced between the Christian prince and the godly community; the Jacobean vision of the godly commonwealth was produced through a transaction between those opposite poles, a transaction which worked very much in favour of the Christian prince and the cause of external order.

For the relationship between ecclesiastical authority and the godly community which was inscribed within episcopacy was entirely different from that contained within presbyterianism. Where presbyterians derived, at least in part, the power exercised by ecclesiastical governors from the people and gloried in the role of active consent and collective decision making, within both the individual congregation and church synods, conformists did their best to expel all such considerations from their account of how the church should be governed. John Bridges would admit that there was a sense in which ecclesiastical power had been given first to the whole congregation or church, but he insisted that in practice the exercise of that power was proper only 'to those persons in or of the church' who 'are of God or man lawfully called thereunto'. Such people were not 'so properly called the church's delegates as God's delegates or ministers' since they represented 'God therein not the church'. On that basis while it might be advisable for bishops to gain the consent of other ministers before they exercised their powers of ordination or excommunication, those powers remained an episcopal monopoly and the search for consent could not be taken to constitute any sort of formal limitation on their exercise by the bishop acting quite alone. (47)

Thomas Bilson admitted that at first the government of the church had been so proportioned that 'neither the presbyters should do anything without the bishop nor the bishop dispose matters of importance without his presbyters'. In the early church, when there had been neither a Christian prince nor church councils to regulate the activities of the bishops, such an arrangement had been the only way in which the 'bishop's will' could be prevented from becoming 'the rule of all things in the church'. However, even then this process of consultation had never implied that the bishop was subject to the collective judgement even of all the presbyters united against him. On the contrary, the bishop was always sovereign, his powers were his and his alone.

Bilson then proceeded to explain how, as Christianity spread and the church acquired the services of both the Christian prince and church councils, things had changed. For together the prince and the councils had been able to regulate the behaviour of the bishops far more effectively than the local presbyteries. After all church councils were composed of the most learned and experienced ministers drawn from all over the church, men uninvolved in the local feuds and factions which all too often dominated the presbyteries. As for the prince, was he not the head of his people and as such far less likely to be swayed by unworthy personal motives than lesser authorities? Thus the role of local ecclesiastical authorities became increasingly the mere enforcement and application of laws and orders made by the Christian prince and church councils. This the bishops were far better able to do than the presbyteries and so, over a period, the role of the presbyters in regulating and limiting the powers of the bishop withered away almost to nothing. (48)

Again, ever since Whitgift the conformists had

been prepared to admit that at one stage bishops had been elected by the laity. Bilson even went so far as to ground this practice on the 'principles of nature' according to which, he argued, every church had the right to elect its own pastor or governor. However, the practical experience of 'factions, schisms, tumults, uproars, murders and what not' which were incident to such popular elections had led the Christian prince to curtail and then entirely to remove the rights of the people to choose their own pastor. In so doing, as Whitgift, Bilson and Hooker all agreed, the prince had been acting entirely within his rights as the head of the commonwealth, in both removing the occasions of such disorder and ensuring the appointment of able and respectable men to episcopal office. (49) Always, therefore, the thrust of the conformist position was away from popular consent and collective decision making as mechanisms for avoiding abuse and tyranny in the church, and towards the application by a higher authority, which culminated in the person of the Christian prince, of human and divine law.

Nor was the break between the realm of external government and the imperatives of edification based only or even mainly on such essentially politique considerations. It was built into the logical structure of the conformist case. Ever since Whitgift's attack on Cartwright's affinities with the Anabaptists the claim that the presbyterians confused Christ's spiritual government of the invisible church with their own government of the visible church had been central to conformist polemic. Such an accusation had fitted easily enough with the erastian relativism which had been Whitgift's dominant mode of argument in favour of episcopacy. However, the argument was used with no less enthusiasm by the next generation of conformist writers, who were firmly committed to the assertion of the iure divino defence of bishops. Thus according to Bancroft the presbyterians misapplied to the discipline 'all those places of scripture' 'which are written of the spiritual government of the Holy Ghost in the hearts of the faithful'. Sutcliffe agreed; the puritans confused 'Christ's eternal kingdom' with the 'external government of the church'. (50)

And yet, as we have seen, one of the major attractions of the iure divino case for bishops was the way in which it allowed conformists to apply the same sort of exalted language to episcopacy as the presbyterians used about the discipline. Indeed, some conformists got so carried away that they

215

actually replicated the causal link established by
the presbyterians between the form of church
government commanded in scripture and the process of
spiritual edification itself. Defending the
perpetuity of the powers given by Paul to Titus and
Timothy, Hadrian Saravia claimed that 'if the church
could have been edified without them they should
never have been ordained in the church'. As the ends
for which the powers of bishops were ordained were
perpetual, so must be the office of the bishop
itself. 'For are they not still to edify by these
offices and to grow together into one mystical body
of Christ?' Thomas Bilson appeared to go even
further. In a long passage he reproduced the
presbyterian image of the government of the visible
church 'as the body of Christ' and grounded the
powers of bishops on the fact that Christ had set
'watchmen and leaders over the flock' for 'the
edification and preservation of the church'. (51)

How could such exalted claims be made to fit
with the strict division between the visible and
invisible church which formed so central a part of
the conformist rejection of presbyterianism? Of the
writers of the 1590s Thomas Bilson alone provided an
answer to that question. 'Order' and 'discipline', he
explained, were 'the very nurse and mother of all
peace and quietness' which 'though it be not the life
or spirit that quickeneth the church yet doth it
fasten and knit the members thereof as joints and
sinews do the parts of our bodies.' This of course
was all of a piece with the general conformist
tendency to collapse the demands of edification into
those of external order and uniformity. But it also
ensured that the external government of the church
was too important to be left to human whim. 'We must
not frame what of regiment we list for the ministry
of Christ's church but rather observe and mark what
manner of external government the lord hath best
liked and allowed in his church even from the
beginning'.

That, of course, let in the *iure divino* argument
for episcopacy and yet Christ's kingdom remained too
exalted, too spiritual to contain episcopacy as one
of its central pillars. Thus Bilson continued to
distinguish between 'the external regiment of
pastors and teachers among themselves and over their
flocks' and 'the internal that God hath by his spirit
and truth in the hearts of the faithful'. That was
the real 'kingdom of Christ' and as such was distinct
from the 'outward things in the church which he hath
left to others'. At this point the conformists'

consistent insistence that episcopacy had been
founded not directly by Christ but by the apostles
came into play. It enabled them to maintain the
crucial gap between the external government of the
church and Christ's spiritual body or kingdom; a gap
which they were able to accuse the presbyterians of
trying to close and yet themselves continue to use
the most exalted language about the government of
bishops in the visible church. (52)

Significantly for the present argument the
conformists often ran together their political and
theological objections to the presbyterians' elision
of the visible and invisible churches. By confusing
the decisions of their presbyteries and synods with
the government of Christ himself and by playing up
the role of popular consent and collective decision
making they were in fact making the will of God wait
upon that of man. That way lay genuine spiritual
tyranny. 'I pray, you sirs,' Bilson asked the
presbyterians, 'for God's decrees who shall execute
them. Must the presbyters' voices be asked before
God's laws shall be executed?' 'Take heed not of
tyrannical but of Satanical pride if God's will take
not place in your churches till the presbyters be
assembled and agreed.' Historians who want to argue
for the dominance of consensual forms of decision
making in early modern England would find much to
confirm them in their opinions in the writings of
Elizabethan conformists. Matthew Sutcliffe could not
imagine why 'if three be against two ... the odd
voice should make the determination of three to be
the sentence of the church, especially if the greater
part overcometh the better, which often falleth out'.
Bilson shared his puzzlement; 'doth the whole church
err when falsehood hath for herself ten or twelve
bishops more than truth hath?' (53) For conformists
tyranny was not a function of the presence or absence
of consent or collective decision making, but of the
relationship between the ruler's will and law.
Neither man's propensity to sin nor Antichrist's
power to delude fallen humanity left much hope that
there was any safety to be found in numbers. The
whole history of popery showed that 'three may see
the truth when three hundred may miss it'. (54) Thus
the great advantage of rule by the Christian prince
and the godly bishop was the exclusion of any popular
voice from the process of government. The church
should be both reformed and governed by the will of
the prince, guided by scripture, with the advice, in
normal times, of his godly learned bishops. On this
view the gap between the conduct of external

government and the opinion of the godly community was complete and unbridgeable.

Thus for all that conformist rhetoric about episcopacy aped the scripturalist claims of the presbyterians their position still lacked that edge of essentially eschatological excitement which had characterised presbyterianism. Entirely absent from conformist thought was that hint of transcendence whereby the inward government of the church by Christ merged with its outward government by men and the immanent presence of Christ's spiritual body within the structures of the visible church became itself visible through, even identical with, the external ordinances laid down by Christ.

Of course edification and even transcendence could be pursued within the Jacobean church through the propagation of that evangelical Calvinist piety which still passed as orthodox (at least until the very end of the reign). Anyone seeking confirmation that Jacobean protestants were able to maintain a sense of the godly community as a direct creation of the word preached and the autonomous action of the spirit need only read some of the godly lives written during the period. Nevertheless, considerations of personal godliness and the promptings of godly opinion were rigidly excluded from the realm of external government. From being a means to hand control of the church to the visibly godly and thus simply remove the tension between the national church and the godly community the argument from divine right had become a means to isolate all considerations of personal godliness from questions of external government.

In the hands of evangelical Calvinists this could merely lead to the maintenance of the creative tension between the visibly godly and the elect upon which the experimental predestinarian style of piety fed. In the hands of the opponents of that style of divinity, however, the *iure divino* case for episcopacy led elsewhere. As early as 1588 Walter Travers had pointed out that the claim that the church had never been governed except by bishops rested on an implicit recognition of the Church of Rome as a true church and a repudiation of the Foxeian vision of an underground true church tradition, existing within but not of the popish church. (55) Not everyone accepted the logic of that assertion; under James it was still perfectly possible, with Archbishop Abbot, to combine an acceptance of the *iure divino* theory of episcopacy with a recognisably Foxeian vision of the true church under popery. (56) Others, however, followed the logic of Travers' argument with far greater enthusiasm.

Partly under the direct encouragement of James himself the idea that the Church of Rome was a true church, indeed the true church of which the Church of England represented a reformed continuation, was gaining ground. Others like Laud would take such notions even further and at least imply that episcopacy was necessary to the being of a true church. (57) This was no continuation of the Foxeian tradition but an attempt to effect its closure. That closure was part of a wider attempt to dissolve the tension between the godly community and the national church by subverting the theological assumptions which had underpinned the traditional protestant (and/or Calvinist) account of that community. It is perhaps one of life's little ironies that by the time the Church of England had acquired a self image so inclusively national as to suppress any trace of tension between the godly community and the national church, the effects of that ideology were so divisive as to split the English protestant tradition into its constituent parts for good and all.

Notes
1. Q.R.D. Skinner, The foundations of modern political theory (CUP, Cambridge, 1978), vol. 2, p.210.
2. P. Collinson, The Elizabethan puritan movement (Cape, London, 1967), pp.101-21, 291-302.
3. J.S. Coolidge, The Pauline renaissance in England; puritanism and the bible (OUP, Oxford, 1970), pp.1-54; W. Fulke, A brief and plain declaration concerning the desires of all those faithful ministers that have and do seek for the discipline and reformation of the Church of England (1584), pp.120-1.
4. Dudley Fenner, A defence of the godly ministers against the slanders of Dr Bridges (1588), sig. E3r-4v, T3v-T4r, R3r; Dudley Fenner, A counterpoison (1584), pp.495-6; An humble motion unto the right honourable lords of her majesty's Privy Council (1590), sig. Cr., F4r; W. Travers, A defence of the ecclesiastical discipline (1588), pp.167-8; Fulke, Brief and plain declaration, pp.139-41.
5. T. Cartwright, The rest of the second reply (1577), pp.151-70.
6. J. Whitgift, Works, ed. J. Ayre (Parker Society, Cambridge, 1858), vol. 1, pp.405-6.

7.   A part of a register (1593), p.203.
8.   Fulke, A brief and plain declaration, p.127; J. Udall, A dialogue concerning the strife of our church (1584), pp.85-6, 88.
9.   Fulke, A brief and plain declaration, p.80; Fenner, Counter-poison, p.467.
10.   Fulke, A brief and plain declaration, pp.82-3; Travers, A defence, p.104.
11.   Fulke, A brief and plain declaration, pp.83-4; 86, 107.
12.   Collinson, Elizabethan puritan movement, pp.22-31; S. Brachlow, 'Puritan theology and radical churchmen in pre-revolutionary England, with special reference to Henry Jacob and John Robinson', unpublished DPhil thesis, Oxford University 1978, Chapter 1. For contemporary comment see Whitgift, Works, vol. 3, p.471 or R. Bancroft, A survey of the pretended holy discipline (London, 1593), pp.65-6, 432-3.
13.   Travers, A defence, pp.37, 105, 121; Fenner, Counter-poison, p.426; Fulke, A brief and plain declaration, pp.80-1.
14.   Travers, A defence, pp.13-14; Whitgift, Works, vol. 1, pp.389-90; vol. 2, pp.60-1, 113-14, 425-6, vol. 3, pp.315; Humble Motion, sig. B3r-v; Fenner, Counter-poison, pp.424-5.
15.   Whitgift, Works, vol. 3, p.189; Cartwright, The rest, p.66.
16.   Whitgift, Works, vol. 1, p.382-3; W. Travers, A full and plain declaration of ecclesiastical discipline (1574), p.185.
17.   Travers, A defence, pp.167-8, Fenner, A defence, sig. T3v-T4r, Humble Motion, sig. Cr.
18.   Whitgift, Works, vol. 1, p.390.
19.   Cartwright, The rest, p.18.
20.   S.L. Adams, 'Eliza enthroned? The court and its politics,' in C. Haigh (ed.), The reign of Elizabeth I (Macmillan, London, 1984); D. McCulloch, 'Catholic and puritan in Elizabethan Suffolk; a county community polarises', Archiv für reformationsgeschichte, vol. 72 (1981).
21.   W. MacCaffrey, The shaping of the Elizabethan regime (Cape, London, 1969), p.109.
22.   M. Graves, 'The management of the Elizabethan House of Commons; the Council's men of business', Parliamentary History, vol. 2 (1983); G. Bowler, '"An axe or an acte"; the parliament of 1572 and resistance theory in early Elizabethan England', Canadian Journal of History, vol. 19 (1984).
23.   Whitgift, Works, vol. 2, pp.113-14; vol. 3, pp.186-7; A part of a register, pp.241-2.

24. Travers, <u>A defence</u>, p.136.
25. Martin Marprelate, <u>The protestation of Martin Marprelate</u> (1589), pp.4-5.
26. For Whitgift's division between the visible and invisible church and his accusations of anabaptism levelled at Cartwright for his failure to observe the distinction see Whitgift, <u>Works</u>, vol. 1, pp.183-4. 391; vol. 2, pp.62, 83-4; vol. 3, pp.188, 198; on edification see Whitgift, <u>Works</u>, vol. 1, pp.196-200. Also see Coolidge, <u>Pauline Renaissance</u>, p.44 and generally chapter 2.
27. M.R. Sommerville, 'Richard Hooker and his contemporaries on episcopacy; an Elizabethan consensus', <u>Journal of Ecclesiastical History</u>, vol. 35 (1984).
28. Whitgift, <u>Works</u>, vol. 1, pp.184, 363; vol. 2, pp.263-4; vol. 3, pp.164-5, 176. For Hutton see P. Lake, 'Matthew Hutton, a puritan bishop?', <u>History</u>, vol. 64 (1979); Fenner, <u>A defence</u>, sig. H3r. 'We perceive that they hold it (episcopacy) not as a constitution humane of our laws which may upon good advice be altered but to be of so near conjunction with her majesty as her crown and their rotchets must live and die together.' Also see sig. P4v. 'I think when it cometh to the point they will claim it by human ordinance not contrary to the word (as they say) not yet appointed by the word.' Also see Travers, <u>A defence</u>, p.84. Replying to Bridges' attempt to prove the authority of bishops 'by the scripture', Travers called on him to 'as frankly confess it as they do that maintain the supremacy of the Pope to be due to him <u>iure divino</u> and which necessarily followeth hereof let him deny that princes or any creature may lawfully cause this office to cease to be exercised in the church.' Also see Fenner, <u>Counter-poison</u>, pp.486-7.
29. J. Bridges, <u>A defence of the government established in the Church of England for ecclesiastical matters</u> (London, 1587), p.338 where Bridges embraced the distinction between the bishop of God and the bishop of man. Also see pp.366-71, 1079-81 for the origins of the episcopal monopoly over ordination and excommunication, derived from the apostles and in particular from St. Paul's grant of authority to Timothy and Titus. For the response to Bridges see Marprelate, <u>Hay and work for Cooper</u> (1589), p.29. 'Until this beast Dr Bridges wrote this book they never as yet durst presume to claim their lordships any otherwise lawful than from her majesty,' Travers, <u>A defence</u>, pp.84-5. For Knollys' reaction see W.D.J. Cargill-Thompson, <u>Studies in the</u>

<u>reformation</u> (Athlone Press, London, 1980), pp.94–
130, where Cargill-Thompson points out that the
sermon to which Knollys was reacting was preached by
Bridges and not Bancroft. As Margaret Sommerville has
pointed out Bridges also set out the <u>iure divino</u> case
for bishops in his book against the discipline of
1587. For Hooker on the relative novelty of the <u>iure
divino</u> case see his <u>Laws of Ecclesiastical Polity</u>,
VII, xi, 8.

    30. See for instance Whitgift, <u>Works</u>, vol. 2,
pp.92–7; T. Bilson, <u>The perpetual government of
Christ's church</u> (London 1593, (ed.) R. Eden, Oxford,
1842), pp.2, 33–5.

    31. For such a gloss on Jerome see for instance
Bridges, <u>A defence</u>, pp.285, 389. Bridges had earlier
espoused the Whitgiftian position and cited Jerome to
prove that episcopacy was a tradition of the church
introduced after the time of the apostles. See his
<u>The supremacy of Christian princes</u> (London, 1573),
pp.359–63. For a similar gloss on Jerome to bring him
into line with the <u>iure divino</u> case see Bilson,
<u>Perpetual government</u>, p.290. For an extended
discussion of the <u>iure divino</u> case as it was
expounded by the likes of Bilson, Bridges, Saravia,
Sutcliffe and Bancroft see W.D.J. Cargill-Thompson,
'Anthony Marten and the Elizabethan debate on
episcopacy' in G.V. Bennet and J.D. Walsh (eds),
<u>Essays in Modern church history</u> (London, 1966).

    32. Bilson, <u>Perpetual government</u>, pp.393–405;
Travers, <u>A defence</u>, pp.77–82.

    33. Bridges, <u>A defence</u>, p.9; R. Bancroft, <u>A
survey</u>, 'to the reader'; M. Sutcliffe, <u>An answer to a
certain libel supplicatory</u> (London, 1592), sig. B4v.

    34. By the 1590s, however, they had all
switched to the <u>iure divino</u> position. For Bridges see
above fns. 29, 31; for Hutton, Lake, 'Matthew Hutton'
and for Whitgift's position in 1594 see J. Strype,
<u>The life and acts of John Whitgift</u> (Oxford 1822),
vol. 2, p.170.

    35. H. Saravia, <u>Of the diverse degrees of the
ministers of the gospel</u> (London, 1592), 'To the
courteous reader' sig. C3v., p.41, 62; R. Bancroft, <u>A
sermon preached at Paul's Cross</u> (London, 1589), p.17;
M. Sutcliffe, <u>A treatise of ecclesiastical
discipline</u> (London, 1590), p.68.

    36. Sommerville, 'Hooker and his contemporar-
ies'. For Fenner see <u>Counter-poison</u>, p.492.

    37. Collinson, <u>Elizabeth puritan movement</u>,
pp.385–431; for Hooker see <u>Laws</u>, VII, xi, 8.

    38. Hooker, <u>Laws</u>, VII, xvii, xix, xx, xxiii,
Saravia, <u>Diverse degrees</u>, pp.196–201.

39. Whitgift, Works, vol. 3, p.10; Travers, A full and plain declaration, pp.124-7; Saravia, Diverse degrees, passim; Bancroft, A survey, pp.236-7, 246, 232-3; A sermon preached at Paul's cross, p.24.

40. The one possible exception is Bancroft who in an aside in A survey, pp.235-6, might be taken to imply that tithes were due 'by the word'. The passage, however, is ambiguous.

41. L. Andrewes, Sacrilege a snare (London, 1647), passim, esp.p.10. 'I came hither to preach not to dispute and therefore betake myself to the more received opinion that tithes have their force from the imposition of the church.' Also see Andrewes, Of the right to tithes (London, 1647). I owe these references to the kindness of Dr Martin Dzelainis.

42. G. Carleton, Tithes examined and proved to be due to the clergy by a divine right (London, 1606), passim.

43. Carleton, Tithes examined, 'To the archbishop of Canterbury'; R. Eburne, The maintenance of the ministry (London, 1609), 'To James by divine providence lord bishop of Bath and Wells.' Carleton's tract also carried an epistle to the reader by William Cowell, one of Bancroft's chaplains, writing from Lambeth House, which also serves to reinforce the impression of a pseudo-official campaign.

44. For Selden's tribulations over his History of Tithes see J. Selden, Table Talk, ed. E. Arber (London, 1905), pp.4-6, and D.N.B.

45. For a comparison of tithes and the sabbath as based both on the promptings of natural law and reason, which provided the general propositions that maintenance should be paid to God's ministers and time set aside for his worship, and the specific dictates of scripture, which laid down the precise proportions of one day in seven and a tenth of each professor's income, see W. Sclater, The minister's portion (London, 1612), p.34. For sabbatarianism in general see K. Parker, 'The English sabbath', unpublished PhD thesis, University of Cambridge, 1984.

46. J. Sommerville, 'Jacobean political thought and the oath of allegiance controversy', unpublished PhD thesis, University of Cambridge, 1981 and J. Sommerville, Politics and ideology in England, 1603-1640 (Longmans, London, 1986), chapter 1. Also see K. Fincham and P. Lake, 'The ecclesiastical policy of James I', Journal of British Studies, vol. 24 (1985).

47. Bridges, <u>Defence</u>, pp.1080-1.

48. Bilson, <u>Perpetual government</u>, pp.393-405.

49. Whitgift, <u>Works</u>, vol. 1, pp.371, 466-8; vol. 3, pp.211-13; Bilson, <u>Perpetual government</u>, pp.434-49; Hooker, <u>Laws</u>, VIII, xiv, 7.

50. Sutcliffe, <u>A treatise</u>, pp.226-7; Bancroft, <u>A survey</u>, p.399.

51. Saravia, <u>Diverse degrees</u>, p.79; Bilson, <u>Perpetual government</u>, pp.33-4.

52. Bilson, <u>Perpetual government</u>, pp.35, 48; Sutcliffe, <u>A treatise</u>, pp.7, 221, 217. Also see Sutcliffe, <u>De presbytero eiusque nova in ecclesia Christiana politeia</u> (London, 1591), p.63.

53. Bilson, <u>Perpetual government</u>, p.51; Sutcliffe, <u>A treatise</u>, p.149, Bilson, <u>The true difference between Christian subjection and unChristian rebellion</u> (Oxford, 1585), p.271.

54. Bilson, <u>True Difference</u>, pp.207, 534.

55. Travers, <u>A defence</u>, pp.108-9.

56. G. Abbot, <u>A treatise of the perpetual visibility and succession of the true Church in all ages</u> (1624), passim.

57. <u>The works of ... William Laud</u>, eds W. Scott and J. Bliss (Oxford, 1847-60), vol. 2, <u>Conference with Fisher</u>, pp.194-5, fn.u. Citing Jerome's opinion that 'ecclesia autem non est quae non habet sacerdotes' Laud commented that 'in that place most manifest it is that St Jerome by sacerdos means a bishop'. Tackled with this opinion at his trial Laud replied that 'the passage in my book is an inference of St Jerome's opinion no declaration of my own and if they or any other be aggrieved at St Jerome for writing so they may answer him'. <u>Works</u>, vol. 4, p.307. Laud, therefore, hedged his bets on the subject, but as his famous letters to Joseph Hall reveal his was an exalted vision of episcopacy, which was designed to concede as little as possible to the foreign reformed churches. (See <u>Works</u>, vol. 6, pp.572-5.)

INDEX

Aaron 105, 117, 120
Abbot, George 218
Abraham 105
Acworth, George 150
Admonition controversy 185
Ahud 135
Albigensians 169, 171
Aleander 21
Alfred 180
Africk, Thomas 14
Allen, Edmund 91, 93
Alwaye, Thomas 54, 55
Amersham 3, 4, 6, 14, 15, 17, 23
Anabaptists 134, 215
Andrewes, Lancelot 211-12
Angrogne 177
Anne of Cleves 56, 58
Anselm 175
Antichrist 15, 46, 68, 80, 82, 86,
    87, 162, 164-5, 166, 167, 168,
    170, 171, 172, 173, 176, 180-
    1, 182, 185, 209, 217
Antwerp 24, 44, 54
Aristotle 139
Armachanus 168
Ascham, Roger 63, 64, 66, 67
Ashford, Agnes 16
Agnes, Richard 11, 16
Askew, Anne 40, 48, 65, 69, 83
Astley, Katherine 66
Athaliah 116, 131, 139
Augsburg, Confession of 44, 57
Aylmer, John 70

Baal 119
Bacon, Nicholas 44

Bainham, James 55
Bainton, Sir Edward 39, 40, 49-
    50, 70
Baldwin, Archbishop 181
Bale, John 22, 40, 59, 79-81, 83,
    85, 89, 90, 125-8, 130, 140,
    162
Bancroft, Richard 209, 210, 211,
    212, 215
Barentine family 8
Barlow, John 50
Barlow, William 7, 50, 56
Barnes, Robert 11, 23, 24, 38-9,
    45, 47, 81
Barrett, John 2, 3, 8, 11
Bartlett, Isabel 11
Bartlett, Katherine 14
Bartlett, Richard 4, 11
Bartlett, Robert 4-5, 11, 13
Basle 120
Becket, Thomas 175, 181
Becon, Thomas 70, 107, 111
Beele, Thomas 20, 23
Bembridge, Thomas 154-5
Berkeley, Sir John 156
Betts, William 52, 53
Bible, the Great (1539) 46
Bilney, Thomas 22, 55, 81
Bilson, Thomas 208, 209, 214-15,
    216, 217
Bishops' book (1537) 58
Blage, George 48, 69
Boleyn, Anne 36, 39, 41, 43, 46,
    47, 49, 50, 51-6, 66, 69, 70,
    71
Boleyn, Thomas 52

225